Risk Bandits

Rescuing Risk Management from Tokenism

Rob Hogarth and Tony Pooley

BALBOA.
PRESS
A DIVISION OF HAY HOUSE

Balboa Press books may be ordered through booksellers or by contacting:

Balboa Press
A Division of Hay House
1663 Liberty Drive
Bloomington, IN 47403
www.balboapress.com
1 (877) 407-4847

Cover design: Carolynn Walsh

Print information available on the last page.

ISBN: 978-1-4525-2984-4 (sc)
ISBN: 978-1-4525-2985-1 (e)

Balboa Press rev. date: 08/19/2015

Contents

Foreword

Don't Take This Any More

This book puts on record some unpleasant truths about organisations and their current standards of managing risk based on our experience as risk professionals since the early 1990s. In the words of Howard Beale in the 1976 movie 'Network', we're 'as mad as hell and we're not going to take this anymore.' We're not asking you to stick your head out of the window and shout it out but hopefully a small, but critical, number of board members, audit and risk committee members or CEOs will demand an audience with their risk manager and genuinely probe how much trust they should put in their organisation's risk management framework. Why would you bother? . . . Let us explain.

The nonsense spoken, and the resultant waste of resources that occurs, in the name of risk management in organisations around the world is mind-blowing and our experience, including the occasional candid conversation with a worried director or executive, tells us that much of executive management already knows this. However, as with the naked emperor, they are reticent to speak out because no one else seems to notice, and anyway, what would they do if risk management really were worthless? There are stock exchange expectations and regulations on risk management, we can't just opt out!

Battling Risk Bandits

We are putting our experiences on the record now to help equip you to recognise the potentially critical weaknesses in your organisation's risk management process and the risk bandits who consistently fail to address them. If you are at the top of your organisation, you didn't get there without making important decisions so you will be well equipped to make a call on risk management effectiveness after reading this book. However, to cut to the chase, the simple painful but inescapable truth is that we can't just go out and buy good organisation risk management in a box no matter how much we'd like to. The components of a good system are explained in this book in order to allow you to make risk management work for your organisation … but only if you give a damn in the first place.

This would have been a brave book for us to write a few years ago because our careers may well have been cut short as a consequence. However, to retain our credibility with readers we must concede there is little bravery involved in writing this book now because with some talent, even more luck and the minimum of banditry we've reached a point in our careers where we enjoy the great luxury of working for whom the hell we want to. In regard to our credentials for building this paper pulpit, we have learned that neither of us could have done it alone but together we constitute one hell of a risk guru.

Our guess is that many of our readers will conclude that much of what we say is true but that it doesn't apply to *their* organisation. We would remind such readers that in the last decade or so, the first initial of the listed companies that have identified blatantly high risks, concluded that their defences are fine and moved confidently unprepared into the perfect storm, would fill more than an alphabet. Try it for yourself, we'll start you off with AIG and complete the alphabet with Zavvi. Our guess is you won't even slow up until you reach the letter X. We suspect that every one of them would have spoken proudly of their risk management capacity if asked in the months preceding their downfall.

Oh, a reality check at this juncture; good risk management can't fix all of the challenges that an organisation faces. The best risk manager in the world, assisted by Merlin the Magician and Glinda the Good Witch of the South (perhaps not so much reality after all), couldn't have avoided the infamous financial disasters of the early 21st century in organisations with a moral void at the executive level.

Director Discomfort

If directors' understanding of financial statements were on the same level as their understanding of organisation risk management, share trading would have become extinct decades ago. Analysts can look at a balance sheet and reasonably assume it is professionally prepared to a strict and proven formula; the numbers within it are supportable by credible data, and that it is consequently auditable. Pick on any aspect and seek demonstration of accuracy and there will be a trail that can be followed. Valuations are carefully applied and all transactions are accounted for. All values will be aggregated to defined outcomes like total assets and shareholders' funds. This is not to say that the resulting conclusions are never contested, but that they are based on a transparent process that provides a basis for reasoned argument.

Organisation risk profiles are, however, supported by risk registers, most commonly in the form of a simple descriptive spreadsheet, completed by people with no prescribed professional qualification and with no ability to follow any trail other than to determine whether a bunch of people sat down in a room and actually said what has been recorded. There is no control over the way the risk events across an organisation are broken down and as a result duplication and omission is rife. The data, irrespective of how it was generated, can only be aggregated to a trite organisational output that offers little as a basis for meaningful executive management or board review. It's probably more reassuring for investors to conclude no one really looks at such risk registers because it would be considerably more worrying to think someone at a senior level actually found them plausible.

Of course, directors will dutifully partake in the truckload of training recommended by their professional association but most will exit the training knowing a lot more about the consequences of getting risk wrong (paranoid) than about how to manage it (empowered). This is not a useful state in a world where promising returns rarely arrive without substantial risk as their travelling companion.

Some directors may calm themselves by placing their trust in executive management and the apparent compliance with standards. If so, such individuals should prepare for a shock as they read on.

Spotting Risk Bandits

For the moment let us move the focus from those who have oversight of risk management to those who implement the process. When we talk of "risk bandits", we refer to risk professionals who take their organisation's pay cheque or consulting fee and deliver little return to investors for their services. They're less akin to bank robbers (too much risk in that) and more akin to confidence tricksters, although not in receipt of personal gain other than their ego and remuneration.

Sadly, whilst some bandits know full well they're peddling snake oil, many actually think they're doing something meaningful. They come into a meeting room full of people, "solve" anything from a score to a hundred complex risk scenarios in a day and leave the room genuinely thinking they've done a great job. We regard even those deluded souls as bandits because ignorance is no excuse in the eyes of corporate law.

Many readers may find that much of what we have to say in this book is unpalatable. It may be unpalatable because so many resources have been committed without benefit or meaning, or simply because it means you've been duped. But the sourest taste of all is likely to come from accepting that somewhere in the back of your brain you've suspected this all along.

Here are a few symptoms that may help you detect this organisation health issue:

- When asked what are the top three things they worry about, your organisation-managers' answers never coincide with what the risk register says they should be worried about

- Your organisation's Chief Risk Officer (CRO) understands a whole lot more about assurance than about risk management (audits aplenty, but of what?)

- You assume that risk management is like accounting, engineering or law where the letters following the practitioner's name guarantees a level of competence

- You, or your organisation's executive management, would never say it aloud but regard risk management as simply a compliance or cover-your-ass issue (a largely justified conclusion if we look at what passes for risk management in most organisations)

- Your organisation sees risk management as an attempt to prevent headaches, rather than deliver success (what is the difference between "reducing production interruptions and producing more?" or "reducing losses and increasing profits?")

- Your organisation becomes comfortable that the risk of potentially disastrous events are well managed (we should always have a sense of chronic unease about such disasters, continually checking that we haven't missed something)

Of course there's ample intellect within the executive management team of most organisations to understand what makes a good risk framework; they just don't make the time. Instead they allow inept practices to continue unabated. They simply can't be asking themselves the basic question … 'Why don't I refer to the risk register more often if I really believe in it?'

The most common truth, of course, is that they don't believe in it, and yet that single piece of personal honesty will become the critical first step to creating an organisation risk management framework that enhances shareholder returns and demonstrates genuine corporate responsibility.

Beating Banditry

Some organisations have stepped above the pack and are already getting much more from their risk management activities than their peers. The most successful have the strong support of a CEO who has taken the time to really understand the difference between the wheat and chaff of risk management. Nevertheless, if the CEO isn't the sponsor, it's OK to push forward on a single front such as a better risk methodology, creating a direct linkage between risk assessments and audit activities, or by establishing a top-down risk-events hierarchy before allowing the bottom-up work to commence. However you intend to start, the objective of this book is to present options for an overall approach that will rescue risk management from tokenism and make it a reason for investors to queue for equity in your organisation.

Notwithstanding the above, it's our belief that the primary responsibility for making this change happen is held by the CEO and the preferred use of this book is to allow directors to support and guide a CEO that is already knowledgeable in risk management. In reality however, this may not occur swiftly enough for a board that is determined to deliver both substantial growth and rock-solid governance in a short timeframe. In such cases we are hoping the book may help the board to ask the right questions to light the way for an otherwise talented CEO.

If you are flicking through the bookshelves to see if this book is for you, try answering the following question to help you decide. 'Do I feel lucky?' For directors of most organisations, luck may well be playing a bigger part in their current success than they'd like to think.

What Lies Ahead

"Risk Bandits" is in two parts separated by a short Intermission.

Chapters 1 to 6 look at the tokenistic nature of risk management in most organisations including companies seeking commercial returns and not-for-profit or public sector enterprises. The lack of value extracted, or in fact any significant impact on risk levels, in organisations is analysed. The links to compliance, process-focused standards and regulations are explained and the flow on impacts to the ill-defined role of boards in risk management are highlighted. Finally, the tricks of the trade used by internal and external risk bandits are exposed. An account is provided as to why these tricks are so well accepted and why they not only fool some executive managers and boards into believing that the current state of risk management is useful, but also fool the risk bandits themselves. There is no apology for the criticism in this first part of the book; we call it as we see it—largely tokenism.

Chapters 7 to 10 move into constructive mode with practical solutions put forward to assist executive managers and boards rescue their organisations from risk management tokenism. A practical approach to genuine organisation risk analysis is explained using non-technical language and high school maths. Having properly built the basics, a step-by-step guide is provided for executive managers and boards to extract real value from organisation risk management including their role and the types of reporting they should be demanding. Finally, two practical case studies are presented from the detailed risk-assessment level to show how the results are used to enhance organisation-wide performance management.

Navigation Guidance

As "Risk Bandits" is written for directors and executive management of organisations, a familiarity with organisation risk management is assumed rather than specialist knowledge. The content has been carefully sequenced to build understanding from this base. Don't be put off by the 99 Figures and the threat of complex maths—technical aspects are explained, the maths is not advanced and Figures are designed for speedy visual interpretation. Alternatively, readers may care to dwell only on the detail in the Figures of greatest interest.

Where detailed content in a chapter can be speed-read without losing the plot for later discussion, these sections are identified immediately beforehand. Readers then have the option to either press on or take the time to build more context around the discussion.

Preface

The Rip Van Winkle Syndrome

If Rip Van Winkle awoke from a 30-year slumber today, imagine the difficulties he would experience in coping with such a different world. At the start of the 1980s he would have bought his favourite artist's latest record on vinyl, watched McEnroe and Borg battle at Wimbledon with wooden racquets, and wondered whether any of his friends and family would survive the escalating nuclear arms race. Today's world would be an absolute revelation to him but, if he was a risk professional, he could at least re-start work tomorrow without missing a beat. His outmoded tools of trade are still in use, and if his workplace still existed, his absence might even have gone unnoticed!

It's a Failure in Governance

"Risk Bandits" is motivated by the reflections of two ageing contrite risk practitioners, an accountant and an engineer, who got to the same point—total dismay with our profession! It exposes organisation risk management as a failure in governance occurring in most medium to large organisations, be they commercial, not-for-profit, or public service enterprises.

This failure has only a little to do with how organisations deal with the potential of specific hazardous events. The real rub is how organisations delegate risk taking to the right people and strategically manage the balance of taking on an appropriate level of risk in order to generate an attractive return. For simplicity we refer to this risk/return focus as enhancing shareholder value, even if the organisation is not a listed company. Shareholder value in this sense includes social responsibility along with profit, as objectives for an organisation.

The missing ingredient in the governance pie is the way risk management is used in making decisions. Not just risk treatment decisions but weighing risks, with both positive and negative potential outcomes considered, in making operating and strategic decisions across organisations.

Risk Registers Don't Enhance Shareholder Value

Rip's outmoded tools of trade are risk registers and risk management plans, and neither enhances shareholder value. Whilst they give comfort to some executive management teams, boards and regulators; it's a false sense of security. Shareholders and other stakeholders deserve better.

Perhaps the biggest question is 'how can this be occurring under the noses of so many clever people?' Some probably recognise this state and are frustrated by the lack of technical progress by the risk management profession. Those who don't recognise the failure are usually unable to achieve clarity in the distinction between risk management processes that deal with individual risks as they arise, and a risk management framework that sits across an organisation to allow personnel to deal with individual risks in a way that adds flesh to a well-considered skeleton.

Offering a Solution to Boards

The way forward is for boards to demand a paradigm shift from their CEO and executive managers. Mr. Winkle will be another 30-years older (but probably not an ounce wiser) if we wait for the risk management profession to lead. "Risk Bandits" exposes the governance failure inherent in the current state and offers boards a way to challenge executives to performance manage the link between the returns from their activities and the exposure the organisation takes on to achieve them.

Acknowledgements

This book is critical of a great deal of what passes for risk management in organisations all over the world and we know that we are inviting a maelstrom of indignation and the associated ejected venom of a very large number of risk professionals. Even though we are confident in justifying what we are putting forward, we are further fortified in facing this storm because of the invaluable input of four individuals who critically reviewed this publication before its release.

Each reviewer had a perspective on the book that we felt would add something to our own and we were right.

Professor Barry Cooper of the Deakin University Business School gave us hard-nosed feedback on our chance of sustaining a busy director's interest and the appropriateness of the content for business today.

Norman Ritchie, Director of the vPSI Group in the US and outspoken critic of unthinking risk assessment, helped us tighten some of our jargon-free descriptions of technical aspects and avoid unintended muddying of key messages as a result of differing English language and cultural interpretations.

Shayne Arthur has probably been personally responsible for the implementation of more of the risk management concepts argued in this book than any other senior risk professional in Australia, and is the antithesis of a Risk Bandit. His detailed input was both valuable and reassuring.

Emeritus Professor Jean Cross of the University of New South Wales is more than a risk academic—her leadership in the development of the first internationally acknowledged standard for risk management in 1995 has been followed by 20 years of intelligent, patient and insightful publications advancing the risk management cause. Jean helped us to be more constructive in arguing a better way.

We thank all of these reviewers for their time, frankness and support, without which this would have been a significantly lesser publication.

Risk Bandits

In Addition

We had our hands full just getting the words right in this book—so we're not sure what we'd have done if graphic artist Carolynn Walsh hadn't created the cover image and made the many technical figures look as interesting as inherently bland diagrams can be. We also thank Prof. Patrick Hudson for allowing us to quote his 'pinning the tail on the donkey' matrix analogy and turning the thought into a persuasive image.

About the Authors

Tony Pooley

Tony was a mechanical engineer in the Oil and Gas industry in the UK before founding the Qest Consulting risk group in 1992. Qest created some significant new developments in risk including the creation of the SQRA™ experience-based risk quantification process.

Tony joined the Newcrest Mining executive committee in 2007, which gave him the opportunity to create and manage an enterprise risk framework from within a listed company for the first time. He recently completed a five-year term on the National Offshore Petroleum Safety and Environmental Management Authority Advisory Board advising Federal and State ministers in regard to offshore oil and gas safety and environmental management and he is an adjunct associate professor in risk management at the University of South Australia.

Rob Hogarth

Rob is an Australian chartered accountant who retired from KPMG in 2009 after being a partner for 29 years. He is now a professional non-executive director being a member of the board/audit and risk committee of eight private and public sector organisations and consults to a range of organisations on financial and risk management.

Rob's career at KPMG in Australia and Asia was focused on business risk, with major functional roles in a range of consulting areas including risk advisory, governance, major projects and sustainability and earlier in external audit and internal audit. Rob's industry experience is primarily in mining, manufacturing and education.

1. From Stagnant Tokenism to Effective Capitalism

Counting Tokens

Most executive managers would admit openly that they see the consumption of resources by risk management in their organisation as a necessary defensive measure for a 21st-century enterprise. But few would see it as a primary vehicle for delivering a substantially enhanced shareholder return, and even less would be delivering on that vision. Yet, in a small number of organisations, risk management does deliver substantially enhanced shareholder returns on a continuous basis. In order to realise this state, however, risk management needs to be taken out of the hands of the defensive minded and handed over to those who don't need a prescribed pathway to work out what delivers most for their organisation. In other words, there is a need to let go of the follow-the-pack philosophy and think freely. Let's see if we can persuade you to do so.

First—a question for readers. How do you react when the shopping precinct and traffic-light predators (aka charity collectors) step into your eye line and shame you into a donation? Perhaps, like us, you get a little peeved because no matter how many donations we make, badges we buy, third world children we support, or raffles we enter, they always want more. It's not even a serious drain on our income, but it keeps us in a kind of *Groundhog Day* where each morning on the way to work, or as we walk to lunch, somebody approaches us for a contribution to something they believe makes a difference … and quite frankly, we're not at all sure that it does.

If we thought raffles and badges were a real game changer, we'd all jump in the deep end. Half our income so that Africa has no more hungry children? What a bargain—where do we sign? But we don't believe it's the case, so we mumble some apple pie and motherhood encouragement to the collector and keep putting the tokens in the collection box. We're buying off the annoying collector and diluting our guilt a little, but it's a long way short of achieving genuine peace of mind.

This is also what has happened to risk management in most organisations. Executive management donated generously to the cause for a long time and

1

had hopes of a no-more-surprises world. After a while, they saw little real change in their business, but it's now neither politically correct nor in some cases legally possible to say, 'Enough! Let's use these resources to better effect'. Like the targets of street collectors, executive management keeps the tokens flowing long after belief in the cause has faded.

Consumed by Process

From 1990 to 2002 the world saw increasing focus on corporate risk management acts, guidance notes and standards. You may recognise some of the titles that became folklore, including Sarbanes Oxley, COSO, Cadbury and Turnbull, and AS 4360 and its offspring ISO 31000 (more on all this in Chapter 2). The corporate world was too sluggish to make risk management its own initiative; it was now a matter of compliance, and corporations through the decades have argued that compliance is a poor route to excellence.

Even the smartest people are prone to stop thinking when the early promise isn't delivered and compliance-capture offers an easy way out. Our risk management champions may never have been the smartest people in the room, but the zombie-like lovers of process—people who want to check what they do against a piece of paper and not real outcomes—have taken firm control. As a result, the risk world is teeming with conveyor-belt facilitators following the simplest possible interpretation of risk standards, and auditors aplenty doing what they do best—checking that we do what we say we do, whether it makes an iota of difference or not.

Compliance isn't the only road to tokenism. An unfounded but passionate belief that your organisation manages its risk brilliantly because it is inherently good at what it does will take you there too. In the early days of the risk management surge (circa 1992), a risk consultancy was engaged by one of Australia's largest companies to undertake a major risk review. The results were to be presented to a regulator to obtain permission to undertake a major development. The chief operating officer was a hard, confident character who laid down the following parameters for the report to the consultant:

'It will cost no more than $80,000, will be two inches thick, and it will promise nothing other than this company will always hire the very best people.'

It never occurred to this extremely talented man that any process he hadn't already adopted could possibly add benefit to his massive project.

The regulator accurately described the resultant report as 'both confused and confusing' and approval was withheld. By the time the second version was completed by the same consultant, but with no parameters other than to get approval on reasonable grounds, the individual had sanctioned several fundamental changes to the project that had been uncovered by a genuine attempt to undertake a thorough risk review. In fairness to that manager, he went on to make the risk process mandatory on all of the company's developments around the world, including locations where no such process was stipulated by law.

The point here is that this larger-than-life character was not afraid to show his confidence (arrogance?), and it was therefore possible to account for it and go on to reach a good outcome. In fact, there is little doubt that the regulator and the consultant were in some degree of conspiracy to bring this outcome about. The problem today is that arrogance and complacency are not outwardly displayed when it involves widely endorsed risk processes or values that find themselves deep in the political correctness zone. It's a motherhood, apple pie and risk management world in the 21st century.

Recognising you have a sickness is the first step to curing it, so let's take a look at some of the many ways the tokenistic approach to risk management in organisations can be detected.

Risk Management in a Box

One-stop packaging is everything today. We pay the required sum and all of our problems go away. In an executive committee meeting at a major resources company a few years back, the tension in the room was higher than normal when discussing the introduction of SAP, a life-changing and expensive enterprise resource-planning IT system. This was somewhat surprising, given that these same individuals regularly discussed massive investments where an inappropriate decision, or lack of one, could cripple the company. The tension was explained when an executive director reminded the committee members that more executive heads have rolled over failed business management systems than over any core business performance issue. When asked why the hell the company was doing it at all then, the answer was much less succinct.

The most likely explanation is that the decision was peer pressure. Most of the top resource companies had made the move, and the company, which had rapidly moved up the stock exchange list, wanted this latest badge of corporate honour to prove it was indeed part of the elite. Whilst the business case was unclear, executives and directors were as influenced by the pressures of the latest corporate trend as any youngster looking to get the latest Nike shoes by protesting that absolutely everyone at school has already got them.

Whatever the real need, the articulation of the project value to all of the people that would go through the pain of its implementation was centred on the efficiencies of an integrated system—a one-stop shop. However—and this was foreseen by executive management—one of the first outcomes was a series of requests from department heads for permission to continue to use their current self-developed databases or bespoke software instead of the relevant SAP module. Mostly, refusal was withheld and many general managers felt the effectiveness of their department had taken a step backward as a result.

A packaged vacation analogy when assessing integrated system software versus bespoke alternatives can provide a useful perspective. Consider the integrated IT system as a 'packaged tour' where you just get yourself to the starting point and don't have to engage your brain at all to travel, eat, sleep, shop and party in London, Paris, Rome and New York. In the bespoke independent travel approach, however, you have to think up front. You set your own itinerary and go to places you want to go when you want to go to them, and you're free to adjust if you see something better along the way. It would be nice to take a survey of executives and directors and find out how many of them go on packaged tours, but we suspect that bespoke itineraries would be the norm. So why would they be less inclined to think for themselves on risk management when wearing the organisation hat?

One reason is that there are some quick wins when you select a packaged tour to the exotic island of risk management. It's a great way for ambitious internal risk bandits to shop if they are too ill-equipped or time poor to actually think for themselves. Frankly, it's a pretty low-risk option, given the CEO and board are unlikely to probe with questions like 'how does this package influence our annual planning?' or 'how does this drive our internal audit program?' or 'why is a delay in an environmental permit an "environmental" risk when it doesn't harm the environment one jot?'

A shiny, slick integrated software solution full of data is also an effective way of convincing external risk bandits (internal auditors, regulators, etc.) that the organisation has mastery of its risk profile. As with the packaged tour, peer pressures are minor, as everyone has the same experience as their travelling companions. It's the smart way to go … if you're a sheep. If you're a pack leader, however, the following option may be of interest to you.

This "Risk Management for Dummies" packaged approach has to be targeted at the lowest common denominator to ensure an adequate market size and it focuses on solutions that are largely independent of the human dimension. It never ceases to amaze us, that some of the biggest companies in the world are happy to accept that the risk management package to meet their needs is the same one that meets the needs of the industrial and commercial minnows. The very same giant organisations that would laugh at the suggestion that a small business bookkeeping package is totally adequate for their complex accounting and financial management needs, will nonetheless assume their risk management needs are identical to the needs of the little guys. Now there's wishful thinking in a big way.

The simplistic nature of the risk assessment "engine room" in most risk-software packages is mind-blowing. It most commonly involves a crude selection of likelihood and consequence with little real definition of causal interfaces. As a result, few assessments will take more than an hour and most less than 15 minutes to nail a risk answer. Whilst this may be good enough for screening out scenarios that are clearly low in terms of the most severe credible consequence, it is delusional to consider it adequate for anything else.

If the above seems to suggest that all risk software is bad we have given the wrong message. It isn't that it's all bad—but even the good packages can't do the job in isolation of a good organisation risk framework—and that in turn involves the smart guys and girls at the head of the organisation taking a very proactive role. It's quite difficult for board members and executives to oversee a process they have only ever looked at from a great height. They first need to understand it at ground level where they can prod and probe it, perhaps like we would a prospective son or daughter-in-law. Ask the questions that they fear may be stupid and they will not only be the brightest person in the room but the most informed too. Board members and executives may not, however, entirely enjoy this experience, but avoiding the early recognition of unpleasant truths is likely to have serious outcomes whether the issue is risk management or cancer.

In summary, the main problem with one-stop solutions is that the organisation's risk bandits believe that they only have to administer the software and good risk outcomes are somehow assured. It's all about process and not results. Risk bandits will know exactly how many risk assessments have been carried out and who was responsible. They will know how many actions were promised and sometimes even the percentage that were completed on schedule. Sadly, they will never know whether the right risk assessments have been undertaken and how they relate to each other and they will never know whether the actions being completed are having any effect at all on the level of risk to which the organisation is exposed. Bandit brains were switched off long before the box was unwrapped … it is up to board members and executives to change things.

Which Risk Management System Do You Believe?

We're now going to ask you to be candid with yourself by giving your honest responses to three considerations. We'll never know what you answered, nor will any of your colleagues so hey, why not go for it? What we're hoping to do is give you an insight into how much, or how little, you walk the risk management talk.

Test 1—Double or Nothing!

You're a CEO who has the chance to buy out your closest competitor. Your market share has always been a little less than theirs but lately they've had poor results and the market in your sector is a bit twitchy, so their share price is illogically low. One of their major institutional investors has expressed their displeasure and has indicated they'd be supportive of any takeover attempt by your organisation. Knowing you have their support means a well-presented case is very likely to succeed.

The efficiency benefits would be amazing and you'd be the clear sector leader, with your nearest competitor a long way back in second place. Finance is freely available and your M&A department say it's a great opportunity to create a dominant brand. However, the risk register has a major acquisition assessed as an "Extreme" risk and the risk-mitigation strategy included setting a firm gearing debt/equity ratio for the business. When you ask the risk manager why it's an "Extreme" risk you are told it's because it would exceed the organisation's gearing guidelines by a large amount and because the two organisations have very different work cultures. She points out that the General Manager M&A was in the risk workshop. You remain keen to proceed because the upside is phenomenal. Do you …

A. Accept the risk register and comply with the findings re gearing and cultural mismatch?

B. Have a new risk assessment undertaken and attend personally?

C. Have a new risk assessment undertaken and advise the M&A GM of your thoughts on gearing and culture differences?

D. Disregard the risk register; everyone knows it's unrealistic anyway?

Answer A would put you in a very small minority and the decision would be admirable, assuming it is a very good risk management system, and plain dumb if it isn't.

Answers B and C are effectively the same, because either way you don't believe the register but want the record to suggest otherwise. These answers would probably be the most common responses, which is sad because they show no belief in the system but a willingness to pretend it means something.

Answer D scores high on honesty but low on responsibility, because once again a poor system is not repaired.

Test 2—What's in a Register?

A second test is much easier; think of a business issue that really concerns you and look for it in your organisation's current risk register. Then answer the following questions:

A. Was there an assessment of your issue?

B. Did the risk ranking reflect your concern accurately?

C. Did the information in the register show the assessment had recognised the critical aspects of the issue and responded to them effectively?

Clearly a "No" answer to any of the three questions is indicative of a poor risk management process that may require a solution. Irrespective of the answers to the three questions; why hadn't you gone to the risk register before we asked you to do so?

Test 3—Where is it Anyway?

How many times have you taken a risk assessment or risk register into a meeting with you?

Would you even know where to look?

Sometimes Management Don't Want to Know

Earlier in this chapter we touched on executive management oversight of risk management, but it's worthy of more attention. The largely superficial oversight of risk management by the executive team (e.g. a few probing questions occasionally in their individual area of professional expertise to let them know they're nobody's dummy) in the great majority of organisations presumably means one of three things:

i.   Executive management believe risk management is well managed and will continue to be well managed without their help, or

ii. They're uncomfortable with how risk is managed but feel it is difficult to exert significant influence from their position, or

iii. They just don't get risk management and find themselves shying away from it as a result

A possible fourth option is that executives believe that there is no substantial risk in their business, but we won't waste our time commenting on that option because they wouldn't waste their time reading this book.

Executives who think risk management in their organisation is well under control by line management and therefore can't add much are in line for a risk bandit badge of dishonour. Investors, who are funding their salaries, sure as hell want them to sweat a great deal over risk on their behalf.

Any investor who has played the market over a period of time knows that unsinkable organisations are even rarer than unsinkable ships. Risk is a malicious organisational gravity—it's ever present and just waiting to dump us on our ass if we take a wrong step. Risk gravity, like terrorism, only needs to get lucky once; and good risk managers believe Henry Ford was spot on when he said the harder he worked the luckier he got. It's time for the executive and board to work harder on their organisation's risk management framework.

For an organisation that is in Category i or ii above there's good and bad news. The good news is board members and executives can learn how to influence a good risk management framework and once the organisation has a good framework on paper it becomes relatively easy to monitor that it's being applied properly. The bad news is that board members and executives have to devote a brief period to really understand the fundamental principles of risk management, not just the simplistic formulas and tools, and challenge the copy and paste generated framework they are probably using right now. Hopefully, the fact that you are reading this book means that you might be prepared to give it a try.

Having the men and women of the executive and board involved in the development of a good risk framework will result in them being provided with the information that allows them to provide real oversight of risk in their operations. Only then will they be confident that they can discharge their duties effectively and lighten the load on the courts at the same time. They say 'shit happens!' and they're right, even good risk management can't always guarantee protection but organisations can earn the right to avoid much of the stench when it hits the fan by showing how appropriate decisions were made based on the information at hand, despite the outcome.

Case Example

The management team for a Formula 1 Grand Prix were interviewing potential consultants to improve risk management after the death of a track marshal in a freak incident in the previous year's race. That event had seen the organisation come under heavy attack during the Coroner's inquest.

With this in mind, the CEO asked the consultant if they had been employed a year earlier would that marshal be alive today. The consultant, unlike all the other candidates, answered that the marshal would still have died—but the Coroner would have found it a lot harder to attack the organisation.

It appears that the CEO knew that this accident was not reasonably foreseeable and that any consultant who thought that it was would not be able to focus available funds to the most effective risk reduction areas. The trend-bucking consultant got the job.

Strategically, Risk is Positioned in a Negative Way ...

After compliance, the biggest driver of risk management in most organisations is as a defence against blame for not dealing with hazards. How much better it would be if the organisation's primary driver were to deliver better returns to shareholders. This situation is quite understandable because the majority of risk management systems around aren't capable of delivering the latter anyway. In truth, simplistic risk management systems are little use in delivering ass-covering too, because a clear basis for the decisions taken is invariably absent.

At first glance, this defensive versus progressive debate appears to be a simple matter of glass half full or half empty, but it's considerably more than that. The outcome for the defensive approach is measured by the reduction in the losses suffered and in the alternative, by the enhancement of shareholder value. Both come directly from the performance difference between before and after risk management and neither changes the validity of the risk management process, but it sure as hell changes what executive management want to see in the way of reporting and the kind of data they need to make decisions. This changes the risk management framework considerably.

Another example—if management wanted to know the projected profitability generated from opex and capex spends and found out that one was returning twice the other per dollar spent—you can see how it might change the business strategy significantly. However, applying risk management in the way most organisations do, from the bottom-up and in whatever chunks deemed fit by each department and using the simplest of risk assessment tools, management will never get to see that picture. They will never be able to directly compare the value of a new project or venture (a risk intensive guess at future value) against investing funds in current assets and programs (capturing what the organisation has historically let slip away).

Of course, all organisations will need a balance of efficiency improvement and new revenue earners, but the mental shift of seeing the whole picture in one go is immense. Organisations spend money to make more money or otherwise improve shareholder value—they are winning more, not losing less—opportunities are seen as the majority of assessments, not a small minority.

Let's get some clarity around the terminology—in the context of an organisation "opportunity" is not the inverse of "risk". "Risk" in an organisation is 'the effect of uncertainty on its objectives'. These uncertainties impact an organisation through events that may arise from circumstances that are hazards (or threats) or they may be opportunities. The event caused by a threat will probably have negative outcomes (consequences) such as unfavourable exchange rate movements causing the cost of inputs to rise. The event caused by an opportunity will probably have positive outcomes such as a favourable exchange rate movement lowering the cost of inputs.

Imagine risk as a coin spinning in the air—it can fall heads or tails. Only when you place your bet can you define what is "opportunity" and what is "threat". Risk is neither good nor bad; it's simply a spinning coin. When time allows it to come to rest, there is no risk, just good news or bad news dependent on the call you made. The outcome of the realisation of the uncertainty is relative to the objectives that were set.

Turning Defence into Offence

In summarising this chapter, perhaps a sporting analogy can help. Competitions are rarely won by an individual or team that thinks in terms of defence and offence (attack) as stand-alone processes. The inability of an individual or team to understand quite how their opponent seemed to absorb an attack and morph it into a position of strength means they are not likely to be winners. Most organisations are in such a situation today. Risk management is not just defence; it is the springboard of attack for the sportsman and the entrepreneur. If your organisation suffers the common affliction of seeing risk management as a passive system, each chapter in this book will play a part in restoring your organisation's health.

2. Organisation Risk Management in a Time Warp

The Basic Process with Lipstick

> 'Where lipstick is concerned, the important thing is not color, but to accept God's final word on where your lips end.'
>
> Jerry Seinfeld

Everyone is familiar with the basic risk management concept; we all use it every day. Whether crossing a road or climbing a mountain we instinctively identify and assess hazards, decide on an action and then get on with it. But when these actions steps are applied within organisations, we move to the realm of risk bandits, where simplistic risk tools are made to look more sophisticated than they really are.

Over the last two decades risk bandits have resorted to cosmetics in an attempt to pretty up the basic risk management process to look like an organisation-wide risk management framework. It has not worked. Organisation risk management is stuck in a time warp, positioned as a separate and distinct framework producing reports rather than as an integral part of governance interacting with organisation strategy and performance management.

For more than two centuries the Brits have had a saying to cover this situation, 'mutton dressed up as lamb'. Originally used by women to criticise peers that resorted to external decoration to mask the ravages of time, men have now joined the queues for Botox and Collagen injections. Perhaps we shouldn't blame the old risk processes for wanting to feel loved but rather censure the risk bandits that rush to apply their wares.

The apparent logic of the basic process used by organisation risk managers is difficult to fault:

- Identify events that may cause variations from achieving objectives

- Assess the range of outcomes and how often they may occur

- Decide whether to accept the current level of control or act

- Implement that decision

Whilst the logic looks sound, the process ignores the context in which an organisation undertakes these steps. This basic process remains unchanged over decades despite the enormous changes in the organisations that adopt it.

Medium to large organisations today are not just bigger and more sophisticated than ever before, they also have greater geographic coverage (and exposure) and adopt a wide range of models to delegate authority (across diverse cultures) to a wide range of operating units (and compounding threats).

This is enabled today by sophisticated information technology in processing and communication that has been revolutionised in the last decade. No organisation used the Internet in the early 1990s now they all do. Organisations now utilise the advantages, and take the risks of, engaging with social media, yet the basic organisation risk management process remains unchanged over this entire period!

The lipstick that has been applied primarily involves putting a loose strategic context around the basic process, setting an organisation "risk appetite" and producing risk reports. The fundamental problem is that it's an overlay to the basic process—an afterthought.

So in practice does the basic risk management process manage risks across an organisation? The answer is: to a limited extent in a few cases, and not one iota in most. This is simply not good enough because this lack of substance results in ineffective control over opportunities, regular day-to-day threats and potential business disasters. Ask yourself, what other process would impact these three areas where you would sit back and let it continue as an endorsed business practice?

The most likely outcome of the basic risk management process is that it becomes a historic data collection exercise that provides static periodic snapshots at best, and a rot-riddled foundation of false security more often than not. The effort is primarily directed at populating risk registers that faithfully record all sorts of details about risks and suggested actions but rarely create real value. Specific risk management action may be prompted by this process but it is seldom proactive in nature nor does it have impact throughout the organisation. The process is focused on the past but risk is about the future.

If risk managers didn't invent the term "herding cats" they certainly know the feeling. They are continually frustrated by operating managers who have been nominated as being responsible for specific risk events because there is misalignment with the concept of what that responsibility really means. Operating managers want to ensure that risk is a part of everyday business (outcome focus) whilst most risk managers are more focused on making sure that any promised risk-treatment actions are completed once a month in time for reporting (process adherence). The risk manager's mindset is more one of compliance than excellence

The bottom line is that the formal risk management process as run by risk managers and exemplified by the ubiquitous risk registers, usually works in parallel with an informal risk management process that is how risk is actually managed across the organisation. If you remember your geometry accurately, that means they never intersect. In some organisations the geometric term "skewed" would be more accurate than parallel, i.e. not only do they do not intersect—they are on totally different planes. Risk managers are often sidelined (whether they deserve it or not) because what they do has little impact on what happens in practice. The formal process may be the form but most decidedly not the substance. Even worse the formal process is the shaky foundation for reporting on compliance with organisation policies and regulatory requirements.

For risk to be properly managed across an organisation the risk/return decisions need to be transparent to executive management and the board. It's like changing variables in a spreadsheet to see the impact on the output— executive management and boards need a process that gives them the encouragement and power to test the sensitivity of risk/return decisions and define an appropriate balance to achieve the organisation's objectives.

Interaction means a real time process that permeates the organisation, not a dust-laden rearward looking tome. How can executive management determine how many resources to throw at quality management in the production line if it doesn't know the impact on the outcome of varying the level of quality management resources? General Motors or Ford would probably struggle in the market if they aimed for Mercedes quality at the price they can attract buyers, but they need to ensure their workforce factor this into their decision-making.

The basic risk management process is, and will remain, basic because it is focused on individual hazards and negative outcomes and not on increasing returns from the activities of the organisation. The lipstick, no matter how bright or how glossy, makes no difference because there is nothing remotely attractive to executive management or board members underneath it. Most risk processes are applying lipstick way beyond the lips' end.

Risk Manager Applications Required… Anyone… Please…?

Risk managers across medium to large organisations come from an incredibly wide variety of backgrounds. IT managers usually come from IT backgrounds; accountants and engineers similarly tend to have roots in their own professions, but risk managers in an organisation can be accountants, engineers, actuaries, insurance specialists, lawyers or internal auditors. They are often unsuccessful line managers who are looking for a new way up the career ladder.

Sometimes the incumbents are qualified in risk management, or have at least done some sound risk management courses, but not often. So what do they do? They look at what the organisation is doing, read some articles that are pitched low enough for them to comprehend and apply their intuitive skills to the basic process … it's not that difficult to get by because few people know what a good risk manager actually looks like!

Whilst this wide gene pool could be a source of freshness and innovation, it rarely happens that way. The aura of directors, executive management and regulators in the background usually encourages a don't-rock-the-boat approach.

The outcome is that most organisation risk managers are risk bandits because they use the basic process and claim it is necessary to go to the lowest common denominator to achieve widespread buy-in. It is depressing that sometimes it is the organisation's leadership that is swelling the ranks of the lowest common denominator. In such environments the time warp not only survives, sometimes it thrives.

Risk Reporting; a Riveting Read, Not!

As with the basic risk management process, the apparent logic of the basic internal reporting to boards and executive management used by risk managers is difficult to fault:

- Provide a current assessment of the risks that the organisation faces

- Identify risks that require action to get to an appropriate risk-comfort level

- Provide a status report on risk management actions

Then why is it that the risk management section of meetings of many audit and risk committees and executive management teams is usually a short presentation, few questions, little debate and a sigh of relief when it's over? Now let's get on with the real substance of the meeting!

One reason is that most internal risk management reporting produced by risk bandits involves information that is largely irrelevant, and is not presented in a form that readily enables meaningful analysis. The reporting itself is often implied by the risk manager and inferred by the executive and board to constitute risk management governance; it's a mutually comforting delusion!

Let's have a look at these uncomplimentary claims!

The risk profile is the customary report of the current assessment of the risks that an organisation faces. It's typically the old likelihood and consequence matrix with bubbles positioned to represent the assessment of risks and is so outdated it was probably first used by Noah to assess which creatures great and small would be most threatened by the flood! What stakeholders thought of the process is difficult to ascertain, although it's rumored that Unicorns were pretty vocal as the floodwater rose.

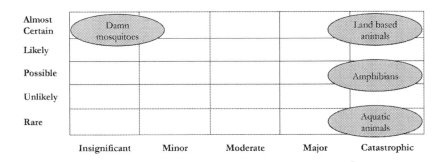

Figure 2.1—Noah's Risk Matrix

The risk matrix is at best a simple screening tool for risk managers. What does this tell members of the audit and risk committee and the executive management team? Does it assist them with the governance over an organisation's risk management? Hell no! It is subjective, process focused and not geared to inform of the reader. Professor Patrick Hudson of Leiden University and creator of the globally recognised Safety Maturity Model calls it 'Pin the Tail on the Donkey' risk assessment and he's not far wrong at all. Ask yourself if you would accept a profit forecast that said costs were "poor", revenue was "good" and profit was "fair" even if the information was presented with traffic light colouring?

It conveys little about the key information needed for proper governance and risk/return decisions. Totally absent is any granularity in the relative importance of each risk within any cell within the matrix. It would also be useful know the level of assessed risk relative to "risk appetite" and trending of risk relative to previous periods.

The second key report is the status report on risk treatment actions. It's typically a spreadsheet that lists improvements that have been promised, with owners and due dates allocated. These risk treatment actions are shown against each risk, often indicating the estimated outcome they will have on the subjectively assessed level of risk … almost always reflecting a drop in risk rating that represents a massive reduction in risk.

These reports are usually very busy, full of ill-defined and often overlapping scenarios, and are at best a stab in the dark whilst wearing sunglasses. Although some useful information to assist governance over an organisation's risk management resides deep within in these horrible reports it is veiled by the almost unhealthy craving to show falling levels of risk assessments that ascribe a degree of achievement in the assessment outcomes that simply does not exist.

Missing is information such as the prioritisation of risk treatment actions based on risk/return considerations rather than subjective risk mitigation without demonstration of worth. Perhaps some current and projected performance data (e.g. revenue, output, etc.) would provide insight into the risk/return action decisions and whether they are really important.

The poor quality of internal risk reporting is a direct result of a process without an effective organisational framework and it's a key indicator that executive management and the board are not in control of their own destiny. They don't know if disaster or a windfall is around the next corner because they are still living within the risk time warp.

Guidance and Standards That Impress Only Their Authors

With apologies to Sir Winston Churchill, never in the field of regulation has so much been written, for the adherence of so many, for the benefit of so few!

Risk management standards, framework definitions and guidance abound. Most countries, most governments, most large organisations and many other institutions have developed extensive documentation of the basis for risk management. These guidance documents are probably too widespread to conclude here that they are all useless, there must be some useful ones amongst them, but we can describe the top three contradictions that illustrate this verbal diarrhea is a major part of the problem.

Forest Versus Trees Contradiction

In considerably more than 90% of organisations the risk forest is managed on a tree-by-tree basis rather than at the forest level with policies and procedures, risk registers and reports all focused on individual risks and not the overall risk position. Indeed, given the overlap of risk scenarios in most registers and risk profile summaries, branch management is a phrase that takes on a new, apt and very worrying meaning. There is no strategy for the forest, only thousands upon thousands of tree inspections and treatments. Those receiving the risk profile report can see the individual trees that are at greatest risk but they can't see if the organisation's risk position is improving or declining.

Risk management guidance documents are intended to improve the performance of organisations yet their foundation is a basic risk management process aimed at individual risk scenarios and not an organisational framework that starts out with the big picture. It's like constructing a railway system by asking residents at each destination where they want to go and giving them the necessary tracks. It sounds great in concept but with no relativity between individual needs it ends up cheap and swift in the planning and wildly expensive and extremely ineffective in the delivery. So does risk management.

Often added as an afterthought are motherhood statements about building a risk culture and embedding risk management. During this phase, risk management is described as needing to be driven from the top of the organisation but the majority of the guidance documents describe a bottom-up process. They are designed to achieve a result on each risk scenario rather than an organisation-wide objective and providing tactical actions across the whole organisation risk profile.

Case Example

The shipping department of a major resource company was very concerned about the reliability of its rail-based product movements and had projects underway to address each of the main worry areas—a flood prone zone here, a bottleneck there. They were working like crazy people to find alternative responses for each problem area, but the real problem was that they had no power over the rail company because they were the only option in that region. The rail company was simply not investing in the line or rolling stock because it only had a five-year government licence and made more money by running a reactive breakdown-based maintenance program than a preventative program.

When the company introduced a meaningful framework and detailed risk assessments they found that transportation could undermine their entire regional operations and posed a much bigger threat to them than the production issues on which they had been focusing. This was because a major production breakdown was an evident painful event, but transportation problems came from scores of moderate events that added up to a far greater issue. Executive management took control of the situation recognising that the shipping department were not empowered to call for a government policy change to give the rail company a tenure that would make asset investment more appealing. It led to the creation of an industry group to lobby government with the backup option of building their own railway to compete with the government's operator.

Glass Half Empty Contradiction

Risk management guidance documents include regular reminders that risk management involves the upside as well as the downside but the focus of all detailed discussion is on hazards and negative outcomes. Had Kipling lived in the risk management era the sign above the Wimbledon dressing-room door would surely have talked of 'Threat and Opportunity' instead of 'Disaster and Triumph'.

In risk management process terms they are one and the same thing—a coin spinning in the air as mentioned in Chapter 1—with the only difference one of current versus future state. "Disaster" is assessed on the basis of protecting what we currently have and "triumph" on the basis of protecting what we hope to get. However, Kipling reminds us we must treat those two imposters just the same and we almost always fail to do so. Upside and the risk/return context doesn't rate a genuine mention in most frameworks and accompanying strategic decisions regarding the allocation of resources is buried by the liberal use of templates to drive a mechanical process.

Deduction Versus Evidence Contradiction

Risk management guidance documents require attestation from lower and middle management that everything is working and the production of historic snapshots of the results of the basic risk management process as supporting evidence. These snapshots and sign-offs are usually provided to executive management and the board even though performance data might indicate that such conclusions are not even remotely justified. The performance data relating to how controls and mitigation actions are impacting key decisions is not required by risk management guidance documents yet it provides the best evidence of how risk management is working. As a result, executive managers and directors continue driving whilst looking only in the rear view mirror, giving scant regard to what's charging towards them.

The generic risk management guidance documents that are probably the most universally used by risk practitioners are the various COSO[1] framework guidance documents, which is the US risk traditionalists holy book, and ISO 31000[2], the Johnny-come-lately European model that has overrun the rest of the world. There are strong diverging views on whether they compete or complement each other, so they are overviewed below.

COSO: a Catalogue Dressed Up as a Framework

The COSO framework is widely used, particularly in the US. Its background helps explain its positioning.

COSO was organised in 1985 and has developed recommendations for public companies and their independent auditors, for the US Securities and Exchange Commission (SEC) and other regulators, and for educational institutions. Its mission is 'to provide thought leadership through the development of comprehensive frameworks and guidance on enterprise risk management, internal control and fraud deterrence designed to improve organisational performance and governance and to reduce the extent of fraud in organisations'.

The COSO Enterprise Risk Management Integrated Framework was issued in 2004, driven largely by a need to address fraudulent financial reporting. Its foundation is the previously issued internal control framework and so it is 165 pages of compliance-based, complex and multi-layered detail directed at prescribing controls for events with negative outcomes. Its financial focus is a direct result of having been authored by auditors, accountants and financial specialists. COSO has commonly been applied to

---

[1] The Committee of Sponsoring Organisations' of the Treadway Commission—COSO is sponsored jointly by five major professional associations headquartered in the United States with representatives from industry, public accounting, investment firms, and the New York Stock Exchange.

[2] ISO 31000:2009 Risk management—Principles and guidelines issued by ISO, the International Organisation for Standardization. ISO is an independent, NGO made up of members from the national standards bodies of 164 countries that develop and publish International Standards.

internal controls and fraud deterrence but its use for risk management is in decline, particularly outside the US.

The infamous COSO framework 3D cube is a psychedelic Borg spaceship that attempts to summarise the framework and is widely criticised for its failure to do so:

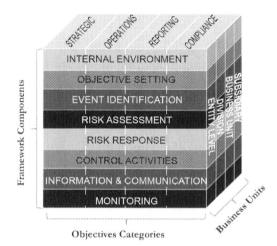

Figure 2.2—COSO Risk Framework Cube

A mechanistic approach is taken—an organisation's enterprise risk management is effective if the framework components are functioning across the organisation's objectives and operating units so that risks are within risk appetite. The objectives categories are strategic, operations, reporting and compliance. The framework's eight components are shown below:

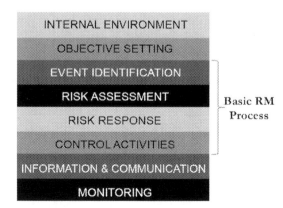

Figure 2.3—COSO Risk Framework Components

The COSO spaceship and its supporting framework remain firmly in the time warp. The basic risk management process is topped and tailed with lipstick for some organisational context but does not constitute a strategic process. The detail below the process is comprehensive and provides a control catalogue as a large checklist, that only its mother could love. The framework suits regulators because they think it drives a compliance response that is evidence based. The response is however driven by risk managers who are not connected to day-to-day risk management activities, and the involvement of executive management with COSO goes as far as learning how it's spelt and, just occasionally, what the acronym stands for.

ISO 31000: an Opportunity Missed

ISO 31000 is not a prescriptive set of rules but a set of principles and generic guidelines on risk management that can be adopted by any organisation. Utilisation of the standard allows an organisation to assert that they have a risk management system in place consistent with the international standard.

The "International Organization for Standardization" is the world's largest developer and publisher of international standards covering areas as diverse as defining the tolerances and loading for ball bearings to requirements for sleeping bags. However, ISO 31000 is designed for self-regulation where compliance is voluntary and is not used for certification or audit purposes. An organisation cannot be held to be negligent because of non-compliance with ISO 31000. Unfortunately, unsubstantiated compliance claims are pretty safe territory because its concepts are very broad and there is no checking process anyway. However, misleading assertions about compliance by publicly owned or facing organisations may be the subject of a legality debate in some jurisdictions.

Despite countless risk bandits in consulting selling "compliance" services, the standard itself clearly states that '**This standard is not intended for certification, regulatory or contractual use**' and the word "compliance" does not even appear in the document.

ISO 31000 was largely sourced from the Australia/New Zealand standard AS/NZS 4360:2004 which was first published in 1995 and was then increasingly adopted around the world. It became international standard ISO 31000:2009. It is not specific to any industry or sector and aims to provide a universally recognised standard to replace the huge volumes of risk management guidance documents existing across organisations, sectors and regions.

There are three core elements to ISO 31000:

- Principles for managing risk

- Framework for managing risk across the organisation

- Process for managing risk which consists of the following steps within an environment of monitoring and review and communication and consultation:

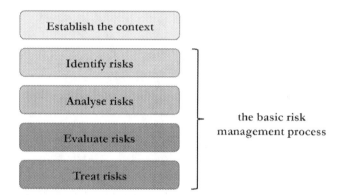

Figure 2.4—ISO 31000 Risk Management Process

The conversion of AS/NZS 4360:2004 to ISO 31000 in 2009 was an opportunity to take forward the good work done all those years ago in Australia and New Zealand and bring the risk management profession out of the time warp. The opportunity was largely missed. The flexibility in the standard, to allow tailoring of its use, has seen risk managers not only continue to produce the lowest common denominator but also assert compliance with an international standard. Many organisations assert, albeit without ISO endorsement, that they are 'in compliance with' or 'consistent with' yet all they have done is to copy ISO definitions and jargon and apply beginner level risk assessment.

Whilst the strategic and organisational context around the framework in ISO 31000 is markedly better than the COSO framework, it is not driving an improvement in the positioning of risk management as an element of governance, including strategy and performance management. Rather the formal risk management process in many organisations asserting compliance continues as a separate and distinct activity from day-to-day risk management. After all, the ability to show a certificate (e.g. ISO 9000 on quality management and ISO 14000 on environmental management) or imply you have one (ISO 31000 on risk management) has created far more smugness than excellence in the last couple of decades.

ISO 31000 and its predecessors have been both a contributor to, and a victim of, the organisation risk management time warp. A fundamental problem with the risk management process as outlined in ISO 31000 and applied by most organisations is that it is set up to help risk managers do one thing only. That is—list things that might happen unexpectedly and decide whether to do something about them or not. This was fine in 1995 when risk management in organisations was a new idea, and when a primary aim of the standard was to demonstrate that there was a common process applicable to both engineers and financial managers. It applied to risks defined as 'the chance of something happening'.

It is not fine 30 years later as Rip Van Winkle awakens. The definition of risk has changed to 'the effect of uncertainty on objectives' but little else in organisation risk management has moved forward. Organisations now need to deal with risk in the majority of decisions they might want to make—the speed, complexity and geographical spread of these decisions would have been unimaginable 30 years ago. Risk management standards and their application have simply been left behind.

The outputs of many organisations using the ISO 31000 framework and process include the puerile risk profile matrix, risk registers and risk reports described earlier in this chapter. Yogi Berra (the famous American baseballer and coach known for his to-the-point quotes) wouldn't have been confused, he'd have seen straight away—it was deja vu all over again.

Stock Exchanges and Regulators in a Fog (Opportunities Mist)

The featherweight impact of regulations on organisation risk management progress is best shown by an analysis of risk management related company regulations and stock exchange listing requirements. In broad terms these requirements fall into two categories, those relating to financial reporting risks and those relating to corporate governance.

Financial reporting regulations are of course designed to ensure that shareholders are provided with reliable financial reports. In most jurisdictions this involves not only complying with accounting standards but also that internal controls are effective in the systems producing the source financial data. Some regulations recognise the link of these controls to risks and add effective risk management to the requirements.

The regulatory approach of adding risk management to the internal control mix tends to reinforce a focus on dealing with hazards (or threats) and potential negative outcomes with a view to ensuring the safeguarding of assets or protecting investors' capital. Whilst this focus may be appropriate for financial reporting regulations it sometimes flows on to the corporate governance regulations where this one-sided focus is less appropriate.

The second category of risk management regulations relating to corporate governance is where regulators struggle. Some adopt a very narrow approach to corporate governance as being about structures, systems and controls and that produces a focus on hazards and potential negative outcomes. The more enlightened approach is that corporate governance is about directing an organisation to achieve its objectives so that structures, systems and controls are just part of the overall risk/return decision framework.

The role of the board in risk management is also part of this second category of regulations where regulators struggle. Should they be 'part of the process?' or 'approve it?' or 'review it?'' or just 'oversee it?' Let's apply the reasonable person test.

If you as an individual invested a significant percentage of your wealth into a company's shares, what sort of regulatory requirements would you expect as to how those funds are used? As the management of those funds is delegated to the board then shouldn't it be the board that take on responsibility for how the funds are used? But what should that responsibility be? Is it reasonable for the responsibility to be limited to having systems in place to not lose it? Surely it should be more than that! Do hospitals just aim to not kill patients with golden staph, or to render them healthy again? Do professional gamblers simply aim not to lose, or maximise profit?

You have invested knowing that there is potential for gain or loss because that's how commerce works. So it is reasonable—nay essential—to expect the company to take on risk but in the context of getting a commensurate return. It is often said that you can't regulate good decision-making. It is possible, however, to regulate that decisions are based on sound systems that optimise the risk/return balance rather than just defending the current status. So let's look at the regulations.

Below is an analysis of risk management related company regulations and stock exchange listing requirements in the US, Australia and the UK using the two categories, those relating to financial reporting risks and those relating to corporate governance. The analysis excludes specific industry regulations such as those in place in most countries for the banking and finance sector. In summary it looks like this:

	Financial Reporting Risks	**Corporate Governance**
US:		
Approach	Prescriptive overkill	Principle based underkill
Outcome	Pass or fail test result	Little comfort for investors
Australia:		
Approach	CEO / CFO sign-off	Generic principles
Outcome	Boilerplate disclosures	Boilerplate disclosures
UK:		
Approach	Narrow requirements	Enlightened principles
Outcome	Compliance disclosures	Extensive disclosures

Figure 2.5—Summary Of Risk Management Regulatory Approaches

This range of approaches and outcomes means that the action that is needed to break free of the time warp in organisation risk management in this global age is highly unlikely to come from regulators.

Navigation Guidance

Readers not wishing to understand the detail behind any or all of the country approaches summarised in Figure 2.5 can speed-read the next few pages without losing the plot for the remainder of "Risk Bandits". Rejoin us at 'Professional Snouts in the Trough'.

US: Overkill/Underkill Imbalance (Odorous Sox)

SOX, the pet name for the Sarbanes-Oxley Act 2002, has done for risk management what the movie, 'Jaws', did for shark conservation.

SOX was a reaction to a number of major corporate and accounting scandals such as Enron and WorldCom when the US in 2002 enacted a wide range of measures implemented by the SEC. The key requirement fitting neatly into our first category, financial reporting risks, is that management of listed entities and their auditors must sign-off on the adequacy of the company's internal control on financial reporting. It's called a SOX 404 sign-off as it is required by Section 404 of the SOX legislation (along with Section 303). What's so bad about that, you might ask.

The main problem with SOX 404—despite the SEC trying to simplify it—is the mechanistic nature of the process. Thousands of pages of rules and guidance describe a top-down process involving a risk assessment of the significant financial information flows and an assessment of the controls using a recognised framework such as COSO. The SOX 404 assessment involves testing the design and operating effectiveness of each of these controls. It's a pass or fail result! A material weakness and you fail.

So how does all this relate to the organisation-wide risk management process, particularly in regard to being part of a world where time elapses and evolution occurs? The SOX 404 sign-off only relates to controls over information flowing into the financial statements, and whilst this delineation is problematic, it does mean a good part of the strategic, operating and compliance information flows are outside its scope. Nevertheless financial reporting controls are still a significant component of the overall risk management and control structure in any organisation so the SOX 404 work is relevant to risk management across the organisation, although not in its entirety. There are three key aspects to the impact on the organisation risk management time warp.

Firstly, SOX 404 drives a mind numbing mechanistic approach for the sake of compliance. Some consultants and even management have tried to portray SOX 404 as a base from which to extract value—to use a good Aussie expression—they must be dreamin' mate!

Secondly, performance data around the impact of these controls is ignored, yet this information could provide a much better indication of operation of controls.

Thirdly, SOX 404 is only concerned about whether each control is effective, not whether it's appropriate for the level of risk—the risk/return decision. It's a bit like setting acceptance criteria for a brake without knowing whether it is being applied to a sedan, race car or semi-trailer. Does anyone expect or even want semi-trailer brakes on their company car? The SEC is focused on the processes to ensure companies accurately disclose what has happened to your money. There is no focus on the adequacy of processes that determine how your money was spent. It's hospital performance measured on the lowest number of mistakes and not the highest number of healthy people leaving the wards.

Enough of SOX, let's look at our second category of US risk management related company regulations and stock exchange listing requirements, those relating to corporate governance. The contrast of the approach to this aspect relative to SOX is staggering, as we move from overkill to underkill.

The SEC approved rules relating to board leadership structure and the board's role in risk oversight require disclosure of 'The extent of the board's role in the risk oversight of the company'. The guidance suggests this might include how the board administers its risk oversight function, such as whether the individuals who supervise the day-to-day risk management responsibilities report directly to the board as a whole or to a board committee or how the board or committee otherwise receives information from such individuals.

Also relevant are the New York Stock Exchange (NYSE) corporate governance rules that require the audit committees of its listed companies to 'discuss policies with respect to risk assessment and risk management'. The related commentary includes 'While it is the job of the CEO and senior management to assess and manage the company's exposure to risk, the audit committee must discuss guidelines and policies to govern the process by which this is handled'.

So for NYSE listed companies, the board is only required to disclose its structure and role in risk oversight and discuss risk management policies. There is no requirement to be part of it, approve or even review it so most listed companies go for the minimalist approach with their disclosures even if the board do get involved and approve or review risks. Had the White Star

Line directors been on board the Titanic they could have complied with NYSE current rules and 'Nearer my God to thee' would still have been the last song they ever heard.

Separately the SEC does require companies in annual 10-K reports (which are available to the public), to make quantitative and qualitative disclosures about market risk and discuss the 'most significant factors that make the company speculative or risky'. These disclosures are increasingly informative but of course are focused on hazards and negative consequences and generally little is disclosed about the relative importance within the wide range of different disclosures. As a result, annual report readers will recognise some as standard industry risks which are there simply there to cover all eventualities, no matter how minor or obvious, and may well assume the "real" exposures are of similarly small import.

Australia: Generic Principles, Unclear Impact

Australia's parallel to SOX are the Corporate Governance Principles and Recommendations issued by the ASX Corporate Governance Council (ASX CGC). The Third Edition of these principles was issued in March 2014 effective for balance dates beginning on 1 July 2014. The ASX CGC was convened by the Australian Securities Exchange (ASX) as an independent council, comprising mainly of professional bodies, to develop and issue principles-based recommendations on corporate governance practices (the Principles).

ASX listed entities are required to report against the Principles on an "if not, why not" basis—if they are not adopted then the reason must be disclosed. The Principles have become the generally accepted benchmark for corporate governance guidelines in Australia and are also widely used by organisations outside listed entities such as government bodies as well as medium to large unlisted companies, professional bodies and associations.

Principle 7 contains the risk management recommendations under the generic principle that entities 'should establish a sound risk management framework and periodically review the effectiveness of that framework'. Principle 4 contains a recommendation in relation to reporting on risk management.

Recommendation 4.2 works together with Section 295A of the Corporations Act 2001 for our first category of risk management related company regulations, financial reporting risks. The relevant aspect of the recommendation is that the board should disclose that they have received certification from the CEO and CFO that the financial statements are founded on a sound system of risk management and internal control and that the system is operating effectively. This disclosure is not audited.

In a sense Recommendation 4.2 is shallower than SOX 404 being principles based and in not requiring formal procedures to produce a sign-off. However, it is also broader than SOX 404 in that the coverage of the risk management system is included in the sign-off in addition to internal controls. Also following a change in the Third Edition of the Principles the sign-off is no longer limited to just financial reporting risks.

The impact of Recommendation 4.2 (and its predecessor, Principle 7.3 from the Second Edition) is disappointing—disclosures about the certification are compliance boilerplates with very few describing any departures or mentions of risk management systems being under-developed. The level of work behind the certification is under-whelming. Some CEOs and CFOs sign-off based on their day-to-day knowledge, some receive completed questionnaires from process owners and very few go any further. But almost every company signs-off with a clean bill of health. The extension of coverage beyond financial reporting risks in the Third Edition has been introduced without a discernable whimper from listed entities—evidence that it is generally given only scant attention.

It simply is not credible that every risk management system is sound and operating effectively, whether in relation to just financial reporting risks or more generally. Certainly not the formal risk management system run by risk managers, perhaps it is the informal "we know this business like the back of our hands" risk management systems that are sound and operating effectively. After all the CEO and CFO are more involved with this system than the formal system!

Recommendations 7.1 and 7.2 fall into our second category of risk management regulations—corporate governance. They state that entities should have a committee to oversee risk and that the board or its committee should review the entity's risk management framework at least annually to satisfy itself that it continues to be sound and report such a review has taken place. Interestingly, Principle 7 refers to a sound risk management

31

framework (such as ISO 31000 or COSO) whereas Recommendation 4.2 refers to systems.

These Principle 7 recommendations illustrate the narrow approach to corporate governance as being about structures, systems and controls and provide shareholders with little useful information about how risk management is used to manage risk and return. The commentary to Principle 7 states that it is the role of the board to set risk appetite, oversee the risk management framework and satisfy itself that it is sound. However, there is no requirement to disclose the results no matter how dismal, only that it has occurred.

As with Recommendation 4.2 (and its predecessor, Recommendation 7.3, from the Second Edition) the disclosures for Recommendations 7.1 and 7.2 are compliance boilerplates with very few describing much detail or any departures. Whilst all listed entities should be in a position to be able to state that they are managing business risks, very few could show how their formal risk management system actually achieves this outcome.

The Third Edition of the Principles has also introduced a new recommendation on risk, being Recommendation 7.4, which requires disclosure of any material exposure to economic, environmental and social sustainability risks[3] and how the entity manages or intends to manage those risks. It's amazing that disclosure of these longer-term risks is recommended but no mention is made of disclosure of other risks that are more immediate and probably have greater exposure. The commentary suggests that a Sustainability Report could be used to satisfy this requirement—it's a giant leap for mankind to suggest that these reports have any relationship with risk management. For many organisations they are the finest example of air brushing, creating a look that is easy on the eye but we all know the reality is something different.

UK: Focused Laws, Codes and Principles

In the UK, the relevant company regulatory regime for risk management derives from the Companies Act 2006 and The Corporate Governance Code (the Code). They are given authority under the London Stock Exchange

---

[3]   "economic sustainability", "environmental sustainability" and "social sustainability" are defined to be within the concepts used in sustainability reporting.

(LSE) listing rules and the Code is implemented by a regulator, the Financial Reporting Council (FRC). The Code, which is also widely adopted by organisations that are not listed, recognises that corporate governance is not just to provide accountability to shareholders but also to manage the company effectively to deliver long-term success.

In our first category of risk management related company regulations, financial reporting risks, the UK requirements are limited. Apart from the usual sign-off on the presentation of the financial statements and accounting standards, the risk related sign-off for directors is that they are responsible for safeguarding the assets and hence for taking reasonable steps for the prevention and detection of fraud and other irregularities. This is a classic regulatory focus on dealing with hazards or potential negative outcomes with a view to ensuring the safeguarding of assets or protecting investors' capital. Boilerplate disclosures are sufficient.

Fortunately, the second category of risk management regulations, corporate governance, are extensive in the UK and lead the way for the US and Australia. These disclosures are normally included in a separate corporate governance statement or strategic review, which is subject to audit review.

The Code, which was updated in September 2014 applying to accounting periods beginning on or after 1 October 2014, adopts a principles-based approach in that it provides general guidelines of best practice in good corporate governance. Listed companies disclose how they have complied with the Code or explain where they have not applied the Code, referred to as 'comply or explain'. This is similar to the Australian approach but the impact of the UK's guidelines on disclosures about risk management is more extensive.

The key relevant part of the Code is 'Section C2: Risk Management and Internal Control', which includes as its main principle: 'The board is responsible for determining the nature and extent of the principal risks it is willing to take in achieving its strategic objectives'. In contrast to the US and Australia, there is recognition that risk management as part of corporate governance goes beyond structures and avoiding hazards to achieving objectives.

Underlying the main principle are two provisions that are relevant to this discussion:

- Provision C.2.1: 'The directors should confirm in the annual report that they have carried out a robust assessment of the principal risks facing the company... The directors should describe those risks and explain how they are being managed or mitigated'.

- Provision C.2.3: 'The board should monitor the company's risk management and internal control systems and, at least annually, carry out a review of their effectiveness, and report on that review in the annual report. The monitoring and review should cover all material controls, including financial, operational and compliance controls'.

The Code requires more than confirmation that reviews of the risks and systems have taken place, it also requires descriptions of the results, the risks and treatment actions.

In addition the FRC, also issued in September 2014 a landmark guidance entitled 'Guidance on Risk Management, Internal Control and Related Financial and Business Reporting' (the Guidance). The Guidance sets out clear responsibilities for the board in relation to risk and internal control including:

- Ensuring the system design is appropriate

- Determining the risk appetite

- Agreeing how principal risks should be managed and the operation of controls to manage risks

- Monitoring the underlying systems to be satisfied they are effective including specifying the flow of information to the board, the extent of delegations and the levels of assurance that it requires

- Integration of the systems with the strategy, business model and business planning processes

The regulations in the UK result in quite extensive disclosures on risk management that are generally tailored to the specific circumstances of each company rather than the boilerplate disclosures common in Australia. This greater transparency on how risk is managed does, however, have a downside, the time-warped nature of risk process becomes much clearer. Much of the disclosure is about the basic risk management process wrapped in risk ownership allocation and committee review structures. The focus is generally on hazards not performance management.

The Companies Act also requires companies to publish a "Strategic Report" that must include a description of the principal risks and uncertainties facing the company. Boilerplate disclosures in this area have prompted FRC concern. Some companies disclose specific mitigation actions against each hazard, but very few explain how they performance manage risk and return 'to deliver long-term success' which is the foundation of the Code.

Professional Snouts in the Trough

As with the wide gene pool of organisation risk managers described earlier in this chapter, risk management professionals emerge from an unbelievable melting pot of backgrounds, skills and vested interests. Professions claiming risk management as their own include accountants, engineers, actuaries, academics, insurance brokers, internal auditors, safety managers plus of course risk managers themselves. Each profession has its own slant on risk management and professional associations, and in many cases multiple competing associations within a profession, protecting the interests of their members. Professional rivalry thrives in the form of lightly veiled turf wars. Herding cats has moved to the forest, now there are three dimensions in which they can roam!

Not only do multiple professions have their snout in the trough from a delivery viewpoint, the users of organisation risk management delivery, such as audit and risk committee members, are as scattered as free-range felines too. These users also have professional bodies that include business councils, directors associations, company secretary bodies, investor and investment analyst groups, and specific interest groups such as property owners, financial service providers and corporate governance guardians.

These wide ranging and competing interests make consultation difficult and consensus pretty much impossible. This is not surprising when you consider that an assessment facilitated by an engineering risk professional may be presented to an accountant and lawyer dominated risk committee by an insurance risk manager. Consultation groups formed to progress organisation risk management inevitably design a camel. Regulations around the world and ISO 31000 do not include technical specifications that are requirements to assert compliance for a damn good reason. The result, however, is that regulations and ISO 31000 are generic with no mandatory features other than broad steps. Whilst the steps are valid—if you don't do them all then you will have a bad result—they are not an automatic route to success—you can do them all and still fall short.

The "warring tribes" nature of risk management professionals helps sustain *Groundhog Day* in organisation risk management.

The Time Warp in a Nutshell

Risk management across most organisations is akin to a couple of weary Cyclopes leading the blind out of the maze. The pair has the same number of eyes as a fully sighted person but remain devoid of depth perception.

Organisation risk management is frozen in time because it is positioned as a separate and distinct activity—and sometimes several distinct activities—requiring a separate and distinct framework. To work effectively it must become an integral part of governance interacting with strategy and performance management. Risk managers, organisation executive management, risk professionals, standard setters and regulators are all missing the mark. Hell, they are not even aiming at the same target.

The current organisation risk management effort is primarily directed at developing a risk history book based on the premise that the only things that might bite us in the future are the things that have had a nibble in the past.

The underlying process is comatose—it does not evolve because it's not interactive as organisations undergo massive change. There is little momentum external to the process to move it forward because the audience for its reports are comfortable not to rock the boat, founded in the belief that this rubbish is all risk management has to offer. Compliance is the iron lung that keeps it breathing.

3. Who's In Charge?

Risk Tennis

'Yours!' That's the call from a doubles player in tennis when relying on their partner to take the shot, but when both partners yell 'Yours!', the point is lost. So it is with the formal risk management system in most organisations—most of the executive management rely on someone else to take the lead and the one that typically does is a risk manager with ample enthusiasm but not the talent to hit a winner.

Figure 3.1—Risk Tennis

The risk manager is in charge of the basic risk management process, executive management teams are spectators more than players and boards are bored. Of course there is a nominated executive that the risk manager reports to, but no one in real power is actively taking control of the risk management framework across the organisation. Shareholders and other stakeholders look on from outside the action and like tennis fans feeling it is bad form to make a noise until the point is lost. Only the occasional '*ooh!*' and '*aah!*' escape their lips.

That's Not a Framework

Many risk managers lay claim to driving the risk management framework across their organisation but all they are doing is topping and tailing the basic risk management process with some organisational cosmetics. This normally involves generic policies, superficial plans and overly detailed procedures for overly simplistic processes, role definitions and rollout procedures, and reporting and monitoring. It's reminiscent of Crocodile Dundee pointing to the inadequacies of the mugger's knife—that's not a framework!

Most guidance documents describe a risk management framework as including a logical structure to organise risk management tactics and resources across the organisation. But it should also be an integral part of corporate governance interacting with the organisation's strategy and performance to direct the organisation to achieve its objectives as part of the overall risk/return demand within its market. When was the last time you 'saw how much return your organisation got for its risk dollar?' or 'saw a non-risk professional get promoted for their risk management achievements?' or 'saw a department reduce their budget this year because previous risk work has increased efficiency and reduced losses?' Any of these and many other examples would indicate a meaningful framework, but instances are rarer than rocking horse poo.

A risk management framework across an organisation must move beyond the basic four steps of risk identification, analysis, evaluation and treatment to become part of organisation decision-making. This can only be achieved by a systematic identification of all the activities and decision points in an organisation that might drive a significant variation from organisation objectives. The organisation's risk management framework should be a substantial part of corporate governance, providing guidance and driving authority to deal with risk in these activities and decision points.

If you are successful enough to be buying a house worth $3 million, then you would probably want to insure it. If the annual premium is $2,000 it is probably not a difficult decision to go ahead but what if the annual premium was $200,000? You'd probably assess your other expenditure needs and conclude that it's not economic—this is a risk/return decision and is an obvious process to go through when the decision is made in a personal context.

But what if this decision is made in a medium size or larger organisation? How does a middle management person know how to assess the risk versus the return on behalf of the organisation? The personal view of that manager is not the context of the decision—it's the context of the organisation that is relevant.

Risk managers often deal with this complication through the concept of "risk appetite", which generally means the amount and type of risk that an organisation is willing to accept. The concept is vague and the subject of widespread debate as to how it is defined and implemented, there is no generally accepted approach and painfully convoluted definitions abound. It is focused on hazards and negative outcomes and not on the balance of risk and return.

The fundamental problem is that organisation risk appetite is an overlay to the basic risk management process to help make the basic process fit the organisation context; in essence it's a retrofit. It needs to be part of the design of a risk management framework as an integral part of corporate governance. It should interact with the organisation's strategy and performance to direct the organisation to achieve its objectives as part of the overall risk/return decision framework. More on risk appetite in Chapter 5.

A sound organisation risk management framework selectively applies the basic risk management process within these activities and decision points to achieve the risk/return balance that best enhances shareholder value. It goes beyond delegation of authority and policies and procedures to performance management. More on using risk in performance management in Chapter 8.

Risk Managers: Snake Oil Sellers

The assurance provided by most risk managers to boards and executive management has as much genuine impact on corporate health as snake oil had to those looking for miracle cures in the *Wild West*. This is because it fails to build on the basic risk management process, preferring the altogether more relaxing route of cosmetic enhancement. Not only does it fail to inform and manage risk/return decisions it fails to come to grips with the informal risk management activity that occurs in the organisation. But it gets worse, the basic risk management process adopted by most organisations—asserting consistency with ISO 31000—is fundamentally flawed.

Figure 2.1 illustrated Noah's risk matrix, with bubbles positioned to represent the assessment of risks. Many organisations use this as their sole tool to assess the level of risk based on a subjective assessment of the likelihood and consequence parameter tables.

Let's look at an example to demonstrate the problems.

Think of a large agricultural product processing plant located in a remote area, near agricultural producing land. An expected risk would be the "non-availability of critical spare parts". If the parts are not available then production of say $4 million a day is disrupted until a replacement can be delivered and installed, but the cost of carrying spares for all potential failures on site can be prohibitive. The risk/return decision of the holding of spare parts is likely to be significant to the plant. The likelihood and the financial guidance part of the consequence parameter matrix might look like this for this organisation's current risk framework:

Consequence ➡	Insignificant <$10k	Minor $10k to $100k	Moderate $100k to $1m	Major $1m to $10m	Catastrophic > $10m
Likelihood ⬇					
Almost Certain Multiple times per year	Medium	High	High	Extreme	Extreme
Likely Once per year	Medium	Medium	High	Extreme	Extreme
Possible Every 1 to 3 years	Low	Medium	Medium	High	Extreme
Unlikely Every 4 to 10 years	Low	Low	Medium	High	High
Rare (More than 10 years	Low	Low	Medium	Medium	High

Figure 3.2—Risk Matrix Extract

In such circumstances it is likely that the plant production team and the spare parts stores team have detailed data about the failure rate of parts based on maintenance regimes and work with suppliers for emergency back-up to determine the appropriate holding on site.

In the risk assessment workshop the risk manager wants to force this situation into the risk register, risk profile and status report. Using the above matrix the risk manager suggests that on average the most expensive part fails every two years because this has occurred twice in the last four years and if they did so the lost revenue for three days production would be $12 million based on the average lost production last time it occurred. The Production

Manager informs the workshop that the "mean time between failure" for these parts across all their plants is currently about six years and usually a replacement is in stock or quickly available from suppliers nowadays, so the consequence for the one in six-year event is far less than $12 million. The workshop has another 15 risks to assess in the remaining two hours so further debate is curtailed at the risk manager's suggestion that the worst-case scenario be used 'to be on the safe side'.

The bubble placement in the likelihood/consequence matrix would be "Extreme" in this case, in one of the two shaded cells in Figure 3.2, rather than "Medium" (when the parts are in stock) or "High" (when the supplier provides a replacement within two days) if the Production Manager is right. The site production and spare parts teams are bemused—this doesn't feel right to them because they've fixed the problem that caused the previous two events—but they don't object, perhaps because the risk manager is on a mission from the board. They know the risk assessment won't be considered when the spare parts purchasing decision is made eventually anyway!

The risk manager's assessment is a superficial estimate of one outcome ignoring the real dynamics of the scenario that might cause different parts to fail in future and the new controls in place along the multiple cause and effect pathways that might avert a production loss. The risk status report to the board would list an action to reduce the assessed level of risk by increasing spare parts stocks because it is beyond the organisation's risk appetite. Yet the production and spare parts teams have a sophisticated decision-making process that is probably effective in practice but it is not linked into the organisation's risk management governance framework.

There is another piece of risk banditry in this example that is well disguised by the seemingly unchallenged acceptability of the risk matrix as a risk assessment tool. Look at the graduations on the "Likelihood" scale— each step down the column is roughly three times less likely than the previous step. Who decides which factors to use on these graduations? Of course it's the Risk Manager who has designed the ruler to measure the 100-metre dash—he can simply compress or expand the scale to suit his own fitness but executive management or the board rarely challenge it. Matrices with a factor of three are common for "Likelihood" especially in the so-called "Enterprise Risk Management" practice, but so are matrices using a factor of ten or more. This arbitrary scale is not noticed because the risk matrix is unrelated to the decision-making process.

To return to the snake oil, let's look at why risk managers like to allocate "owners" to individual risks. It makes sense doesn't it? It means there is some accountability in managing those risks.

True in theory but a muddle in practice and often used by risk managers to make it clear that they don't manage risks, their role is "all care and no responsibility"!

Allocation of ownership of risks is usually done by:

- Functional responsibility such as the head of an operating unit or support function being responsible for the risks in that area, or

- Level of assessed risk where "Extreme" risks are allocated to the board and "High" risks to executive management and so on, or

- Consequence basis (e.g. maximum financial parameters, multiple fatality events, etc.) which is the same as level of assessed risk but the likelihood is not factored in, only the maximum exposure

This risk ownership allocation process is symptomatic of the lack of a formal yet value-adding framework in risk management across most organisations. After all who is going to take meaningful ownership of a risk that they feel is influenced too often by the risk manager, as in the spare part example? The allocation allows the risk manager to duck responsibility for individual risks and to be elevated as the drover to herd the cats. Sure, the drover will play the corporate game by following up action plans allocated to owners, but it is likely to be a process check (was it completed?) rather than a value or effectiveness test.

A properly constructed organisation risk management framework would distinguish the important responsibility aspects involving considered delegation to risk owners, control owners and, where necessary, specific action owners. The role of these "owners" is:

- A "risk owner" has day-to-day operational responsibility for taking on a risk and so should have the skills and authority to do so and not just to tick-off the risk manager's action list. Each risk is likely to have multiple control owners

- A "control owner" is the person responsible for the integrity of a specific prevention or mitigation action or control for a particular risk. For example, the environmental scientist seeking an environmental permit for a new production line is a control owner but the risk may relate to production delay not to environmental harm

- An "action owner" is responsible for the implementation of a single action relating to the improvement of a control, where necessary. For example, the project planner who is assigned to reschedule the production expansion to allow more lead-time in gaining the environmental permit

The allocation of responsibility for risks should therefore be part of the whole governance framework of an organisation. Allocation may be to risk owners, control owners and action owners based on the circumstances. It should occur as part of the delegation of risk/return decisions and their application across the organisation, not to help the risk manager show movement—any movement—at the cattery.

Management: the Wise Monkeys

Executive management in most organisations play the wise monkey role in relation to the formal risk management process—they are passive observers. They don't take ownership but they don't criticise too much—a little prodding like a doctor who has already decided you are not seriously ill. It's a necessary evil for compliance, a bit like external audit. They resent the cost and time involved but dare not seek to change as efforts to extract value may be viewed with suspicion by the board. The risk manager is seen as a protected species, with a skill set that is too complex for others to understand and of course with the unspoken endorsement of ISO 31000. Resistance is futile!

C-level managers, when asked what keeps them awake at night; certainly don't think back to the risk profile compiled by the risk manager or even their own risk register. They informally manage the relevant aspects of the organisation using risk/return decisions outside the formal risk management system. Whilst this informal process may work quite well in pockets, there is no attempt or desire to capture such thinking in a formal, transparent and collegiate process that fits into an organisation-wide framework.

But who in the executive team wants to be the risk manager's boss? Most CEOs make their choice clear by not making it a direct report. At least the audit and risk committee chair may get additional compensation for the role.

There is a huge variation across organisations in who has responsibility for the risk manager. It's one of those functions many executives try to duck. Risk management cuts across an organisation so it does not neatly fit into the typical functional structure.

Most commonly in organisations, risk management is given a home in the compliance area under the CLO (Chief Legal Officer) or the CFO (Chief Financial Officer) where it is focused on financial reporting. If risk is seen as safety dominant in an organisation it may find itself under HR, People and Communications or whatever the fashionable label might be at the time of going to press. This structure provides a clue that the risk management function is likely to be more form than substance. Interestingly, the CLO is usually the executive responsible for the establishing and maintaining the delegations of authority (DOA) across an organisation. Unfortunately, the DOA is usually specific to decision-making authority and rarely is used to delegate risk taking.

Some organisations have created the executive role of CRO (Chief Risk Officer). The CRO is more common in the financial sector where risk is often quantified into value at risk and rules abound from central banks and international capital adequacy standards. Whilst the appointment of a CRO means that a member of the executive team has a specific responsibility for risk, the effectiveness is entirely dependent on the level of engagement with the rest of the organisation. It is a great first step, but certainly doesn't guarantee a good outcome especially if it results in even less involvement by other executives.

Some organisations have created the role of CAO (Chief Audit Officer) to bring together risk, internal audit and related cross-functional review activities. There is much debate as to whether risk and internal audit should be separate—if the CAO is responsible for risk management won't the internal audit function be checking on itself? This is really a moot argument because rarely does the risk management function manage the risks, it just provides a simplistic process and tries to marshal the cats within it.

Occasionally, the COO (Chief Operating Officer) is the member of the executive committee to whom the risk manager reports. This is likely to produce more genuine risk management activity rather than form filling but often falls short on the governance and compliance side. This approach may put Dracula in charge of the blood bank because "High" risks might be interpreted as poor operations' management by the CEO or board so they won't see any in the COO's reports.

What this variety in reporting lines in practice tells us is that there is no clear cut answer and hints that risk management is an unwanted parcel looking for a victim when the music stops. It's part of the risk tennis syndrome and illustrates the size of the challenge to manage risk across an organisation. Unfortunately it also means the concentrated focus that is needed to create a meaningful organisation-wide risk management framework is unlikely to come from executive management.

Boards: Bored with Risk

The boards of most organisations struggle with what their role should be in relation to risk management. Board charters are imprecise and often motherhood statements and surprisingly many corporate governance principles provide little help. As we saw in Chapter 2, regulators and stock exchanges have a wide variety of views. The risk section of board meetings for most organisations focuses on poorly presented and rearward looking data prepared by the risk manager and gravitates to a compliance role rather than a focus on governance of the organisation. Boards receive a false sense of security from these reports. They live in fool's paradise if they really believe the reports (ignorance is indeed bliss) but we suspect many see little option other than to choose to do so. No wonder boards get bored with risk.

Survey after survey of boards consistently shows that they are largely dissatisfied with the risk management process within their organisation. Some boards have formed Health and Safety Committees to closely monitor policies, procedures and performance in that area. Why is that necessary? Sure board members want to do the right thing, especially where personal liability of individual directors is involved, but why not rely on the organisation's risk management framework? They can't place reliance on this framework so some boards feel bound to dip down into the detail.

Opinion is split on how boards should operationally handle risk management. One school of thought is that overseeing risk management is a whole of board function and should therefore be done by the whole board. Others believe it is such a specialist area that it's best attended to by a specific purpose committee, which we are referring to as the audit and risk committee. Whilst this operationally-focused debate rages, the much more important strategic question receives very little attention. What should the board's role be in relation risk management?

- Should boards just oversee a process and the risk profile or should they help identify and manage risks?

- Should boards review risk assessments and management plans or formally approve them?

- Should boards sign-off on internal control systems?

- Should boards also focus on risk upsides?

The range of approaches to these issues in practice is staggering. Let's have a look at some examples of prominent organisations from publicly available data on their websites.

Firstly, the world's largest (or second largest depending on the share price of the day) organisation by market value, Apple[4]:

'Review and discuss with management:

- management's program to identify, assess, manage, and monitor significant business risks of the Corporation, including financial, operational, privacy, security, business continuity, legal and regulatory, and reputational risks;

- management's risk management decisions, practices, and activities …'

The committee on behalf of this board reviews but does not approve the program. It also does not set the framework, management does.

Secondly, the world's largest mining company, BHP Billiton[5]:

'At least annually, the Committee will review the effectiveness of the Group's systems of risk management and internal control, identifying and managing risks that are material to the achievement of the Corporate Purpose and the Group's strategy and plans. The Committee will seek assurance from the CEO that … the Group maintains a system to identify, assess and manage

---

[4] Apple Inc.—Audit and Finance Committee Charter (December 2012)
[5] BHP Billiton—Risk and Audit Committee Terms of Reference (January 2015)

risks that are material to the achievement of the Corporate Purpose and the Group's strategy and plans'.

'The CEO, the CFO and their nominees will present … The procedures for identifying material risks and controlling their financial impact on the Group and the operational effectiveness of the standards and procedures related to risk and control, including the submission of the Group's risk profile to the Committee twice per year for its endorsement (supported by regular assurance reports)'.

The committee on behalf of this board reviews the effectiveness of the system for identifying and managing material risks but does not approve them. It obtains assurance from the CEO that the system is in place and endorses the risk profile twice a year.

Thirdly, a key part of the network of one of the world's largest NGOs, World Vision Australia[6]:

'The Board is responsible for considering and approving strategies and policies to ensure appropriate risk management, and monitors compliance of the Risk Management Policy and Guidelines. The Board has delegated its oversight of the Risk Management Policy to the Audit Committee including review of the effectiveness of World Vision Australia's internal control framework and risk management processes'.

This board approves the strategies and policies and also monitors them, but only for compliance.

Finally, the governing body of one of the world's great cities, the City of London[7]:

'The Audit and Risk Management Committee oversees the City of London Corporation's systems of internal control and makes recommendations to the Finance Committee relating to the approval of Annual Statements of Accounts. The Committee also oversees the City Corporation's risk management strategy, anti-fraud and corruption arrangements, to ensure that the Authority's assurance framework properly reflects the risk environment'.

This board oversees the risk management strategy and internal controls but does not approve them.

---

[6] World Vision Australia—Statement On Corporate Governance (2012)

[7] City of London—Audit and Risk Management Committee, Purpose of Committee (2014)

It is clear that there is no generally accepted view on the role of boards in organisation risk management. Many prominent organisations such as sporting bodies and international agencies don't even disclose the role played by the board. It seems that a minimalist approach is the norm, doing no more than is required by law or at least disclosing only the minimum. The individual's posterior is considered—or perhaps just hoped to be—best protected in this way; but is it defensible?

Let's consider the question of what the board's role in risk management should be using the principle of what is reasonable for shareholders, noting that directors act in the best interests of shareholders to achieve the organisation's objectives. We get a vastly different answer to this question depending on whether we take a minimalist approach or an approach based on sound corporate governance. Remember that we are thinking of corporate governance as being about directing an organisation to achieve its objectives so that structures, systems and controls are just part of the overall risk/return decision framework.

	Minimalist Approach	Corporate Governance Approach
Objective	Documentation of avoiding negative outcomes	Achievement of organisation's objectives
Focus	Minimising harm	Optimising shareholder return
Assurance approach	Review management reports	Approve framework and monitor compliance and performance

Figure 3.3—Board Risk Management Approaches

Why is the minimalist approach to the role of directors acceptable? Whilst the above examples of the stated roles no doubt meet the minimum expectations of their regulators, why don't directors go further than the minimum? How can boards seek sign-offs from lower and middle management but not be prepared to provide them themselves? It's all part of the 'Yours!' philosophy, the lack of clarity as to who is responsible for ensuring that risks are actually managed to enhance shareholder value. As we saw in Chapter 2, stock exchange guidelines allow, and in some cases encourage, the adoption of the minimalistic interpretation.

Even if boards do go further than the minimum it's not usually disclosed. There is reluctance within boards to be in the firing line of accusations that they should have caused action to occur on a specific risk. This is understandable when the board has low confidence in the formal risk management process within their organisation. The reluctance to be specific on risk management externally might dissipate if the board were comfortable internally with the organisation's formal risk management process.

The 'Safe Harbour Provision' in the UK and the 'Business Judgment Rule' in the US should assist boards to be more specific about risk management in external reports. However, most boards would be reluctant to rely on these defences as they have little confidence that their organisation's formal risk management process would hold up to legal scrutiny. The formal process should readily meet regulatory tests such as 'knowing information is misleading' or 'reasonable monitoring' or 'following up red flags'—the bar is not set very high.

Whether the boredom of boards with the formal risk management process is a cause or an impact of the limitations of the formal process is not clear. As most boards comprise astute experienced people there is cause for optimism that boards can be an agent of change. Chapters 8 and 9 attempt to identify some pathways for that to happen.

The Risk in Shareholder Value

Whilst owners of organisations have the most to gain from sound organisation risk management, apart from closely held shareholdings, they usually lack the power to push the organisation into moving into the modern risk management world. Owners come in variety of forms, such as individuals, companies, institutional or government shareholders or association members. For convenience we refer to owners of all organisations as shareholders.

Whilst being a shareholder involves risks that are quite separate from the risks faced by the organisation itself—such as changes in the investor's funding costs and liquidity—the organisation's entity level and business risk impacts flow through to shareholders. How does this impact shareholder value?

Shareholder value in commercially oriented companies is intuitively easy to grasp, a return through dividends and capital gains on shares. Some commercial investors also add that this return must be generated responsibly, some go further and say ethically. For other organisations, within the meaning of shareholder value, financial viability is an objective that stands alongside, what is sometimes called "public value", being service delivery to the community, members or other stakeholders. Examples include government departments, sports clubs and not-for-profit NGOs.

We do not see many examples of shareholder calls for changes in the organisation-wide risk management framework. There are however, instances of specific risk management changes brought on by shareholders such as the inputs to executive remuneration packaging. Another example is hedging by gold companies, which is worth a look.

An individual shareholder in a gold mining company manages his or her portfolio within their own risk parameters for aspects such as rates of return, ethics, liquidity and alternatives for the use of funds. But they invest in gold mining because they are seeking the upside and are comfortable with the downside in that sector.

In the 1990s a lot of gold mining companies started hedging against a fall in the gold price, some of this was driven by the need to secure project finance, as financiers were concerned that a price fall would make projects uneconomic. Hedging generally involves removing downside but forgoing upside. Many shareholder institutions were unhappy—they were seeking exposure to the gold price. They had two alternatives—sell their shareholdings or get the companies to change the practice.

Gold hedging is now not common for gold mining companies as shareholders won the day. The alignment of organisational and shareholder objectives was restored—but no thanks to executive or board vision—it took external pressure to achieve it. Shareholders effectively said to boards, 'you are paid to get the optimum risk/return balance right and you patently failed to do so'.

This example helps illustrate why organisation risk management often fails to "enhance shareholder value". If risk management, is managing 'events impacting the achievement of organisational objectives' then the symmetrical flow-on impact to shareholder value does not occur when the objectives are misaligned. There are two obvious situations where this misalignment happens in organisations.

Firstly, where the organisation's risk management activities do not generate the optimum balance of risk and return. Directors of most organisations receive no information as to whether this is occurring because it's not measured—if the optimum balance is achieved it's because of good people doing good things despite the process.

The second situation is where organisations don't communicate the nature of organisational risks to shareholders. Most organisations are bad at this—small surprise given that they can't even communicate well internally in relation to risk management.

Shareholders usually make decisions about the alignment of objectives before the investment decision is made. This assessment can range from gut feeling of an individual investor to sophisticated analysis by institutional investors. If the objectives are assessed as not aligning then the investment will probably not be made—but the organisation won't even register the share price impact as a result. It's all a bit Darwinian with natural selection of shareholders that are aligned with the organisation's objectives. Apart from closely held corporations, shareholders of most organisations are rendered spectators but with only an interrupted view of the risk management main game.

Sway from Other Stakeholders

If shareholders lack the power to push the organisation into moving into the modern world on risk management, perhaps other stakeholders have more direct power?

Some of the changes driven from organisation to organisation through the supply chain around product quality, human rights, environment, health and safety are good examples of the power that external stakeholders can exert on risk management in an organisation. Other examples are the impact of social media on corporate behaviour through brand damage as well as financiers requirements on environment and social impacts on project financing. Generally, however, this stakeholder influence is only targeted at specific risks, rather than risk frameworks, and usually just focused on negative outcomes.

It is a similar story with the impact of insurance brokers on their customers. They usually focus on hazards as part of insurable risk and loss control; whilst they encourage embedding of risk management into business processes they don't impact the organisation-wide framework. Insurers are also the worst possible example of driving whilst looking in the rear view mirror; actually perhaps they are the best example. The industry has been slow to take a position on the impacts of climate change, will they wait to see if the impacts are significant or will they set a base in the market for increased premiums over time? It's not so much a question of whether climate change is real it's more about dealing with the uncertainty.

Some industry bodies establish guidelines for members in dealing with risk management. Governments often go further and have specific risk process requirements for the organisations within their control. Unfortunately, these guidelines and requirements inevitably reside in the risk management time warp.

Perhaps there is hope that ratings agencies or investment analysts may have a broader impact on risk management across organisations. Standard & Poor's (S&P) have had in place for over five years a process to assess organisation-wide risk frameworks of financial institutions and insurers. This was initially focused on risk metrics such as pricing models and value at risk. This now appears to have been expanded to risk-framework maturity assessments and to non-financial institution issuers of equity or debt instruments.

It appears to be still very early days for ratings agencies and investment analysts in having a role in risk-framework assessments, but one can't help but wonder if would they perform the role any better than they have performed in their traditional roles in recent years? In any case, there is little evidence that they are yet having any meaningful sway on organisation risk management across the companies they assess.

No One is In Charge Unless ...

The conclusion from this chapter is that for most organisations no one is in charge of risk management. Risk managers administer the process—unfortunately that process is flawed—but it's in their own interest to keep it simple. Executive management usually manages individual risks quite well as part of their day-to-day activities but have little involvement in the formal process and dare not criticise it. The board is either deluded that the formal system is working or is dissatisfied but unsure what to do.

This vicious circle continues unless the board demand change from their executives. This does not mean the board have to increase their detailed involvement; it's more about setting objectives and oversight of implementation. Hopefully as this happens and boards become satisfied with internal risk management impacts they will be more comfortable with meaningful disclosures for shareholders.

4. Risk Management Fads and Fashions

Survival of the Cutest

Peer pressure on what is fashionable in risk management was highlighted in Chapter 1 when discussing integrated software solutions, but now let's look at how little these fashion changes are improving risk management. In almost every case where a "new solution" in risk management has been found, the need for improvement has been accurately identified but the resultant "solution" has been designed to be attractive, simple to understand and targeted to the widest possible audience. As a result, it fails to effectively address the need that was originally identified.

It really does amount to consumerism at its most effective. Like fashion it only takes an imaginative tweak here and there. 'Collar a little longer sir?' or 'shall we do away with it altogether this time around?' High wasted and braces … no, even better, high wasted, braces *and* a belt. Our grandfathers must have been fashion icons years ago and we were too young to recognise it.

In the early days of the risk management tsunami there was a short-lived fight between the risk matrix and the "risk nomogram". In those days both were paper-based exercises. The contest was much like the famous battles between VHS and Beta for video recording supremacy in the 1980s and between eight-track and cassette tapes for car audio supremacy in the 1970s. Whilst popular belief today is that Beta and eight-track were the better quality systems, it was VHS and cassettes that won the day. The winners were judged on marketing prowess, not suitability for the job at hand.

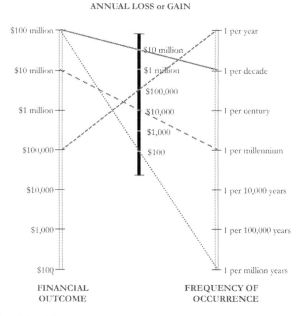

ANNUAL LOSS or GAIN

Figure 4.1—Risk Nomogram

In many ways, and providing you weren't an investor of the losing system, it really didn't matter. Both were seen as sound and revolutionary compared to what had gone before. The step-up for the public was real no matter who won and lost.

Perhaps that was also the case with the risk matrix v. risk nomogram battle, even though the latter, with a bit of careful construction, didn't restrict users to crudely sized cells and very ambiguous descriptions for consequence, likelihood and risk values. In addition, it laid down the foundation for assessing cost/benefit (and ALARP[8] for safety risk) when considering what to do and just as importantly, what not to do, in regard to potential risk reduction measures.

The early use of the nomogram most commonly assumed three variables: "Severity", "Exposure" and "Probability" and, whilst logical, the "Exposure" and "Probability" estimation was often difficult to interpret for risk workshop teams which reduced its attraction. Nevertheless, with some better clarity in defining the variables, by the end of the 1980s, with the help of computers, the nomogram's greater inherent potential could have been realised with ease.

---

[8]   ALARP stands for "as low as reasonably practicable" and means the cost involved in reducing the risk further is clearly disproportionate to the benefit gained.

Today it is alive in only a few quarters but Noah's risk matrix and its visual appeal to the workforce meant it won the battle without breaking a sweat. It was greatly assisted when the first edition of the Australian and New Zealand standard AS/NZS 4360—the predecessor to ISO 31000—was released in the early 1990s with only one example of a risk assessment methodology in sufficient detail to be readily applied. Few readers took heed of qualifying text elsewhere that it was but one option at the lower end of the sophistication scale.

So we have just argued Darwinism over the suggestion in Chapter 2, that Noah invented the risk matrix and got lost in the bubbles. Nevertheless, to ensure that we don't spoil a good metaphor we will continue to sparingly attribute its invention to Noah.

It Comes and Goes

This chapter started out by explaining that most risk management fads and fashions are prompted by a genuine need, even if the proposed solution fails to deliver in the end. Let's have a look at some of the needs.

Need 1—Executive Management Can't be Expected to Monitor Everything

So how can executives and directors detect and monitor risk "hot spots"? It was decided that we needed a "heat map" to give executive management an at-a-glance indication of where to focus their oversight. This particular innovation was introduced by the most respected risk authorities (at least as perceived by executive management) and the big four accounting firms, management consultants and major risk software developers kept the executive and board happy for years with it.

What springs to mind when thinking about the heat map is that it is a magic trick designed, not for kids, but for busy executive management and boards. In the movie 'The Prestige', Cutter, a magician's right hand man, is played by Michael Caine and he describes the three steps in a great magic trick. Imagine Caine's cockney accent pronouncing, 'The first part is called "The Pledge". The magician shows you something ordinary: a deck of cards' (or a risk matrix perhaps?). 'He shows you this object. Perhaps he asks you to inspect it to see if it is indeed real, unaltered, normal. But of course … it probably isn't'.

The second act is called "The Turn". The magician takes the ordinary something and makes it do something extraordinary. Enter the heat map. 'Now you're looking for the secret … but you won't find it, because of course you're not really looking. You don't really want to know. You want to be fooled'. So far in the magician tale, the heat map is shaping up to be a great trick. Executive management aren't really looking, they don't really want to know. What they do know is that it's unreasonable to ask them to look a dozens of risk events on the risk matrix in what looks like a wall built of a child's building blocks. A far more sophisticated diagram is needed where they only need to focus on a small red area in the top right hand corner. How very appropriate for such busy people and how very impressive is the trick that delivered this solution.

Sadly, there is no third part of the heat map trick, "The Prestige". This is where you dramatically turn the extraordinary back into the ordinary; it served no purpose because nobody really wanted it. The simple truth is the heat map was never a great feat in the first place. Figure 4.2 helps you spot the hidden step, but you probably already knew it.

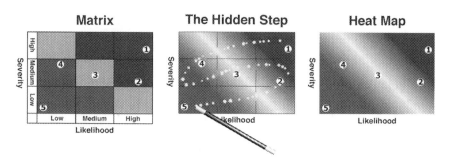

Figure 4.2—Heat Map Prestige

Some of the heat map providers had a greater degree of finesse than others, for example changing the edges of the risk contours from straight lines to arcs to imply mathematical precision, but in truth the heat map never was a great trick, just a transient distraction at a little fairground. It's not even the matrix on steroids, at best it's the risk matrix with designer labelling compliments of the big accounting and consulting houses.

The solution never even tried to change the quality of the assessment for the higher risks and never sense checked what came out of the matrix workshops. It simply regurgitated whatever fodder had been thrown into its computer chip.

The question is 'why didn't anyone see it as such?' Perhaps they did and just didn't care, but the big end consulting firms certainly knew their audience well and perhaps, they knew that they didn't have to be such great magicians to be successful.

Sadly, whilst the identified need to provide executive management with Google Earth oversight (including zoom) of the corporate world of risk was very real, it was never going to be sated by the heat map.

Need 2—To Ensure that Opportunities Don't get Excluded

Much of the fanfare about ISO 31000 on its launch was that it recognised that risk management had to maximise "opportunity" as well as manage "risk". Many consultants and risk managers over recent years have failed to explain exactly how risk assessment delivers opportunity. The only genuine approach we have seen is to assume that the organisation has committed to delivering the opportunity and wants to do a risk assessment on it to ensure the potential rewards don't disappear before they are realised. It's a plain old risk assessment of a hypothetical problem, not a brave new world.

It is of course possible to set an opportunity matrix similar to a risk matrix with consequence and likelihood of positive outcomes plotted as bubbles. This is hardly risk management—as noted in Chapter 1 in the context of an organisation "opportunity" is not the inverse of "risk". If risk events are properly assessed, in some cases the consequence or outcome may be positive or just a lower negative outcome net of positive impacts. This is clearly part of risk management but it's not delivering "opportunity" it's simply valuing the risk outcome of a decision.

Perhaps what the consultants and risk managers are really trying to achieve—albeit unclear if true—is the change from a defensive frame of mind to the entrepreneurial state covered in Chapter 1. If so, the concept is way beyond the broad steps covered in any depth within the ISO 31000 process so the proponents are going to have to move outside of the sheltered zone if they want to progress.

However, it is more likely that some risk practitioners are trying to capture the commercial opportunity represented by the "risk and opportunity" phrase to make some supplementary consulting income. The thinking goes a bit like this … If I can use prompt words to help identify risk events—part of hazard identification in the Risk Analysis step in the ISO 31000 basic process—why can't I provide a different set of prompts to identify opportunities? Whilst we are not saying that this can't be done, in fact we know it can, we are arguing that risk management professionals should learn to do their day job properly before they start to chase pastures new.

Nevertheless, risk bandits can't be accused of overestimating the intelligence of their clients as it has brought them considerable reward to date, so why not go for it? Our response to them is that it won't produce the best value for the investor. We must concede however, that we really don't fancy our chances of changing their approach.

Shortly we will start to unpack how the opportunity side of the risk fulcrum can be effectively realised.

Designer Labels and Content

We, as the authors of this book, make strange literary bedfellows. Rob has a Big Four pedigree and knows the behaviours and needs of the boardroom very well. Tony is an artisan who understands in detail the delivery methods of risk management and has developed risk tools that have been used around the world. It is no surprise to either of us that we never met in our long careers in the same city until 2007, because we know that the client representative that buys the services of one rarely buys the services of the other.

It might be said that Rob provided credibility-critical services directed at risk management oversight to his clients and Tony provided accuracy-critical services directed at risk management mechanics to his clients. These are not uneven values. KPMG origins go back to 1870 through William Barclay Peat and for well over a century their credibility has shown itself to be well earned. The KPMG, or any Big Four, logo on a finding adds considerable gravitas to any client that commissions a review.

Tony's risk company Qest Consulting lasted for just 13 years before being acquired by a large infrastructure-engineering firm. It was only ever known to people involved in risk management activities but it did work for some of the world's very biggest organisations and acquired Det Norske Veritas (DNV) risk operations in Australia to make it the highest profile Australian risk firm early in the 21st century. It was good at assessing and addressing risk, and little else.

Put in the simplest of terms, sometimes it would be smarter for clients to hire Rob and sometimes it would be smarter to hire Tony, depending on what they needed. The trouble was, to get a great overall framework they needed both of us—or two people like us. However, when the risk industry grew at its fastest, we were all flat out making money and the risk framework was simply seen as a specification on how to do risk assessment, rather than helping an organisation to actually see a more complete picture of the operations and to steer it with the help of risk management.

In all honesty, if we wind the clock back a decade, we didn't even know what we didn't know about each other's contribution to good risk management, which presumably makes it a quite fashionable unknown unknown! The introduction of this book is really quite accurate in its assessment of the two of us together as constituting one risk guru. Consider this, if we were considered among the best in their respective roles, and have only recently worked out a better way, then there can be little surprise that risk management isn't anywhere near the place it needs to be. It is very sad however that the time it has taken to start the awakening has been so slow that most of the best people in management believe that risk management died in the same train wreck as Santa, the Easter Bunny and the Tooth Fairy.

We do believe in the future of risk management and thankfully there are still a few remarkable executive managers out there that are listening.

Quality v Quantity of Risk Management

One fad that never totally dies is that more is better, and risk management has entered this phase big time. More assessments, more actions, more critical controls, more audits, more reports. What this means is that the investment in risk management is higher than ever before and the ROI is at its lowest.

The risk matrix and its cosmetically enhanced variant, the heat map, have been the major culprits in this focus on quantity. Shallow risk assessments can be done quickly with these tools so the temptation has been to go for bulk to avoid accusations of not considering all risks.

Most organisations spend enough on risk management already; it just needs to be spent far more wisely. People in these organisations are doing risk assessments that overlap other risk assessments, risk assessments of causes (e.g. "loss of key people") and control failures (e.g. "insurer refuses to pay") instead of risk events (e.g. "change in market share", "project schedule variation", "take-over different to market value"). Many organisations also risk assess things that don't need assessing because it's plain for the eye to see the issues. For example, there is no requirement in most jurisdictions to do a risk assessment for a job safety assessment (JSA) yet the majority of organisations call for it. If you still believe everyone understands the risk matrix just review a hundred random JSAs, it will probably bring you to tears. And while time is spent on needless assessment the time being spent answering the simple question 'what can go wrong and how can I avoid it?' is reduced.

Many organisations have risk registers today with hundreds of assessments included, but an organisation that defines more than 40 or 50 risks as material, each with a handful of critical controls associated with them, won't have the time to monitor anything effectively. Risk reduction actions are also often a shambles. More than half the commitments to risk reduction will make little difference to the level of risk faced by the organisation, and many will make none at all. You may have seen risk register entries that say '*consider* the benefits of a predictive maintenance system', '*raise the commitment* to debt recovery activities' or '*undertake a review* of expenditure overruns'. They commit to absolutely nothing that will actually reduce risk levels and hinder any focus on measuring the impact of these commitments. It's all about being seen to be doing something, anything, almost regardless of impact.

From an organisation point of view there are only three kinds of risk. Those that are high risk and should make our eyelids twitch; those that are low risk but should they actually occur, would cause all hell to break loose (they won't have an anxiety twitching effect but they probably should do); and those that can't really hurt us a great deal no matter what happens. Most risks are in the last category and they are the only ones we can forget about in the organisation risk register. Let lower levels of the business control them as they see fit, they're the ones we can afford to act responsively to. It's the ones where we need to be proactive or very watchful that we need to focus on at the senior level and 40 risks isn't too many for any board to have a decent handle on, given effective distillation of results and progress.

The Workshop Fad

Workshops can be like committees in devolving responsibility to shield individuals from criticism when designing a horse with humps and the capacity to spit. Most risk management processes involve extensive use of workshops and in recent years the workshop fad has become a favourite tool of risk managers.

Risk workshops can usefully achieve three objectives:

- Provide information to participants because they probably won't read poorly presented irrelevant risk information. At least in a risk workshop participants usually feign interest

- Engage participants so that they feel part of process and perhaps even get on board with the output

- Induce interaction of participants so that a range of skills and experiences can be applied to analysis more efficiently than through separate one-on-one meetings or individuals separately reviewing documents

Risk bandits have, however, taken the workshop fad to another level—in many organisations the risk workshop has become the primary risk assessment tool. The positioning of bubbles on Noah's matrix is often determined in a workshop, let's ignore the facts and run with consensus opinion. It's a festival of democracy! You may have even seen electronic voting devices used to speed up the process even further.

These workshops facilitate reaction-based assessments from people who often don't have familiarity with the details necessary for analysis. Like democracy, we celebrate the fact that everyone affects the outcome, regardless of knowledge. As with democracy, sometimes those that talk the loudest or have the most power sway the opinion to the detriment of the quiet person that may have a very important point to make. It's a bit like the judging of diving at the Olympics where the highest and lowest scores from judges are dropped and the rest averaged. But what if the low scoring judge had the greatest insight and saw something the others missed?

It gets worse! Risk workshops are often facilitated by an external risk bandit brought in by the internal risk bandit manager under the guise of objectivity and specialist expertise. In reality it's a further shield from criticism. The consultant often lacks detailed knowledge of the organisation and usually does not distribute any pre-analysis information before the workshop. This not only ensures participants have an open mind for the discussion but also that any analysis is uninformed.

There is no doubt that risk workshops, in support of detailed analysis and interviews, have a useful role in identification of risks and specific aspect analysis at the detailed level or in review at the executive management or board level. The extension of the workshop to being the primary tool for risk assessment by some risk bandits ensures the level of precision of the output is insufficient for any meaningful use. It is strong evidence that the risk process is being used to demonstrate compliance and not to enhance performance.

Fashions in Risk Assessment Engines

The subjective positioning of bubbles on a likelihood and consequence matrix to represent the assessment of risks, first floated for prospective passengers of the Ark, is the most commonly used example of what is referred to as "qualitative risk assessment". Despite the irreversible loss of the Unicorn species that was about to happen Noah probably had no better option than to undertake the flood risk workshop with a matrix. However, most directors, audit and risk committee members and executive managers are today informed on their biggest risk issues by bubbles on a matrix. They must surely wonder—'is this really all there is?'

There is an alternative to qualitative risk assessment but it's just not as fashionable. It seems that the Emperor's new clothes and rudimentary risk assessment both have qualities that are *'invisible to those unfit for their positions, stupid or incompetent'*.

---

[9]   Hans Christian Anderson, 1837

This alternative is generically called "quantitative risk assessment" and, whilst it takes various forms, it assigns objective values (dollars and non-financial impacts) to the components of the risk assessment in order to calculate a quantified outcome (predicted loss/gain per annum). At its simplest level risk can be calculated as likelihood x consequence (we prefer the terminology frequency of a range of outcomes). For example, a risk event that occurs three times every four years with a cost of $6 million has a value of $4.5 million (75% x $6 million), which means that the average annual loss from that event over a substantial period of time is expected to be $4.5 million.

Another illustration would be the thought process you would go through if your brother in returning the $5,000 that he borrowed gave you a choice of two options:

• Option 1—take the $5,000

• Option 2—take the contents of either his right or left pockets, one pocket has nothing in it and the other has $10,000

In deciding which option to take, your thought process would probably be that Option 1 gives me the certainty of getting my $5,000 back but Option 2 gives me a 50% chance of getting $10,000. You implicitly calculated the "risk value" of both options as $5,000 by multiplying $5,000 by 100% and $10,000 by 50%.

Whilst the predicted value is the same for both options, most people are likely to take Option 1 because the loss aversion theory and the endowment effect tell us that people put a higher value on an item they own than an identical item that they don't own. In other words, the $5,000 of your brother's that you may gain is worth less to you than your $5,000 that you stand to say goodbye to forever.

In an evenly matched situation this is fine, probably advisable. But what if your brother raised the ante to $50,000 in his pocket, with your loss still limited to your subconsciously overvalued $5,000? Now there is a tussle between emotion and good business sense, especially if you are going to make multiple risk decisions.

Of course if $5,000 was everything you had in the world and your life would change dramatically if you lost it—you are entering an area that is way outside your risk appetite. This means you should pass up on this great deal, even though you will almost certainly be much better off if you made such decisions on a frequent basis (as in organisations) because of the uncontested science in the "Law of Large Numbers".

This is the difference between risk-based decision-making and consequence decision-making, both of which are valid business decision options that pivot around your risk appetite.

We return to this in Chapter 7—let's go back to quantitative risk assessment. As quantitative risk assessment requires estimates of complex interactions between variables; cause and effect type flow diagrams are useful to plot the variables. The most commonly used tools for the mathematically precise, quantitative risk assessment (which captured the acronym "QRA" back in the 1960s), are the fault tree and event tree. These can become complex diagrams and software is often used in the analysis.

The good news is that there is a middle ground between QRA (mathematical modelling) and qualitative risk assessment (Noah's bubbles and the like) and it provides most of the benefits of QRA whilst being less complex and resource consuming.

It was originally called "SQRA" (an acronym for "semi-quantitative risk assessment") when devised at the end of the 20th century. However, whilst ISO 31000 does not clarify what precisely is meant by semi-quantitative risk assessment, its sister document IEC/ISO 31010 on risk assessment techniques has confused the situation by describing it as follows:

'Semi-quantitative methods use numerical rating scales for consequence and probability and combine them to produce a level of risk using a formula. Scales may be linear or logarithmic, or have some other relationship; formulae used can also vary'.

As a result, semi-quantitative risk assessment is an ill-defined and valueless label because it now refers to almost anything with numbers (such as multiplying values of one to five for both likelihood and consequence in a five x five matrix to give values of one in the lowest risk cell and 25 in the highest). The harm in doing this is covered in Chapter 6, but for the rest of this book we will refer to the genuine middle ground quantitative alternative as "risk value assessment".

Risk value assessment provides an output of a calculated risk value driven by detailed analysis of the risk by drawing on the experience of people within the organisation, tempered by any available external data. Risk value assessment involves a relatively simple process involving a structured approach to the analysis of the mechanics of the risk, rather than complex mathematical models based on actuarial global failure data. Qualitative risk assessment can be retained as a useful screening tool to determine which risks should be subject to a quantitative approach, although arguably better options do exist for screening.

The structured approach of using chronological flow diagrams in both risk value assessment and QRA provides valuable insight into how risks arise in an organisation. This is illustrated below using a high-level (conceptual) "bowtie" diagram, remembering that a risk is defined in ISO 31000 as 'the effect of uncertainty on objectives':

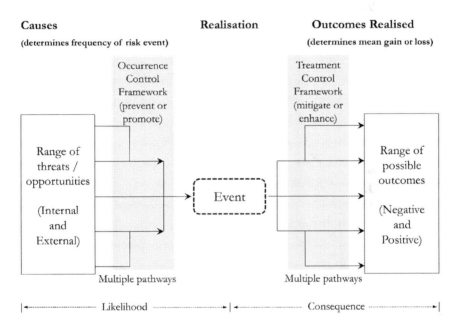

Figure 4.3—Organisation Risk Mechanics

In an organisation, risk events arise from a range of causes (threats or opportunities) that can be mapped as following multiple pathways to depict key relationships amongst cause and effect variables. Along these pathways the causes possibly encounter occurrence controls that an organisation puts in place to prevent (or at least reduce) threats and promote opportunities.

The risk event is the realisation of the uncertainty posed by the threats and opportunities and has a range of possible outcomes of differing severity. The range of outcomes can also be mapped as following multiple pathways to depict the encountering of treatment controls that hopefully an organisation puts in place. These controls mitigate the severity of negative outcomes of events and enhance the positive outcomes.

The use of the terms "occurrence controls" rather than "prevention controls" and "treatment controls" rather than "mitigation controls" caters for the upside from "opportunities" as well as the downside from "threats".

To illustrate organisation risk mechanics let's return to the spare parts example from Chapter 3 with a large agricultural product processing plant located in a remote area:

- The causes (threats) are circumstances such as part failures, parts reaching their useful lives and other destructive forces

- The risk (event) is the "non-availability of spare parts"

- The occurrence control framework over these causes would include: regular inspections, a maintenance regime and warning systems that identify a potential breakdown

- The outcomes of the event could be lost production ranging from a few hours to many days plus any flow on costs

- The treatment control framework over these outcomes would include sister-plant back-ups, supplier warranties and loss of profits insurance

Quantitative risk assessment assigns objective (in this case monetary) values to the components of the risk assessment by calculating the same metrics of likelihood (frequency) and consequence (outcome) used in the qualitative approach. As illustrated in Figure 4.3, it is rarely as simple as assumed in qualitative assessment because of the range of causes subject to occurrence controls and the range of outcomes subject to treatment controls. A quantitative risk assessment (QRA or risk value assessment) calculates the frequency of a risk event after the impact of occurrence controls, the probability that each outcome actually occurs after treatment controls and the weighted average loss or gain from the possible range of outcomes.

The objective is to calculate a monetary outcome that we call "risk value", which is the calculated prediction of annualised impact from a risk being realised. It also enables the benefit of implementing controls based on the achieved reduction in risk value compared to the cost of those controls.

Chapter 7 provides a step-by-step explanation designed for risk dummies, including the assessment of non-financial factors.

What differentiates qualitative risk assessment from quantitative risk assessment is that the former estimates relative positioning, usually conducted by risk bandits in a matter of hours through collaborative workshops involving people from a variety of groups within the organisation. Estimates of likelihood and consequence are plotted on Noah's matrix and participants do not invest a lot of time trying to calculate a precise valuation of risk being realised and the impact of implementing controls. Remember the crudity of the risk matrix scales, with usually only five categories to cover the entire frequency range. Consider a proximity equivalent with "in your city"; "continent"; "solar system", "galaxy" and "universe". If you lived in Johannesburg in South Africa and had one friend in Pretoria and another in Cairo, you may well feel the distance between them is worth knowing about before filling up the old SUV. As far as the matrix is concerned you are just popping around to visit your African mates.

Another way to compare qualitative and quantitative risk assessment is in terms of likelihood and consequence "couplings" or "pairings". In the risk matrix the likelihood and consequence of each risk is depicted as a single point within a range set by the "X" and "Y" axes of the matrix, a bit like a floating bubble. In quantitative risk assessment the likelihood and consequence coupling is:

- Likelihood—the total frequency of the causes of a risk event
- Consequence—the outcome severity of each risk event, being the weighted-average loss or gain from the possible range of outcomes that occur for virtually every organisational risk

Risk bandits say the benefits of a qualitative approach are that it overcomes the challenge of calculating precise figures, and the process is much less demanding on staff, executive management and the board. They can relate to the end result because they were involved and the output is pretty cute if you like heat maps.

What the risk bandits don't say is their qualitative assessments are so vague as to be meaningless for decision-making and their conclusions are constructed on a foundation of maybe a half dozen of the hundred or more cause, occurrence and treatment jigsaw pieces. They ignore the mechanics of how these pieces fit together in playing a part in all risk events whether they occur rarely but hurt like hell when they do or occur often but are annoying rather than hurtful.

Quantitative risk assessment can involve significant research, each risk can take from a day to several days to assess. To some it seems like a black box or sleight of hand and they don't trust it, to others it's threatening because they simply don't have the skills to join the revolution. Whatever the reason, not everyone immediately relates to quantitative risk assessment and risk value. Risk managers should be explaining risk in crisp measurable units to their executive management and board, not roughly plotting bubbles on a chart. The heat map may help children to understand risk, but please stop before they reach their teens—it's likely they would lose interest a lot sooner than risk bandits ever did.

Quantitative risk assessment advantages include:

- It is relatively difficult for individual employees to apply undue influence, e.g. those who support or oppose particular initiatives
- It can be readily used in decision-making, e.g. what should be the holding of spare parts in our remote plant example?
- It enables risk/return decisions about particular controls, e.g. is it worthwhile paying suppliers to hold certain spares?
- It allows executive management and boards to determine which risks are the most material and how well they are being managed over time, e.g. should we even be worrying about plant failures because the demand for the product from this plant is likely to dissipate within five years?

Before we leave QRA, a word of warning is timely. Risk bandits are most commonly found plying their trade using qualitative risk analysis via the risk matrix and heat map. Occasionally they feign quantitative risk analysis so beware; poorly produced QRA can be as inaccurate as the matrix but much more persuasive. Occasionally terms like fault tree, cost/benefit analysis, etc. will roll of their tongues as though they had QRA in their DNA, but you will know the talk from the walk by the end of this book.

Managing Risk Pods

There doesn't seem to be a good collective noun for risks—group or collection is a bit underwhelming whilst portfolio, herd or school is a bit over the top. We like dolphins so we will invoke some poetic licence and call them pods; it may even create a new fad.

So how does the use of qualitative risk assessment versus quantitative risk assessment impact the management of a pod of risks in an organisation?

As explained in Chapter 2, most organisations do not make use of risk pods in governance; rather governance is focused on compliance sign-offs. This is a direct result of risk managers undertaking qualitative risk assessments and then providing risk matrices, heat maps and risk management spreadsheets that are believed, or at least not rejected, by the board, audit and risk committee and executive management. They are unusable for governance and of dubious value for compliance.

Qualitative risk assessments are a key driver of risk banditry—even though they are quite acceptable when used within their limitations—to ISO 31000, COSO, assorted regulators and most risk management guidance documents. Pods of risk bubbles on a heat map do not allow boards, audit and risk committees and executive management to make decisions. No wonder most meetings to discuss risk management are focused on the description of the risks and the placement of the bubbles, what else can they be used for?

A pod of risks based on quantitative risk assessment is a graph of the risk value of each risk and the impact of controls and mitigation actions. If need be, decisions can be made around acceptability of the level of risk, implementing new controls and mitigation actions and the delegation of authority to take on risk. This process not only supports compliance sign-offs, it enables risk to be used as a key part of the governance framework.

The Residual Appeal of Inherent Risk

Amongst risk practitioners and even at executive management and board levels, debate rages as to whether an assessment of "inherent risk" (assumes no management imposed controls are in place) is useful or whether the focus should be just on "current risk" (with existing controls in place) and "residual risk" (after new controls or improvements). Some organisations like to see the full spectrum of the impact of no controls, existing controls and possible future controls, being:

Inherent Risk → Residual Risk → Target Risk

Inherent risk is not even mentioned in ISO 31000 whereas residual risk is defined as 'the risk remaining after treatment'. However, inherent risk remains popular across the "COSO belt" in the US because COSO does make a distinction. The proponents of using inherent risk as well as residual risk argue that the advantages are:

- It provides perspective on the significance of individual causes (threats and opportunities)

- It helps identify the existing controls that are the most critical as they will have the greatest impact on the reduction from inherent risk to residual risk

- It assists internal audit to focus on these critical controls as part of their review of systems

- It adds context to the risk assessment by seeing the impact of existing controls that may prompt consideration of additional controls

The concept of inherent risk is thought to have originated from financial statement auditors where they focus their attention on the most likely areas of misstatement. For example, "obsolete inventory" for a retailer or "non-recoverable receivables" for a wholesaler. Whilst strong controls in areas of high inherent audit risk may reduce an auditors' work, these controls are not assumed and are tested before audit work can be reduced. So inherent audit risk to a financial statement auditor makes a lot of sense as a key aspect of their work design to conduct the audit as efficiently and effectively as possible—but is it useful in organisation risk assessment?

If you have got this far in this book it won't surprise you that we think that for most organisations, particularly those using qualitative risk assessment, the consideration of inherent risk is an irrelevant dream. Its intent is good, i.e. do not take existing controls for granted, but it's a concept that is easily delivered through another part of the organisation risk management process—assessing the integrity of critical controls.

In practice trying to apply inherent risk is complex, way beyond the capacity of qualitative risk assessment. The COSO concept of no management controls implies that existing controls from outside the organisation should be included. So the inherent risk of injury to employees from car accidents can include traffic rules and car manufacturer safety measures such as airbags but not management controls such as defensive driving training and requirements to lock mobile phones in the boot. This definition is very unclear and probably created by those favouring a nanny state. Why would externally provided equipment be excluded from the assessment when it is the driver that must administer or maintain it?

Imagine if you can, an airline trying to assess the inherent risk of a plane crash with all of its financial and safety outcomes. Airport flight control and the plane's body and engine specifications, instrumentation and computer safety systems are included but specific airline operating protocols, pilot competence and maintenance programs are not. Do we assume then that 'all aircraft and engine designs are of equal quality?', 'all runways of the same length?' and 'all flight controllers equally well trained?' Are we right to say "pilot competence" is excluded because individual companies have varying standards when minimum industry standards exist?

In our experience, most inherent risk assessments assume the worst because it can be argued that this is the safest approach. It also allows risk bandits to show how effective the internal controls are compared to the inherent case. Using Noah's original transportation approach to risk assessment, the inherent risk bubble is almost always located very much in the top right hand corner of the matrix—but what have we learned?

If you think the matrix is precise enough to distinguish the impact of controls from an inherent risk assessment, then to quote John McEnroe's eloquent questioning of a confusing ruling at Wimbledon in 1981, 'you cannot be serious!'

The inherent risk rating is an ineffective solution to a very important challenge—the identification of, and a focus on, the most important controls. The implicit question is 'how do organisations keep a strong focus on controls for a risk event that is accurately assessed to be very low risk because of extremely low likelihood yet would be absolutely disastrous if it occurred?' The effective solution was referred to in the discussion about the $5,000 dollar loan earlier in this chapter. If the consequence of an event is something the organisation cannot contemplate then the integrity of individual critical controls must be monitored and assured <u>irrespective of the risk value</u>. This approach meets the intent of the "inherent risk approach" without putting people through the agony of trying to apply it.

To reiterate, the concept of assessing the impact and integrity of controls for high-risk value events, and for events with intolerable consequences irrespective of risk value, is fundamental to a meaningful risk assessment. To do so involves separating the impact of occurrence controls on the frequency of risk events and the impact of treatment controls on outcomes. Chapter 7 explains how this can be done.

Before leaving inherent risk we need to address the lingering residual appeal to some board members and management that it can demonstrate the cost/benefit case for existing controls. This is of course a very expensive backslapping exercise unless there are controls that the organisation would seriously consider removing if they weren't cost effective. In such rare cases, the increase in the level of risk if the control were removed should be calculated and then compared with the cost saving of removing the control. Assuming a meaningful assessment is undertaken (i.e. quantified) such thinking deserves applause, but there is no need to carry out "inherent risk" assessments across an entire organisation for the purpose of assessing a limited number of specific controls.

Navigation Guidance

Readers not wishing to be dwell on some real-life amusing examples of risk junk can speed-read the next few pages without losing the plot for the remainder of "Risk Bandits". Rejoin us at 'Darwin Was Right'.

You Want Cute?

This chapter started with the proposition that often with tools used in risk management, it's survival of the cutest not necessarily the most effective. This debasement of Darwin's insightful explanation of evolution has generated a race to the bottom to develop cute tools that risk bandits throw into reports to divert attention from the lack of substance. To prepare readers to resist this "cutism" here are a few of our favourite things (apologies to Julie Andrews) that executive mangers or directors may have thrown at them. All professions have jargon-rich dimensions where a genuine concept is simplified and wrapped into a single catchy word and sold as the latest development. Some examples in risk management are given below.

"Vulnerability" refers to the susceptibility of an organisation to react and deal with risk events. It is intended to focus on strategic capability rather than individual controls. Vulnerability therefore appeals to some executive management and boards because of the big picture focus on aspects such as scenario planning and financial strength. The level of vulnerability is usually noted against each risk or the really cute trick is to colour code the border of each bubble on Noah's matrix.

Vulnerability is of course another qualitative assessment overlayed on an already imprecise qualitative assessment. It is really an attempt to identify whether occurrence and treatment controls are in place and operating as designed, thereby impacting frequency and outcomes of risk events. It begs the question why not just include this assessment as part of the assessment of impact of controls in completing the risk assessment? Strong "scenario planning" and "cash reserves" are good examples of controls that impact such an assessment. This concept should not survive due to its limited usefulness but cuteness still sells.

A second favourite is "Velocity" which refers to the speed of change of a risk. It can relate to the speed of change of causes (threats and opportunities) and also to the elapsed time between causes and the occurrence of the risk event. Its purpose is to identify those risks that need to be reviewed more often than others because they are changing more often.

Velocity is a qualitative assessment and is also usually noted against each risk or the same cute trick of colour coding the border of each matrix bubble is sometimes used. The concept has merit as risk assessments need to be current and a metric is needed to set priorities for updates. Interestingly, it may not be cute enough as its use is somewhat limited.

"Horizon" is also another concept that is sometimes adopted in risk reports. It attempts to illustrate the immediacy of risks and to distinguish from today's key risks those that are emerging on the horizon. The horizon is usually shown by adding time as a third dimension on Noah's matrix thereby putting a thick coat of paint on an unstable Ark hull to make it look a lot better and leak a little less. This failed attempt at cuteness hopefully consigns it to extinction.

Another favourite is "Maturity Benchmarking" which is one of those terms that many professions like to use to portray a move to best practice by its members. Risk practitioners often present a risk maturity assessment against a benchmark of "basic" moving through to "advanced" or "strategic". This gap analysis of today versus where the organisation wants to be is presented in a cute table with more bubbles, and some arrows and red highlighted gaps. It is usually accompanied by either a self-administered pat on the back by the delusional front-runners or a request for more budget by the laggards.

As cute as the maturity assessment might be, it's pretty close to useless. The assessment criteria that are used mainly relate to tools and processes and some evaluations are so subjective they could be better described as emotional. But don't forget the benchmark for "advanced" still revolves around use of the matrix supported by endless pages from spreadsheets in small font listing qualitative risk assessments and existing and proposed management actions. Do directors really think this is advanced and the goal for the organisation?

Very rarely does maturity benchmarking in risk management involve performance outputs. Risk managers usually do not drive these maturity-benchmarking exercises; they are too busy chasing those pesky cats. Yet there are many other risk related performance outputs that could be benchmarked between competitors without creating problems in confidentiality or competition laws.

The survival of the cutest rule is likely to apply to these maturity assessments. Risk bandits love them as they generate either glory or excuses and perhaps more budget. Ongoing work on the cuteness of the presentation yields a much better return than consolidating the formal risk management process with what happens in practice.

Shape shifting is as rife in risk management as on 'Deep Space Nine' in 'Star Trek'. In the beginning there were the simple little cells of the matrix, then the curved risk arc (no Noah pun intended) took over from the boring straight lines on the heat map, the Borg cubism of COSO followed and now we proudly present … the "risk wheel"!

The risk wheel is the final example of our favourite cute risk tools; it is perhaps the height of "cutism". Whilst these wheels are, perhaps surprisingly, the same shape, they come in different sizes with a range of uses that drive different terminology to describe the segments between the spokes, the wheel rim, the hub and for really cute risk wheels, a rim around the hub. Of course bright colours can fill the different portions as part of the packaging.

A common version is the basic risk management process transformed from the apparently boring vertically oriented list in Figure 2.3 into a cute wheel with arrows showing different entry points for newly identified risks, risk updates and analysis of incidents. Risk bandits use this tool to give the impression that the process has some sophistication; 'let's run this incident through the risk wheel' is the call. But of course the same old unsophisticated risk matrix sits behind the risk assessment.

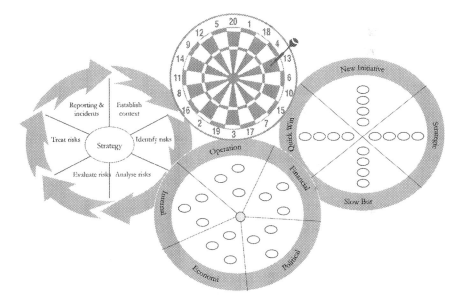

Figure 4.4—Risk Wheel Cutism

Another version of the risk wheel uses the segments between the spokes to depict areas or sources of risk, such as "economic factors", "internal capability" and "political influence". You can imagine the fun risk bandits have in naming the segments in the outside rim and hub rim; let the creative juices flow. To prompt discussion in workshops this is a useful tool but risk bandits take it was beyond its design capacity by using it to illustrate completeness of risk identification to audit and risk committees who don't realise there is little else behind the analysis.

The final example of the risk wheel is where risk treatment actions are placed in the different segments between the spokes which are labelled around the rim according to impact such as "quick wins", "new initiatives" and the very impressive "strategic vision". Distance from the hub indicates importance and the treatment actions are sometimes placed in Noah's coloured bubbles to display the level of risk to which these treatment actions relate. There is little basis, other than just an impression, as to the location and colour of the bubbles but it looks very cute. The irony is that it looks like a dartboard, which is appropriate given the haphazard method of locating the dart-resembling bubbles.

Just before leaving this topic, and to prove we may be ageing but are still vaguely in touch with the 21st century, readers might check their smart phone on the train journey home tonight and find the risk wheel app. It might be good for a laugh but it's unlikely to make you miss your stop.

Darwin was Right

This chapter has illustrated how in the survival of risk management tools and processes; the fittest are the cutest. The cutest fads and fashions survive because they are fit for the simplistic compliance approach that is so widely adopted. Qualitative risk assessment, driven by the risk matrix and heat map, is almost universally accepted and defended because its output looks cute and is labelled to appeal to busy executives and board members. Unfortunately, these tools are too simplistic for anything other than rudimentary application and are used way beyond their capacity.

The alternative, quantitative risk assessment, lacks "cutism" but can power the extraction of real value from risk management for an organisation. Risk value assessment provides a practical approach to quantitative risk assessment.

5. ERM: Not There Yet!

Comparisons are Better than Clichés

"Enterprise Risk Management", or "ERM", has become the common use term for any risk management framework across an organisation. It is a cliché, the term is overused and carries an undeserved sense of effectiveness as it suffers from the process / framework confusion described in Chapter 3. Risk management standards and guidance documents imply ERM is an accepted body of knowledge. In practice it's little more than jargon and yet another concept retrofitted to the basic risk management process.

To avoid confusion, this book refers to "organisation risk management" as the generic term for a genuine risk management framework across an organisation compared to the cliché, ERM, as the collection of terminology and concepts dressed up to look like a body of knowledge. The distinction is important; our definition of organisation risk management is a live and business integrated framework whilst ERM is just more lipstick.

Insert Organisation Context Here!

Imagine a family-owned lamp import and wholesale business where the owners employ a few staff (Confucius take note, sometimes 'few hands make light work'). The owners make the key decisions such as buying, pricing and exchange cover, intuitively assessing the financial risks. They would largely communicate these decisions verbally. The basic risk management process works well in this context.

As the business expands beyond lamps into furniture and commences its own offshore manufacturing, it lists on the stock exchange. A board and executive managers are appointed and a whole range of strategies, policies and procedures are formalised. The business decisions are now being made by a range of people with differing authority levels applying corporate policies using laptops and smart phones to access and process data and communicate across the globe. The decision makers do not know the shareholders well enough to understand their view on risk taking, so there was a need for them to temper their personal views on risk and apply the organisation view.

The change in the family owned business means the basic risk management process is outgrown and an organisation risk management framework is necessary. If you asked risk managers how they insert the organisation context, most would say through the application of ERM. ERM in this sense is very broad generic term, and whilst it is defined in COSO it doesn't even rate a mention in ISO 31000.

COSO defines ERM as '…a process effected by an entity's board of directors, management and other personnel, applied in strategy setting and across the enterprise, designed to identify potential events that may affect the entity, and manage risks to be within risk appetite, to provide reasonable assurance regarding the achievement of its objectives'.

'Yours!' No one is in charge, and the focus remains on hazards and negative outcomes.

Fortunately ISO 31000 does a little better, whilst it does not refer to ERM, the framework for an organisation is one of the three key elements of the standard, as described in Chapter 2. It also recognises the organisation context in the definition of risk management, 'Risk management is an integral part of all organisational processes… [It] is not a stand-alone activity that is separate from the main activities and processes of the organisation. Risk management is part of the responsibilities of management and an integral part of all organisational processes, including strategic planning and all project and change management processes'.

Before looking at how ERM is applied it is important to dig a little deeper into how the organisation context applies to risk management.

The Top and Tail Retrofit

How does your organisation process expenditure? This is not a trick question, we ask it because it's probably a process that is easy to relate to and it is also probably purpose built for the organisation.

If the organisation has multiple sites it is likely that commitments for expenditure are documented and approved under delegated authority levels at various locations through some form of purchase order or contract. The delivery of the goods or service is probably subsequently separately authenticated. The payment of the invoice by cheque or funds transfer is likely to be done centrally after the purchase, receipt of delivery, pricing and terms have been checked and approved.

It's the same basic process, undertaken by a single person, that we use to pay domestic bills but because it relates to a multiple location organisation with a high volume and many employees it's more sophisticated and there are organisational procedures to follow, controls in place and performance management budgets and reporting. The basic process has been significantly upgraded to fit the organisation and it's more than topping and tailing, the process is designed to be both effective and efficient across the organisation.

Now let's look at how the organisational context is dealt with in ERM. In Chapter 2, the four steps highlighted in Figure 2.3 were defined as the basic risk management process. Both COSO and ISO 31000 produce an overlay to these four steps to help make the basic risk management process fit the organisation context; in essence it's an aftermarket modification. Just as an aftermarket turbo charger and media system for a car undermines the engine management system and dashboard control functions that deliver safe and reliable driving, aftermarket risk management frameworks undermine an organisation's core business functions.

The COSO Borg spaceship (from 'Star Trek') is an attempt at an organisational framework; let's highlight the components:

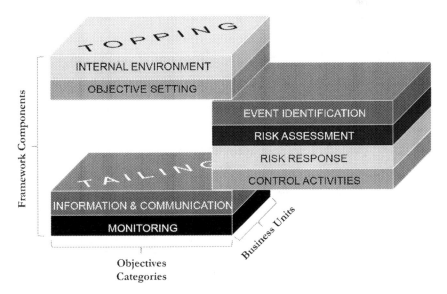

Figure 5.1—COSO Topping and Tailing

The topping is the organisational context around objectives and locations and the tailing is reporting and follow-up. Compare this to our expenditure process example and how that is transformed into an organisation-wide framework. Risk management is about making decisions and how that is done in an organisational context is ignored by COSO.

The main elements of the ISO 31000 top and tail retrofit can be seen from the following summary:

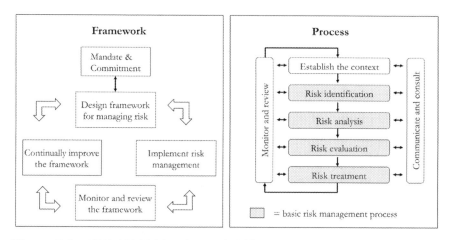

Figure 5.2—ISO 31000 Topping and Tailing

The topping is the organisational context and the mandate and the tailing is the reporting and monitoring. This is not to say there is no value in doing this; after all the ISO is basically saying organisations should consider their business objectives for a specific risk assessment (topping) and keep an eye on how things are going (tailing) without helping them through the process. However, as with COSO, ISO 31000 does not transform the basic process into an organisation-wide framework, because it is focused on the application of the risk assessment steps and not on what should be the framework's primary role of supporting the organisation's core business functions.

This has occurred because the Standard's authorities have treated the topic of risk in the same way that most organisations have done—give it to some "risk experts" and leave them alone to do the job. No wonder practitioners fail to see the bigger picture if those setting the standards have made the same mistake. As a result, risk management remains in the pre-Copernicus era because it still regards risk management as the centre of the organisation's universe and expects the core business to orbit around it.

In essence, employees across an organisation when facing an action or decision involving taking on risk do not know *"what"* to assess and *"when"*, they just know *"how"* to do it. In terms of the expenditure process employees know *"when"* (every time they need to spend the organisation's dollars) and *"what"* (issue a purchase order) in addition to *"how"* (in line with the purchase order procedure). If the transaction value is a certain amount they go down one path, if it's higher than a specified limit, there's a tougher road to travel. It's quite crisp and there is minimal confusion.

With employees applying the four steps in the basic risk management process across the organisation however, things are far less definitive. For example, when the stores supervisor in our remote agricultural product processing plant from Chapter 3 sees holdings of critical spare parts have fallen he knows how to fix it, he can order more spares or make sure the supplier has a holding within agreed delivery lead times. But how does he know what action is right for the organisation and when to take that action? If he looks at the risk matrix or risk register he will see an "Extreme" risk and will probably seek approval to replace the spare parts. This action may result in the best risk/return balance for the organisation or it may not; he has no way of knowing.

The organisation-wide expenditure framework is specifically designed to provide a common answer for all situations no matter which employee deals with the action. In the risk management process when an organisation relies on ERM they can't achieve common answers to the same set of circumstances because so many things remain ill defined.

Tolerance for Risk Appetite

Reference has been made to "risk appetite" as being an important part of ERM. It is a useful concept that at first glance seems straightforward but actually is quite complex. It has been misused by risk bandits to the point where many directors and executive managers have been misled and struggle to work with it. As an observant client, who spoke limited English, once said—there is "confusement!"

COSO defines risk appetite as 'the amount of risk, on a broad level, an organisation is willing to accept in pursuit of value'. Other definitions abound but they are similar enough to stick with COSO. COSO goes on to say that an organisation should take three steps with risk appetite—develop, communicate, and monitor and update.

ISO 31000 does not refer to risk appetite but makes a reference to "risk attitude" which it defines as 'the organisation's approach to assess and eventually pursue, retain, take or turn away from risk'. ISO 31000 also refers to "risk criteria" which is defined as 'terms of reference against which the significance of a risk is evaluated'. The objective of the terms are similar in trying to establish a benchmark for the amount of risk for the organisation to make decisions to achieve its objectives.

The key issue for risk bandits in applying risk appetite is that the risk management system that they peddle is not capable of supporting decision-making. This is so because the risk analysis is superficial, usually based on quick qualitative assessments, and decisions such as spare parts holdings in our remote agricultural product processing plant example from Chapter 3, are made outside the "compliance driven" risk management system.

This doesn't stop risk bandits, however, they are happy to suggest that directors and executive managers use crude exceeds-appetite tags such as "Extreme" or imaginary pass marks like "As low as practicable". After some rather vague risk treatment action they tell them what they feel they want to hear, that the formerly "Extreme" risk is now "As low as practicable" and the organisation is therefore within its "risk appetite". Some arrows from bubbles in red territory to orange or yellow on a heat map may imply a substantial drop in risk, which will suffice for those who need to infer that a good state has been achieved.

Let's briefly look at the major difficulties with the concept of risk appetite when applied by risk bandits. Firstly, it re-enforces the focus on hazards and negative outcomes yet risk involves events that may cause both positive and negative variations from achieving objectives. If a movement in exchange rates causes the cost of inputs to improve profit by more than the variation from objectives inherent in risk appetite, is that a risk management breach? Indeed, we may need two inversely coloured risk matrices to avoid showing a strong opportunistic win as a disaster.

This issue is compounded by the second difficulty—risk appetite in a qualitative risk assessment process can't deal with the range of outcomes that a risk event may cause, as displayed in the high-level bowtie diagram in Figure 4.3 in Chapter 4. If some of the possible outcomes are positive or within risk appetite and some are not, does the organisation just assume worst case and thereby implement costly controls or mitigation actions that reduce the upside? This is often not a good business decision across a large portfolio.

When contemplating this question, note that most organisations approve projects based on "P90" basis. This means there is a 90% chance of an acceptable outcome, up to 5% chance of a windfall profit and up to 5% chance of an unacceptable loss (or below target outcome). Organisations may never approve another project if risk bandits use the unacceptable loss outcome to position the bubble on the matrix because it would become evident that a serious loss (catastrophic consequence) would have a likelihood value of one in 20 projects. So, if four projects per year are undertaken a frequency occurrence (likelihood)/outcome severity (consequence) coupling of "Possible" / "Catastrophic" would result in an "Extreme" risk ranking using the matrix table in Figure 3.2 thus concluding all projects are beyond the organisation's risk appetite.

The third difficulty with risk appetite is dealing with the aggregation of individual events or outcomes that in total test the organisation's risk appetite. It is quite possible to have multiple dependent "Moderate" risks that when aggregated would scare the pants of any director interested in his or her longevity. Yet these directors usually see only isolated symptoms, never getting the opportunity to join the dots and seek prevention or at least an effective cure. COSO attempts to deal with this issue through "risk tolerance" which is defined as 'the acceptable level of variation relative to achievement of a specific objective', which can be interpreted as the sum of lots of tolerances = overall organisation risk appetite. This is realistic in concept in that it recognises that at times organisations will have to make uncomfortable decisions, but the reality ends there because without quantification we can't sum up multiple tolerances.

A similar aggregation issue arises when a risk limit or threshold is allocated to operating units within the organisation. Aggregating the individual limits to a group total ignores the reality that many risks across business units occur independently of each other over a range of probabilities. It's akin to adding apples and oranges and getting the wrong end of a pineapple ... it's so difficult to know what to do with it!

Although these difficulties with determining and using risk appetite are significant, the question most often asked in relation to risk appetite is 'how can it be implemented?' In practice there are three methods outside the finance industry where quantitative calculations of "value at risk" work well:

- By risk label—where simplified statements are made such as 'we don't accept "Extreme" risks and we mitigate "High" risks'. This is nonsense because some "High" risks can't be significantly mitigated yet we still want to take them, and some "Extreme" risks, such as gold price fluctuations to our example gold mining company in Chapter 3, are exactly what shareholders are seeking. Equally it means that a major loss may be tolerable when it's a surprise (in the "Rare" row) because the matrix label for the "Major" / "Rare" cell is usually "Medium" or "High" but never demands risk treatment action. Most successful organisations take occasional horrific losses on initiatives because they are more than balanced out by the gains on the initiatives that work. An organisation carrying out 20 projects with a 95% probability of success can be expected to suffer on one of them, for example

- By risk type—where generic statements are made such as 'we have a low tolerance for safety risks and a higher tolerance for financial risks'. This is a more practical option than the first but it does not provide enough of a benchmark against which managers in the organisation can make decisions

- By risk value—where a risk value limit is set for each of the outcomes within a range that have been identified for a risk event. This option is best used when some form of quantitative risk assessment is used and provides directors and executive managers with a total risk appetite value against which to compare total actual risk value

The designation of an organisation's risk appetite needs to be detailed enough to enable it to be used as a benchmark by managers making specific decisions to achieve organisational objectives across a range of pathways leading to or from a risk event. The benchmarks need to fit together at an aggregated level so that decisions across the organisation result in capital and resources being allocated across the organisation to achieve its objectives as part of performance management. A generic statement, a dollar limit or a single acceptable threshold won't achieve this because of the multiple pathways and non-financial considerations such as safety and reputation.

When a board delegates authority to incur expenditure it doesn't just define dollar limits for differing levels of management. Such delegations recognise that different pathways require different controls so differentiation is often made between such aspects as operating v capital expenditure, within versus outside budget in addition to dollar limits. The same concept applies to the delegation of risk appetite.

Conceptually risk appetite is not really the disease; it's a symptom of an underlying risk management process malaise that could yet prove fatal for the risk management profession. Lipstick is not reserved for the healthy; hospital patients will apply it to fool worried family and friends, and morticians are big users too! We return to setting risk appetite in Chapter 8.

Rationale Versus Reason

Sometimes the rationale, or the arguments put forward, for an action are quite different to the reasons, or the real purpose, of that action. An example is a government before an election giving handouts to marginal electorates. The stated rationale is support for the most needy but the cynics amongst us can't help but notice that most of the needy seem to be in the marginal electorates. ERM suffers from this sleight of hand too.

COSO says the rationale for ERM is to 'manage risks to be within risk appetite' but prescribes an approach that has no chance of making that happen. This is reflected in most organisations, the risk management guidance documents state a similar rationale but it is not supported by the implementation approach. The cynics amongst us would say the real reason for ERM in the risk management guidance documents for most organisations is to support declarations of compliance with regulations, stock exchange requirements or standards.

For the rationale and the reasons to coincide the organisation risk management framework needs to be an integral part of corporate governance. We know that sounds a lot like a COSO or ISO phrase but unlike them we will show you how to deliver it before the credits roll! (We return to this aspect in Chapter 8). The framework should guide, interact with, and respond to the organisation's strategy and performance to deliver its objectives as part of the natural risk/return fundamentals of successful organisation management.

Indications that Risk Management is Not Working

Do you remember the Gulf War when for the first time we watched a war live on TV? Peter Arnett on CNN was either very brave or reckless, but he survived to tell the story. When the Iraq war (some call it an invasion) occurred the American military realised the power of media in propaganda. They began the process of "embedding" journalists with the army, which increased their influence over media reporting. "Embedding" became a popular term; it is even in risk management literature.

When you hear in your organisation that we are 'embedding risk management', think back to the American army where an external agent was brought in to create a level of propaganda. In the context of war this is certainly no surprise and perhaps even defendable, but in an organisation context, risk management should not be used just to create reports for executives and the board but to play a major role in the way governance is designed and implemented. The formal risk management process however, is a foreign body that the risk manager is trying to embed, unlike the day-to-day risk management process that employees actually use, probably works quite well and should be captured, improved where necessary and only then, embedded. To be clear, the existing operating processes are likely to contribute more to a good risk framework than the formal risk management process, contrary to what many executives and boards seem to believe.

Other common terms that may be an indication that risk management is not working across the organisation are "ingraining" risk management and developing a "risk culture". These are all part of the retrofit problem described earlier in this chapter. Both terms assume that risk management is some kind of holy water that must be injected into the existing work systems in the former case and into the corporate blood stream in the latter. To us this feels a lot more like voodoo than science.

Chapter 4 described how some risk bandits offer a risk maturity-benchmarking assessment. The key criterion in this attempt at gap analysis is the extent to which risk management is "embedded". This is the pinnacle of risk banditry because the benchmarks largely ignore how risk management is used in decision-making and how performance is monitored. Witch doctors are "embedded" in many villages in developing nations, pity about the survival rate of sick folk though.

Other indicators that organisation risk management may not be working include:

- Meeting fatigue—the focus of executive management and audit and risk committee meetings is on the plausibility of the risk profile and action lists rather than whether risk management is making a strong return for the resources committed

- Loss of appetite—despite plentiful charts and heat maps there is an unclear organisation risk appetite definition and how it is implemented in decision-making is a secret to all but the risk manager who can never quite articulate it to others

- Lengthy risk descriptions—the descriptions of individual risks are not just limited to a possible event but also include causes and/or outcomes. This probably indicates that the risk manager has simply recorded the output of a risk workshop without further analysis and consolidation. This is a prime contributor to oversized risk registers

- Constant bad news—the focus is on hazards and negative outcomes. The absence of loss is celebrated rather than improved profitability and sustainability because opportunities and positive outcomes are not the dominant part of the risk discussion

- Risk managing the problem away—a common use of risk management is to create a documented record that an unwelcome problem isn't really a problem at all. Sometimes it calms executive management and the board, sometimes a regulator or concerned stakeholder and almost always the risk manager

- Micro focus, macro surprise—hundreds of small assessments fill the risk registers yet game-changing threats like "opportunistic takeover attempts" or "compounding currency and commodity price movements" are totally ignored, presumably because no one really believes the basic risk management process can handle the tough stuff anyway

Upfront Design by Board and Management

If engineers and accountants were as sloppy in their profession as the average risk manager, many bridges and organisations would be sitting at the bottom of harbours. Both have structural requirements set out in law and their design has to be approved by regulatory bodies. Not so with organisation risk management, approval of the design is largely left to executive management and directors in an ocean of self-determination, the only significant exception being highly regulated organisations such as those in the finance sector in some jurisdictions.

It can therefore be argued that risk managers are only part of the risk banditry sickness—they are the symptom of lax executive management and board direction—probably because they themselves don't know how and amazingly, as we saw in Chapter 2, risk management literature is little help.

Attributing blame won't solve the problem, executive management and directors need to get involved in the upfront design of the risk management framework for their organisation and not leave it to risk bandits. If they are sent away to do better, they will just do a makeover on the basic risk management process (topping and tailing to their hearts' content).

The design of a risk management framework needs to be an integral part of corporate governance and therefore warrants significant board and executive involvement. Chapter 8 provides guidance as to how this can be done.

Risk-Based Decisions Can be Risky

A common catchcry in both private and public sector organisations are calls for "risk-based decision-making". This gets to the heart of risk management as part of the overall risk/return decision framework. It involves strategic decisions such as capital and resource allocation as well as regular implementation decisions as part of the day-to-day business processes of an organisation. Risk-based decisions focus on the most critical issues and prioritise spending of time, money and other resources in applying the organisation's strategy for achieving its objectives.

Let's look at an example in each of the private and public sectors to illustrate the mechanics of risk-based decisions.

In the private sector, let's use the example of the company dealing with the spare parts in the remote agricultural product processing plant. The objective of the company is to maximise shareholder value and its strategy involves being a low cost and reliable supplier of processed product.

As the cost of production is a key competitive driver there is pressure on the Production Department from the board to make "risk-based decisions" on cost control. We should expect that two typical key risks (events) would be:

- "Non-availability of critical spare parts" (spare parts are prohibitively expensive to hold unnecessarily)

- "Movement in competitors' operating costs" (competitors are known to be investing in new processing technology)

So how would these risks drive the key decisions around the levels of holding of spare parts and research and development (R&D)? As the Production Department budget is too tight to carry all spare parts and undertake extensive R&D, decisions must be taken on a risk/return basis.

Let's take a look at one of these events in detail. The mechanics of the spare parts inventory holding decision would involve:

- Estimating and ranking the probability of equipment failure where spare parts are needed

- Estimating the impact of each of these possible equipment failures on production and other factors such as safety and the environment. These estimates would involve an assessment of factors such as supplier delivery lead times, the value of production disrupted and the flow on impact to customer deliveries

- Implementing controls or mitigations against the most significant impacts through measures such as plant design (e.g. to isolate failures), agreements with suppliers to minimise lead times and arranging back-up supplies

- Prioritising the critical spare parts holdings for on-site demand

Once all this data is compiled how should this risk-based decision be made? How about the risk manager? No he is not in an operating role (other than cat mustering). What about the general manager of the Production Department? Possibly but she doesn't have a view of competing needs across the organisation. The COO has the authority and breadth of view across the company but the only information he has to make the decision is the risk register and the heat map!

The right answer is that "risk-based decisions" have to be part of the upfront design of the overall risk/return decision framework that is delegated from the board. A performance management framework with goals and actual results covering key indicators such as equipment failure rates and lost production impacts should enable the COO to approve the decisions recommended by the general manager of the Production Department and the accountability for these decisions will be clear.

For the public sector, let's use the example of a government Authority responsible for the network of roads in regional areas of a particular state. The objective of the Authority is to maintain an effective and safe regional road network and its strategy involves efficiency in managing a network that enables reasonable road access to all population centres with priority in high quality roads where there is greatest usage.

As government funding is limited, the Authority is under pressure to make "risk-based decisions". Let's assume that typically key risks (events) might include:

- "Rock falls" (which cause road closures and delays and the resulting harm to people or property)
- "Demand for new roads differing from budget assumptions"

So how would these risks drive the key decisions around maintenance of roadside ground conditions and road network extensions? As there is not enough funding to undertake all maintenance and extensions, spending priority must be given to the areas of greatest risk.

As with our remote agricultural product processing plant example, the mechanics of the decision on how to spend the limited budget for maintenance of roadside ground conditions would involve:

- Estimating and ranking the frequency of rock falls using engineering assessments of the ground conditions of all roads

- Estimating the impact of road closures from each of rock fall. These estimates would involve an assessment of road usage and the extent of delays from available detour routes

- Assessing existing prevention or mitigation controls against the most significant impacts through measures such as rock bolts and concrete spraying and fencing

- Prioritising the spending towards the most significant impacts

Once all this data is compiled how should this risk-based decision be made?

The risk manager can't make these decisions, even though these risks are in the risk register, it's a qualitative risk assessment that doesn't help cost/benefit decisions and is not transparent in how the available underlying operational data has been used. The Ground Maintenance Department Head has the necessary operational data but doesn't have a view of competing needs across the Authority. The CEO has the authority and breadth of view across the organisation but can't make the decisions based the risk register and the heat map!

These "risk-based decisions" have to be part of the upfront design of the framework that is delegated from the Minister. A performance management framework with goals and actual results covering key indicators such as road unavailability rates and safety and property impacts should enable the CEO to effectively review the decisions recommended by Ground Maintenance Department Head and again the accountability for these decisions will be clear.

In the public sector the political implications of a rock fall on a public road probably means that the Minister should also be informed of the cut-off on the priority list where the allocated funding runs out for roadside ground maintenance.

In relation to the risk involving the demand for new roads, the mechanics of the criticality analysis for decisions around spending on new roads are similar using road usage analysis and forecasts across the state based on expected demographic changes.

Risk Bandits

These examples illustrate how difficult it is to make "risk-based decisions" when the risk register and heat map come from a quick qualitative risk assessment in a workshop. When operational data is properly used in risk assessments, risk-based decisions can link directly with the overall risk/ return decision framework that has been designed upfront and is delegated by the board. Risk value assessment provides a valuable input to operating risk-based decisions that may involve tools such as cost/benefit analysis and multi-criteria decision analysis.

The significant advantages of this linkage are:

- Interactivity—this linkage becomes interactive as performance data supports decisions and impacts the risk assessment which in turn improves performance and demonstrates the effectiveness (or otherwise) of the risk framework

- Risk appetite delegations—the risk appetite for key decisions, or risk tolerance, is readily delegated both in terms of individual risk events and aggregated risk across the organisation

- Resourcing decision-making—the cost of prevention and mitigation controls is identified so that resourcing decisions about how much and where to spend can be properly delegated and implemented in applying the organisation's strategy in achieving its objectives

- "Risk-based decisions" is no longer a wishful phrase but a hard specification for the design of an organisation's risk management framework that is an integral part of corporate governance

Navigation Guidance

Readers not wishing to delve into how auditors use (and misuse) risk can speed-read the next few pages without losing the plot for the remainder of "Risk Bandits". Rejoin us at 'Much More To Be Done'.

Risk in Internal Audit

Internal audit in many ways has the same mystique or black box aura as risk management. Audit and risk committees and the executive management of many organisations, who have direct control over internal audit, approve a "risk-based approach" in internal audit plans but have little idea what that means—it just sounds logical. Unfortunately, some internal auditors are not too clear either!

Internal auditors who not only accept but also utilise the content of shallow risk registers and heat maps for targeting audit activities should be outed as risk bandits. Internal audit is a key aspect of corporate governance with direct reporting lines to the audit and risk committee and executive management, but rarely do they expose the banditry within an organisation. Instead they contribute to the false sense of security experienced by the audit and risk committee and executive management by using Ark bubbles as a key foundation for their internal audit program. Let's look inside the internal audit black box to show how this works and the likely impact.

A "risk-based approach" by an internal auditor means an organisation's risk management framework may be used in one or more of the following three ways, with an increasing level of sophistication:

- To set priorities—the organisation risk profile is a key determinant in prioritising audits within budget constraints. The logic is to focus the timing and frequency of internal audit coverage on the riskier areas

- To determine focus—when an internal auditor analyses a business process, such as "Spare parts management" or "Procurement", they usually do so by testing the effectiveness of the design and operation of controls that prevent or mitigate the related risks to business objectives

- As the subject of some of their work—where the organisation's risk management processes and framework are reviewed by internal audit

The value of a "risk-based internal audit" is severely limited when the organisation's risk management framework is a compliance-focused variant of the basic risk management process. These impacts are usually well hidden within the internal audit black box so further explanation is needed.

In the first approach described above, when an internal auditor uses Ark bubbles as a key determinant in prioritising audits towards the riskier areas, they are probably focusing on the wrong areas. If the risk assessment from a quick workshop (typically five to 15 minutes spent in analysis of each event) is wrong then the internal audit focus is skewed to provide assurance that those issues that are relatively unimportant are effectively controlled.

In the example of spare parts in the remote plant, if the risk register shows an "Extreme" risk rating when it's actually "Medium", internal audit effort is not being effectively focused. Instead of in-depth business process audits every second year because it's high priority, the spare parts management system could probably be looked at every fourth year, particularly if the performance management framework and reporting is strong.

In the second approach, when internal audit test the effectiveness of the design and operation of controls, this work should be able to be linked in closely with the risk management process. The basic risk management process, even under the ageing COSO, has an important step of implementing treatment plans. Internal audit should be able to look in the risk register, extract details of the controls and treatment plans and go forth and test them with the knowledge that they are doing meaningful work, but rarely can they do this. The controls and treatment plans in the risk register were probably identified for several risk events in a four hour workshop based on what participants could come up with on the spot.

In the example of spare parts in the remote plant, the risk register has not properly accounted for the effectiveness (or otherwise) of controls established by the different service groups in the Production Department such as plant design (to isolate failures), agreements with suppliers to minimise lead times and arranging back-up supplies. If these controls had been properly assessed, then the efficiency and effectiveness of internal audit would be greatly enhanced.

In the third approach, when an internal audit assesses a compliance focused ERM process, the result should be blowing the whistle on risk bandits. The report should say that the process is for show, just to make the board and executive management feel good in the compliance sign-offs but has little impact on how the organisation manages risk and makes decisions. Yeah, right, that ain't gonna happen! The more likely report from internal audit is whether ISO 31000 terminologies have been used plus the completeness (but not accuracy) of risk registers and action lists.

The impact of banditry on the internal audit is therefore likely to be more on its effectiveness than its efficiency in that the auditor will take the same time to do the work and incur the same cost, but the organisation will have advanced its profitability and ethical performance very little. The auditor is not focusing properly and it's going to take the team longer because of the diversions caused by risk bandits.

If you are a director or an executive manager in your organisation ask your internal auditor to explain how they implement the "risk-based approach" and evaluate their response against the above black box enlightenment. You can then decide whether you have a risk bandit in the role.

External Audit and a Risk-Based Approach

External audit proposals and yearly plans also inevitably include reference to a "risk-based approach". Let's look at what this means and what impacts might arise from the use of floating bubbles by the organisation subject to audit.

Unlike internal auditors, the external auditor's work is not controlled by audit and risk committees and executive management. External financial report auditors make their own decisions on how they form a view on the presentation of financial reports but risk does have a key impact on their work.

A "risk-based approach" for an external audit means firstly that risk is used to prioritise work to the riskier areas and secondly that risk impacts the focus and content of their audit work. Risk for the external auditor in both cases is the risk of misstatement of the financial reports. This is related to, but different from, the organisation's risks sitting in the risk profile that are events that may cause variations from achieving the organisation's objectives. So does risk banditry come into play?

External auditors normally will review an organisation's risk profile and gain some understanding of the organisation's risk management framework. Scepticism is a desired quality for external auditors; they look at the organisation's risk profile and framework and make their own assessment as to how they will use them. Their specific role and independence means they are much less likely than internal auditors to be fooled by risk bandits.

Some of the risks of misstatement of the financial reports identified by external audit will be consistent with the organisation's risk profile and risk management framework, others will not. The external auditor focus is on the flow of information and the risk of not detecting any misstatements. If the organisation makes a bad decision because their risk assessment is poor it has little impact on the external audit as long as the information generated is accurate. The spare parts example illustrates the point.

For our remote agricultural product processing plant an organisational risk is "non-availability of critical spare parts". If the organisation gets the spares holding decision wrong then they can carry too many and incur the extra cost or too few and disrupt production. The risk for the external auditor is a little different, the auditor can easily check the quantity of parts through a stocktake and their costing through checks back to purchases—the risk of misstatement in the financial statements for the auditor is the overstatement of carrying value. If excess or obsolete spares are in stock at full value then the financial report may be misstated because the carrying value may not be recoverable from future cash flows, the asset value is "impaired".

The external auditor would normally use the organisation's risk profile to assist in understanding the entity and its control environment and to establish expectations as to transactions, assets and liabilities. Having decided that spare parts has a significant risk of misstatement, because of the judgemental nature of the decision to hold spares, the auditor would then look at the risk management process in place for the "non-availability of critical spare parts".

To his surprise, although the risk bubble is positioned by the risk manager as "Extreme", the Production Department has in place a sound risk management process that mitigates the risk. This process, however, sits to the side of the compliance driven process that is reported to the audit and risk committee and executive management. The external auditor can then decide if it is more efficient to check for overstatement of the carrying value by doing his own checks of spare parts usage or by testing the system used by the Production Department and relying on the output of that system.

The impact of the risk banditry on the external audit is therefore more likely to be on efficiency than effectiveness. The auditor still gets to the right conclusion as to whether the financial report is misstated; it's just going to take him longer because of the diversions caused by the risk bandits.

If you are a director or an executive manager in your organisation you can ask your external auditor for some observations on the risk management framework without impacting their independence. Ask them whether in implementing the risk-based approach set out in the audit plan he was diverted or assisted by the organisation's risk management framework. Also ask where did they rely on controls that are not recognised in the risk register.

You may then have another clue as to whether you have a risk bandit in the role of risk manager and some real evidence that it's costing the organisation money in terms of an inefficient audit.

Much More to be Done

In summarising this chapter, it is clear that there is much more to be done in developing the body of knowledge to elevate the basic risk management process into a framework to manage risk across modern organisations. ERM is not there yet; topping and tailing with organisational objectives, communication and monitoring isn't enough and the application of risk appetite is as vague as the positioning of bubbles on a risk matrix. The widely accepted simplistic approach to the basic risk management process has simply been elevated, in name only, to ERM.

Organisation risk management needs involvement from the board and executive management in the upfront design of a framework that manages the overall risk/return decision framework that is delegated from the board. Organisation risk management needs to be a pro-active part of the organisation's performance management, run by executive management and not by the monitoring and reporting of risk matrix bubbles by the risk manager.

6. The Matrix; Simulated Reality

Did You Hear the Story About...?

The sales manager, the risk manager and an off-duty policeman walk into your office and the sales manager, who is about to retire, presents the following report on last month's sales across five products:

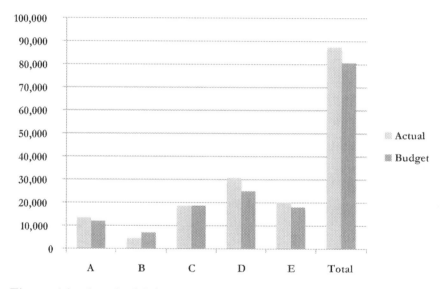

Figure 6.1—Standard Sales Report

You can see at a glance how each product is selling against budget, the relative importance of each product and how total sales are travelling against budget. The overall picture is good enough with actual sales nicely ahead of forecast. However, as CEO you know instantly that you should question whether or not to continue with Product B. On a percentage basis it performs worse than any other but, even if it hits forecast, it would deliver less than any other product. You ask the sales manager whether there is any reason to continue with this product, thank him for his report and the answer to your question and as he walks out you start considering whether the resources used on Product B could be better allocated elsewhere.

Three months later the now-retired sales manager is sitting on a golden beach near his downsized seaside home. He looks at the engraving on his gold watch that says 'thanks for making a difference Joe—from everyone at ACME Products'.

Back at ACME, the former risk manager, has been promoted to sales manager, a direct report to you unlike his previous role that reported through the Company Secretary. He presents his first sales report in his new "concise but insightful" format. Banditry is in full flight in this format that is compiled from the same unit prices and sales volumes as Figure 6.1:

Price / Volume ➡	0-200	201-400	401-600	601-800	801-1,000
$41 - $50	Good	Very Good	(C) Really Good	Really Good	Really Good
$31 - $40	Good	Good	Very Good	(D) (E) Really Good	Really Good
$21 - $30	(B) Good	Good	Good	Very Good	Really Good
$11 - $20	Bad	Bad	Good	Very Good	(A) Very Good
$0 - $10	Bad	Bad	Good	Good	Very Good

Figure 6.2—Revenue Matrix

Everything is "Good" or better—wow this is even better than the performance under Joe. No doubt you'd like to believe this, but the new format unnerves you a little, so you open a spreadsheet and put the same data in old Joe's format and bingo ... you still need to consider serious action re Product B. Now you need to ask yourself 'why didn't I do that kind of check when I first thought risk reports were rubbish?' Before you protest that they are different, have a closer look—revenue is unit prices x sales volumes whilst, as explained in Chapter 4, risk is likelihood x consequence. We think of revenue as a number even though it is the product of two numbers, fair enough. But we have been conditioned to think of risk in an organisation in terms of the two aspects, likelihood and consequence, but the numbers are not usually multiplied because they are ranges and too inaccurate to multiply.

To cover up this shortcoming, the cells in the risk matrix are given captions, just as they have been in the above revenue matrix. The captions and the ranges on the two axes are completely arbitrary but we get an answer quoted as a caption rather than a number. It's the same as saying revenue for Product A is "Very Good" rather than $13,500.

What about the off-duty policeman you ask? Something deep inside him screamed 'arrest this guy' when he looked at the ex-risk manager's presentation. He thought you'd have to act against something so outrageous. Little did he know; it's happening everywhere.

Navigation Guidance

This chapter contains 18 Figures; they are designed for visual interpretation to illustrate the weaknesses in the risk matrix and heat map. It is not necessary to follow the calculations to stay with the plot for the remainder of "Risk Bandits". Alternatively, you may care to dwell on the detail in the Figures of greatest interest.

Dream World Built to Control Us

The 1999 film, 'The Matrix', starring Keanu Reeves, was about simulated reality created by machines to subdue humans. A line from Morpheus in the film has an eerie irony about it:

> 'The Matrix is a computer-generated dream world built to keep us under control'.
>
> Samuel Leroy Jackson

In organisations, risk bandits, rather than machines build the risk matrix, but it does generate a dream world to keep us under control.

Morpheus was also correct when he said 'The Matrix is everywhere. It is all around us'. Risk bandits peddle the matrix and despite it being close to useless for anything other than a high-level guess at the importance of threats; yet it is widely accepted as the tool for risk assessment and presentation of risk profiles. The acceptance of the risk matrix in many organisations has almost developed into an unnatural love affair.

The risk matrix is the foundation of risk banditry; the guessing within wide ranges and applying captions to each cell drive its use as a shonky compliance tool rather than to impact performance within an organisation. It also drives the way risks are described and reported as we analyse below. The wide gene pool within risk management, described in Chapter 2, is enabled by the risk matrix as its use does not require much training or experience. It also allows executive management, usually without complaint from the board, to abdicate rather than delegate the formal risk management system to a risk manager who only has sufficient skills and pay grade to focus on individual risk trees and not the risk forest.

This chapter is about persuasion to try to convince you of the evils of the risk matrix. If you are uncomfortable with the risk matrix, this chapter will help you understand that discomfort, and the revenue matrix above is intended to start that process. If on the other hand you are a risk matrix junkie, please try to read this chapter with an open mind. We think that open minds will be convinced that another quote from Morpheus is correct, 'The Matrix is a system, Neo. That system is our enemy'.

Size Doesn't matter... or Does It?

Is precision in risk assessment important? If risk assessments are an average of uninformed reaction-based opinions from a rushed workshop facilitated by an outsider pinning tails on a multi-coloured donkey—then the answer is clearly no. The use of the matrix reinforces this flight to imprecision, the risk assessment is in the ballpark and that's good enough.

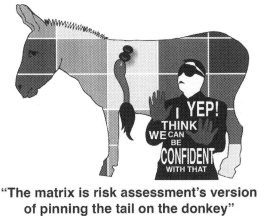

"The matrix is risk assessment's version of pinning the tail on the donkey"
prof. Patrick Hudson

Figure 6.3—Pin The Tail On The Matrix

Chapter 4 explained that at its simplest level risk can be calculated as likelihood x consequence, so a risk event that occurs three times every four years with a cost of $6 million each time it occurs has an expected statistical value of $4.5 million per annum (75% x $6 million). Let's overlay this calculation on the risk matrix from Figure 3.2 to understand the inherent ballpark.

Likelihood	$10,000	$100,000	$1,000,000	$10,000,000	$100,000,000	
						100%
Almost Certain	$10,000	$100,000	$1,000,000	$10,000,000	$100,000,000	
						95%
Likely	$9,500	$95,000	$950,000	$9,500,000	$95,000,000	
						65%
Possible	$6,500	$65,000	$650,000	$6,500,000	$65,000,000	
						35%
Unlikely	$3,500	$35,000	$350,000	$3,500,000	$35,000,000	
						10%
Rare	$1,000	$10,000	$100,000	$1,000,000	$10,000,000	
						0%
Consequence →	Insignificant	Minor	Moderate	Major	Catastrophic	

Figure 6.4—Risk Matrix Ballpark

The boundaries of each cell in this table have a value calculated by the likelihood x consequence, so for example the boundary of the "Likely" / "Major" shaded cell has an approximate maximum value range as follows:

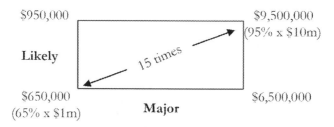

$950,000

$9,500,000 (95% x $10m)

Likely

15 times

$650,000 (65% x $1m)

Major

$6,500,000

Figure 6.5—"Likely" / "Major" Cell Ballpark

This is a huge ballpark! Our example risk value is $4.5 million but the ballpark is $650,000 to $9,500,000 i.e. the highest risk is almost 15 times greater than the lowest risk in this single cell. This means that if the organisation undertook expensive risk treatment measures that reduced the $4.5 million loss per annum by a massive 80% it could remain in exactly the same cell (or ballpark)! Furthermore, the business case for incurring the cost of the treatment measures would hang on whatever subjective grounds the review team come up with because the risk matrix tells us there is zero benefit in cost/benefit terms (i.e. the risk will probably remain in the same cell).

Would the board of any organisation tolerate the use of ballparks like this for decisions such as approving annual budgets, capital projects or transactions? Of course not. So why is the matrix still around? The answer for most organisations is that the ballpark nature is just not noticed because the risk matrix is not really used in decision-making. Size doesn't matter because the whole formal risk management process doesn't matter; it's there to demonstrate compliance not to enhance performance.

For some risks, the calculation is not worth undertaking (e.g. paper cuts and minor travel expense fiddling) and for clear and credible organisation threatening risks (e.g. aircraft crash for an airline) because the figures don't have to be too accurate to justify major investment and focus. But for the majority of material risks size does matter.

The Revenue Matrix in Figure 6.2 is not usable because the organisation needs to know the sales data with some precision, perhaps within 2%. So what is the degree of precision needed for risk assessment? It may be as high as within say 50% but surely it's not plus or minus 750% for each risk!

If risk is applied in an organisation using ballparks why not face up to the fact and not pretend—just don't claim the organisation has a "best practice risk management framework" or that it undertakes "risk-based decision-making". All ballparkism can achieve is a broad level of comfort or discomfort that may well be misleading, it can't be used to drive strategic and operational decisions nor can it legitimately be used to assess resource allocation in strengthening or relaxing controls across pods of risks.

Simple but Neither Understandable nor Effective

Risk matrix supporters argue the matrix is simple, easy to understand and reasonably effective. We only agree that it is simple, in fact so simple that its lack of substance is embarrassing. It's a $5 calculator pretending to be a computer.

If you are worried about ballparkism but your matrix habit is too strong for you to break right now, perhaps introducing a degree of meaningful quantification might help. Unfortunately a common approach to some quantification shown below is not only low on improvement but it is compounding the inadequacies of the matrix. It involves changing the captions in cells in the matrix from words such as "High" to numbers. This is done by captions in the base row and column on the "X" and "Y" axes from one (1) to five (5) with the lowest number representing the lowest likelihood or consequence. Each matrix cell then has a number representing the product of the likelihood and consequence values.

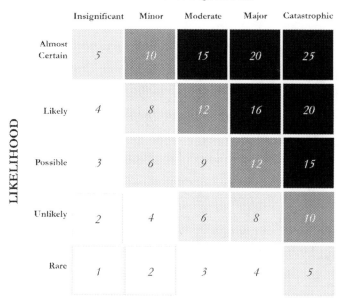

Figure 6.6—'Semi-Quantified' Risk Matrix

Some people call this "semi-quantification" but the only way that is a reasonable description is by interpreting the meaning very literally, i.e. that the risk metric captions are stated in numbers instead of words. Sadly the number captions are even more misleading than the word captions. If this has been allowed to exist in your organisation, someone should be hanging his or her head in abject shame. The numbers are totally misleading for the purpose of prioritising treatment actions on risk events, but they are clearly good enough for some risk bandits to sell to executive management and the board. Let's apply a level of probing that any senior manager or director could have done given sufficient interest.

The bottom left hand cell has a value of one (1) and the top right hand cell has a value of twenty five (25). If you look at the same cells in Figure

6.6 above, which is a typical example of what is used everyday in many organisations, the top right hand risk cell is one hundred thousand (100,000) times and not twenty five (25) times greater than the bottom left hand cell value. If the mid-point of the range is used instead of the maximum the range is only lowered to approximately ninety thousand (90,000) times which is galaxyism rather than ballparkism!

To look at the ballpark compounding effect another way, let us consider a risk profile where the pod of the highest six risks events lie in the top three rows of the "Moderate" and "Major" columns in the matrix in Figure 6.4 above. How can management apply resources to the six events in a manner somewhat proportional to the risk they pose? They simply can't because the range of the six risks in total is $11.6 million to $128.6 million—a difference of $117 million!

Imagine a listed company announcing guidance for next year's profit as $58 million, plus or minus 100%! The reason this does not happen is not the one given by risk bandits, i.e. that there is insufficient hard data available, because there are many unknowns in setting profit guidance too. It's because the risk matrix accepts and encourages the wildest stab in the dark and so it cannot be used for any meaningful decision. One of the strongest arguments for keeping the matrix alive is that it is simple to use and the great majority are comfortable with it. Whilst noting that there is no well-articulated case that it is effective, we do concur that it is indeed simple and that people are comfortable with it. The same could be said about smoking for most of the 20th century. In both cases there was ample evidence of the damage being done but people just didn't want to see it.

Perhaps you think the "semi-quantified" risk matrix in Figure 6.6 is a bit extreme; surely it's hardly used. Enter those words in an images search engine and scroll through the results, it is used by many organisations and there are even risk bandit consultants selling it by lauding its usefulness. If you agree that this form of the matrix should not be used by your organisation, we have agreed the principle that a degree of accuracy is important, and now all we have to do is agree how much precision is needed. So 90,000 times is too much, what about 15 times within an individual cell for each risk as shown in Figure 6.5. If you now feel that is a bit high then your organisation should not be using the matrix.

In a survey of 1,000 American adults, 64% rated themselves as either "Very Good" or "Excellent" drivers. There is absolutely no alignment between the opinion of the drivers about their competence and the factual data (i.e. only 50% of people can be above average) but this overconfidence makes them feel good about themselves and allows them to continue practicing the many illegal motoring acts that are common amongst them[10]. We therefore pose the question; does the smugness of matrix users that they have managed risk well increasingly raise their confidence that risk is under control whilst any rational examination dictates the exact opposite?

In the land of the matrix it is impossible to demonstrate that an event would have occurred if any of the subjectively determined risk treatment actions undertaken were left undone. This is because the claimed gain for risk treatment is never quantified and cannot therefore be tracked. We are convinced that a very substantial part of the risk management expenditure for most organisations provides little or no return. Directors and executive management should be wary of any assumption that a cause and effect relationship exists between risk prevention actions and non-occurrence of risk events because this could involve a waste of funds that could be put to better use elsewhere.

As Easy As Falling Off a Bike

If the limitations of the matrix are recognised then perhaps it doesn't matter so much, as long as it's not used beyond those limitations. Unfortunately, most organisations do use the risk matrix way beyond its limitations. Imagine a consultant risk bandit undertaking a risk assessment of something extremely simple, falling off a bike whilst commuting to work. Let us set the scene …

[10] Allstate Corporation Media Release, 2011, New Allstate Survey Shows Americans Think They Are Great Drivers—Habits Tell a Different Story, P.2

Act 1, Scene 1:   **Curtain Up**

Figure 6.7—Act 1, Scene 1

Two businessmen sit in a small meeting room, with a brightly coloured interpretation of the ISO 31000 risk matrix projected on the wall. In the bottom right hand corner sits a somewhat oversized logo of a risk-consulting firm. The younger of the two men speaks with a slight voice tremble as this is only his fifth workshop as facilitator. He has just finished "setting the context" of the assessment. This didn't take long as there is only one assessment being carried out this day, which means that the hazard identification step has already been completed by the client. The young risk bandit puts his newly learned risk management skills into practice …

RB   'Mr. Punter, how often would you say in your experience your people would fall off their bike when cycling to work?'

Client   'Well, I don't cycle to work personally, but our health and safety log tells us that our people have fallen off five times in the last three years.'

RB   'And what kind of injuries were sustained?'

Client   'Sore knees and grazed arms mostly—on one occasion a woman was sent to hospital for X-rays because a fracture of the wrist was suspected—but they couldn't find anything.'

RB   'So your people fall off five times in three years or 1.7 times each year on average and they sustain minor injuries each time. That's "Almost Certain" or "Likely" in terms of likelihood and "Minor" or "Insignificant" in terms of consequence. Hmmm... that's a "Pale Red" risk if it's "Almost Certain" / "Minor", "Pale Green" risk if it's "Likely" / "Insignificant" but "Blue" risk if it's "Almost Certain" / "Insignificant" or "Likely" / "Minor".'

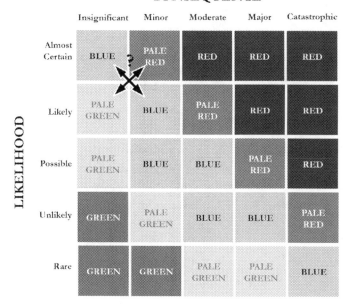

CONSEQUENCE

	Insignificant	Minor	Moderate	Major	Catastrophic
Almost Certain	BLUE	PALE RED	RED	RED	RED
Likely	PALE GREEN	BLUE	PALE RED	RED	RED
Possible	PALE GREEN	BLUE	BLUE	PALE RED	RED
Unlikely	GREEN	PALE GREEN	BLUE	BLUE	PALE RED
Rare	GREEN	GREEN	PALE GREEN	PALE GREEN	BLUE

LIKELIHOOD

Figure 6.8—Falling Off A Bike

Client 'So our risk is "Pale Red", "Blue" or "Pale Green"? What do you suggest I put in my register?'

RB   'Let's say it's "Pale Red", it's better to be safe than sorry after all.'

Client 'What about serious injury or death?'

RB   'No problem—How many times have your employees been killed in the last five years? ...'

Curtain Down

Note that the risk bandit started the conversation with a likelihood question of how often. This is because the likelihood x consequence formula puts it first. However, the likelihood value can only be estimated after the nature of the range of consequences being contemplated has been defined. It's not possible to assess how often a high jumper clears the bar without first asking how high the bar is set. When the bar is one metre the success rate should be close to 100%, at two metres it might be 50% at three metres it won't even be attempted.

The falling off the bike risk event could also have many of the consequences contained in the consequence scale. An entry-level risk bandit probably wouldn't even raise this pesky range of probabilities, and if the client doesn't know better, the risk assessment part of the workshop is now complete.

Act 2, Scene 1:   Curtain Up

Figure 6.9—Act 2, Scene 1

It is two weeks later. Two people sit in a small meeting room, with a brightly coloured interpretation of the ISO 31000 risk process projected on the wall. In the bottom right hand corner sits the exquisitely proportioned logo of a global risk advisory firm. The woman is a partner of the consulting firm and she presents a sophisticated image in both her choice of clothing and the assurance of her dialogue. The man is a client that is revisiting a risk scenario that he took part in recently. He has decided to hire "the best" as doing it on the cheap last time didn't provide him with much confidence in the outcomes.

Client	'I must say I've been looking forward to understanding a great deal more about risk management Ms. Bandit.'
RB	'And I'm happy to share the rudiments of a complex subject with you Mr Punter. For which pushbike consequence would you like us to estimate the risk?'
Client	'Hmmm, this is a different way to start the assessment.'
RB	'Oh really, what do you normally do?'
Client	'Oh, don't worry, I don't think we had the best possible help on the last occasion.'
RB	'Obviously not us then. Actually you'd be amazed at how many poor risk assessors there are around today. Now, as I said previously, which pushbike consequence would you like us to assess?'
Client	'Can't we do them all?'
RB	'Well now, we could but it would take considerably more time and I'm afraid our quotation didn't cover that option.'
Client	'Oh, really? In that case I'd like to cover the serious injury or fatality please.'
RB	'Interesting choice if you don't mind me saying so. Most people go for the most common outcome.'
Client	'Which one would be the higher risk of the two?'
RB	'We won't know unless we do both, and …'
Client	'OK, let me guess … it'll take longer and incur more cost, right? I'll pay for both the most common and the highest consequence options as long as we can finish before 3pm when I have to go to another meeting.'
RB	'As long as you're comfortable with that. Tell me what pushbike incidents have occurred over recent years.'
Client	'Employees have come off their bikes five times in the last three years, four times it caused minor injuries but the fifth one, which involved a suspected fracture, was more painful and took a while to heal.'
RB	'Did the person have time off work? Was it a Lost Time Incident?'
Client	'No—we only lost a couple of hours having an X-ray taken.'
RB	'So all incidents were just minor injuries then—the most common outcome.'
Client	'But it could have been a broken arm as easy as not.'

| RB | 'I suggest you hold that one over until we calculate the risk for the worst outcome.' |

RB   'I suggest you hold that one over until we calculate the risk for the worst outcome.'

Client   'But it won't be the worst outcome, that'll be a broken back or neck.'

RB   'Much as we'd love to, we really can't do everything now can we? Why don't we just complete the two you nominated for now, I'm sure you'll be comfortable that you have a very good grasp of the risk by then.'

Client   'Right, I think I'm getting the hang of this now, we'll forget the bumps and bruises—I can live with them. We'll assess the broken bone/torn ligament stuff, and then the paraplegic/fatality stuff.'

RB   'So you're not going to do the most common outcome after all?'

Client   'Nope!'

RB   'Are you sure?'

Client   'Sure I'm sure, let's go.'

RB   'Tell me about the more serious injuries you've had over recent years.'

Client   'I've already told you, we haven't had any.'

RB   'But at least one of them could very easily have been more serious.'

Client   'So … do we count the might-have-been cases as if they were real?'

RB   'Well, no—but neither can we assess the likelihood of a broken bone or torn ligament with the data we've got.'

Client   'The rules of risk assessment seem to be quite difficult to pin down don't they?'

RB   'Indeed yes, but that's why you hired me to help clarify what is really a quite complicated field.'

Client   'That had been my hope … shall we continue anyway?'

The Partner chose to ignore any possible sarcasm in the client's remark, as she has done on so many previous occasions, and the pair go on to decide that the chance of a broken bone/torn ligament is "Moderate" / "Possible" and therefore a "Blue" risk and the chance of a fatality is "Major" / "Unlikely", also a "Blue" risk. The journey was uncomfortable because the client was forced to guess how often things would occur that the company had never experienced and if, as suggested by the Partner, he agreed to use official public incident data figures, there would have been little point in hiring a consultant at all.

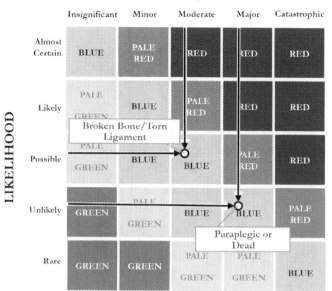

Figure 6.10—Falling Off A Bike, Again

Client 'So we have two "Blue" risks. Are two "Blue" risks worse or better than a "Pale Red" risk?'

RB 'I'm afraid it doesn't work like that.'

Client 'Let me put it another way, if I could treat this risk or a "Light Red" risk, which one should I treat first?'

RB "The "Light Red" one, it's worse than a "Blue" one ...'

Client 'but ...'

RB 'If you'll let me finish sir, and if we did different consequence assessments of the "Light Red" risk we would probably find that there are other risks associated with that one too.'

Client 'I'm not feeling confident Ms. Bandit'

RB 'Oh Mr Punter, you should be extremely confident, after all you're asking much more probing questions than most of my regular clients.'

Client 'You have regular clients Ms. Bandit?'

Curtain Down

Whilst there is a funny side to these two scenes, it's actually rather serious. Scenes like this occur every day in many organisations struggling to deal with a tool that is simply not fit for purpose.

Significant Shortcomings

Some experienced risk bandits know the shortcomings of their risk matrix-centred process but aren't qualified or credible enough to undertake the real stuff. Some are too lazy to even want to. The hypothetical client above has picked up a few significant shortcomings of heat maps or risk matrices; it's worthy of analysis.

Tendency to Round Up

The matrix process isn't anywhere near sufficiently structured to ensure that the frequency of an incident (e.g. falling off a bike) and the probability that the incident goes on to cause the outcomes under consideration (e.g. broken bones and fatalities) are both contemplated within the risk event. Nor does it ensure the relevant outcome correlates with the incident frequency. As a result it is common for risk assessors to conclude that the frequency of the incident (a fall from the bike) is five times in three years (let's say "Likely") and a fatality is quite possible ("Major") and conclude the risk is now a full "Red", not "Pale Red", "Pale Green" or "Blue".

CONSEQUENCE

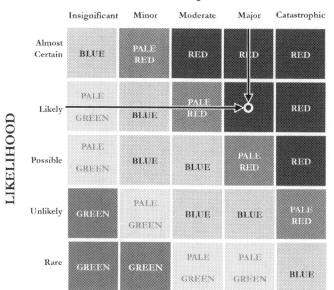

Figure 6.11—Falling Off A Bike, The Finale

If you doubt this occurs regularly, take a good look at your organisation's current risk register—it's unlikely to take you very long to find one!

Simplicity Drives Shallow Analysis

The ballparkism of the risk matrix not only allows risk bandits to get away with shallow analysis of the risks of the organisation, it encourages it. Estimating sales for the month for the Revenue Matrix in Figure 6.2 could be done by a quick chat with the sales and warehouse employees, it doesn't need to be accurate.

The same level of analysis applies to the risk matrix, risk bandits just contemplate as many controls and risk actions as they can and stick them in the risk register. No need to consider their completeness or relative importance just put a few entries in each box in the risk register template and it looks good. Accountants are the brunt of many jokes about double entry but their tools are self-checking, if the trial balance doesn't balance there is an error. No such discipline or self-checking mechanism exists with the risk matrix, so errors and over simplistic analysis simply won't be detected.

Extremely Crude Measurement of Risk

In most risk matrices the likelihood scale goes up in orders of magnitude, i.e. each cell is ten times more likely than the cell below it in line with the ballparkism theory. There is less consistency about the consequence graduations but the steps are significant. In the typical risk matrix in Figure 6.4, the columns are the same width but the scale graduations range from $10,000 to $90 million. At least the Revenue Matrix in Figure 6.1 was drawn to scale. This perverse underlying scale manipulation is simply ignored by, or invisible to, users.

As we saw earlier in this chapter, the typical ballpark within a single cell of the risk matrix is 15 times but across the whole matrix the range is in the thousands, yet Noah's bubbles sit side by side in the same chart enabled by masked scale graduations. Relative importance of risk bubbles on the risk matrix is not just hidden, it's misleading.

It is utter nonsense to consider the risks represented by these bubbles as equal or even remotely similar in significance when deciding on risk improvements. To emphasise this point, for the vast majority of top 500 organisations, all of their catastrophic safety risks (multiple fatalities) and the great majority of their material financial exposures would be in a single cell in the bottom right hand corner of the matrix.

Even if audit and risk committees only consider risk treatment actions for risks sitting in six "Red" cells on a typical risk matrix the relative significance of these risks is likely to be factor of 50+ times between the highest and lowest risk. Yet all these actions are shown as relating to "Extreme" risks and given equal weight.

Assumption that Rounding Up is Conservative

There is no conservative direction in risk assessment because the aim is to prioritise treatment actions. If organisations push all assessments higher they end up concentrating all of the risks in one corner of the matrix and differentiation between those scenarios that are in need of significant treatment resources and those that are less needy becomes even harder.

Imagine you are the new Principal at a school for children with learning difficulties. The fact that any given child is in your school puts that child in the same broad category as all the others, but it is extremely likely that a few of those children will consume far more of your time than most of the others. Now assume that the current approach to allocating resources was to assume every child was at the extreme end of the learning difficulty spectrum—just to be conservative. As the Principal you would swiftly put a stop to the practice. Similarly, the attempt to be conservative using a matrix leads to less effective use of precious resources.

Tendency to Focus on Actuarial Data over What Might be Looming

There is a well-known quotation about over-reliance on past experience when charting the future.

> 'We drive into the future using only our rearview mirror.'
>
> Marshall McLuhan 1911-1980, Canadian philosopher

In the Piper Alpha disaster in 1988, millions of viewers on TV watched as a giant offshore production platform was first consumed by a massive fireball and then, very slowly, melted into the sea with the loss of 167 lives. At a recent conference, Lord Cullen who led the British Government inquiry into the event repeated his view on those that want to overly rely on the rear view. He said 'Major accidents are relatively rare—history does not repeat itself in the same fashion'[11]. Cullen was talking about safety in this instance, but every form of risk contains a similar message. Learn the common trends from the past, but expect them to show themselves in markedly different ways in future. It is critical to remember that many current trends have yet to wreak their full havoc.

Captions, Colours and Criteria are Arbitrary

Many directors and executive managers think the captions and colours on the risk matrix and criteria underlying them are defined somewhere in standards

---

[11] Jeffrey, K., 2013, Lord Cullen—What have we learned from Piper Alpha? Finding Petroleum Sept 16th 2013, http://www.findingpetroleum.com/n/ Review_Lord_Cullen_what_have_we_learned_from_Piper_Alpha/044b5113. aspx

or in well-accepted literature. Wrong—they are set by each organisation's risk manager! A favourite trick of risk bandits is to change the scale or captions on the matrix if all the bubbles float toward the bottom left hand corner or the top right hand corner.

Some audit committees or executive managers are aware that the risk manager has this power and undertake an annual review of the likelihood and consequence scale graduations. Whilst this is good practice, the assumption remains of the use of the risk matrix way beyond its design capacity.

Masking of Extremely High-Impact Low-Frequency Events

Risk managers in setting the likelihood scale of their risk matrix usually start with "Almost Certain" with multiple occurrences in a year and extend to "Rare". The guidelines for interpreting the likelihood tables vary enormously. Whilst some of this variation is appropriate, reflecting organisational differences, much of the variation is not so appropriate.

Many organisations have different risk managers for "business" risk and "Health, Safety and Environmental" (HSE) risk and where this occurs there is often a difference in what is considered "Rare". In safety terms the most common descriptions of "Rare" are 'less than once in 1,000 years' and 'less than once in 100 years' whereas for "business" risk occurrence descriptions like 'less than once every 25 years' and 'less than once in ten years' are far more common. For board reporting, organisations often consolidate the HSE assessments into the organisation's "Enterprise Risk" matrix.

Given the "Rare" bottom row of the organisation matrix only ever has captions of "Low", "Medium" and maybe "High" in the "Catastrophic" column, this structure masks the importance of very low-frequency but extremely high-impact risk events.

The type of events being contemplated here would usually be unacceptable to a board—at least not without assurance of substantial analysis. They may be non-financial events such as safety or environmental harm, however, they could also be financially material, with major corporate fraud and global financial crises as examples. The common organisation matrix likelihood scale is geared to financially oriented everyday operating risks so everything less frequent than, say 25 years, is lumped together. Risks that maybe larger than others by factors in the hundreds are thrown together in the same cell and do not make the board radar because the matrix structure does not throw up an "Extreme" caption. One of the reasons this occurs is that executive managers and directors tend to interpret 'less than once in 25 years' as 'more than 25 years away'. This is a common, but nonetheless potentially fatal flaw in thinking because that 'once' could as easily happen tomorrow as in 30 years' time!

Inability to Deal with a Range of Possible Outcomes of an Event

The last significant shortcoming of the risk matrix and heat map, which was noticed by the observant client, is that most risk events have a range of possible outcomes with severity ranging from tolerable through to disastrous. Which consequence do you plot on the matrix? The highest, the one that gives the highest risk ranking or an average? But there's more! How do you handle different assessments applying the financial and non-financial consequence criteria behind the matrix? A tolerable financial outcome might be disastrous in non-financial terms, safety being a prime example. Remember taking the worst case is not conservative.

Imagine that you are a CEO of a middle tier company servicing a market prone to cyclones. The records going back over a 1,000 years show the occurrence of different categories of cyclones and your team has estimated the impact on EBIT of each cyclone as follows:

Category	1	2	3	4	5
Occurrences	9 per year	9 per 10 years	9 per 100 years	9 per 1,000 years	1 per 1,000 years
EBIT impact per occurrence	$10,000	$100,000	$1m	$10m	$100m

Figure 6.12—Cyclone Statistics

If we assume a loss of $100 million off EBIT would be difficult to survive (either as an organisation or as a CEO or Chairman), how would this be plotted on the risk matrix? Note that these are not different risk events they are differing severities of its occurrence.

Consequence ➡	Insignificant <$10k	Minor $10k to $100k	Moderate $100k to $1m	Major $1m to $10m	Catastrophic > $10m
Likelihood ↓					
Almost Certain Multiple times per year	Medium (1)	High	High	Extreme	Extreme
Likely Once per year	Medium	Medium (2)	High	Extreme	Extreme
Possible Once every 5 years	Low	Medium	Medium (3)	High	Extreme
Unlikely Once every 25 years	Low	Low	Medium	High	High
Rare (Once every 25+ years)	Low	Low	Medium	Medium (4)	High (5)

Figure 6.13—Cyclone Prone Risk Matrix

Difficult isn't it? Is it "Medium" or "High" or should we be worried about the catastrophic Category 5 cyclone? In this case, and using this specific matrix, there are four consequences at "Medium" and one at "High", so we would automatically pick the one that happens to be both highest consequence and highest risk on this occasion. However, it is very likely that the four "Medium" possible outcomes outweigh the one "High" possible outcome, i.e. we are leaving more risk unrecorded than we have included in the register. In addition, had the matrix had a 'once in a 1,000 year' likelihood option, the "Catastrophic" risk would be rated no higher than the others. There simply is no right spot on the matrix because it does not fit the situation of differing possible outcome severities that occurs with most risks.

For these reasons, and many others, the risk matrix can only be used for very crude screening of risk[12] no matter how proficient the user.

Risks Designed to Please

On a number of occasions in this book you have been encouraged to have a look at the risk register used by your organisation. If you get that far, have a close look at say the top five risks and analyse how the risks are described. You are now armed to understand how risk bandits use the risk matrix to 'keep us under control, Neo!'

---

[12] Cross, J. 2012, 'Risk' in HaSPA (Health and Safety Professionals Alliance)—The Core Body of Knowledge for Generalist OHS Professionals. Tullamarine, VIC. © Safety Institute of Australia, P35

How the risks are described? Remembering the mechanics of a risk in the high-level bowtie diagram in Figure 4.3, ascertain if the descriptions include causes, events and consequences. They should be simply risk events as they realise the uncertainty that exists around the achievement of your organisation's objectives. But if your organisation uses the risk matrix then your resident risk bandit will use descriptions including a mix of causes, events, consequences and perhaps even a control failure might be thrown in now and then. The risk descriptions will either be very narrow in describing the cause and consequence around the risk event or they will overlap and need consolidating.

So what is the banditry here? The narrow descriptions of very specific causes and consequences around the risk event are designed to allocate very specific responsibilities to the risk owner. Top marks to the risk manager you might think; we need accountability. But there is a problem, the risk descriptions become so narrow that they ignore the bulk of the totality of that risk. The risk matrix can't cope with ranges of causes and consequences so many risk bandits just pick one and ignore the rest. It's done to make life easier for the risk bandit; narrow descriptions mean less analysis and a smaller herding yard for the cats.

Alternatively, risk managers who dare not change the output of a rushed workshop, allow massive duplication of effort whilst totally missing some critical exposures. This comes about from a lack of control of the relationship between various risk events that inevitably arises in the group dynamics of a workshop using a risk matrix as the basis of assessment. An individual risk event description might look half reasonable in itself but together with others in the register they often overlap, occasionally miss a chunk of the risk pie and always confuse. Overlapping risk descriptions are likely to result in risk owners, management and audit and risk committee members losing any interest in the detail of the risks because it's all just too hard. This is a key reason why the details of risks recorded in the register and risk profile reports are rarely discussed at executive and board level in an organisation and the unchallenged compliance sign-off is the only tangible result.

Some examples will help you detect this shambles in your organisation. Let's start with some easy ones, exchange rate risk and IT risk, then we will move on to something a bit more complex, climate change risk.

How does this sound as a risk description for a small manufacturing company?

"Increased offshore sourcing leading to higher costs as the exchange rate falls"

Yes, the description is accurate but muddled—is the concern "increased costs?", or "offshore sourcing?" or "exchange rate fluctuations?" If it is increased costs then there are many other contributors, some of which may have positive impacts, as the negative impacts of others get worse. If the issue is offshore sourcing then domestic sourcing may bring even worse problems. If the issue is exchange rate then the risk analysis would need to consider both sides of the exchange rate equation, upside and downside, within the cost of product.

The risk manager loves the micro approach because he can allocate ownership of this risk to the purchasing or finance people and he is off the hook. What about foreign currency revenue, expenses and loans? A much better description using the initiating event concept is:

"Foreign exchange gains/losses different from forecast"

This description covers the totality of the risk and relates the uncertainty to the organisation's objectives. This description requires multiple owners of causes and controls so a cunning risk bandit will use the risk matrix to avoid this extra pressure.

The second example is:

"IT system failure resulting in loss of data"

There are similar issues here as the first example, including the many other causes of data loss and the many other impacts of IT failure. A better description is:

"IT system non-availability"

This description brings into play disruptions from causes other than system failures and consequences other than loss of data.

Climate change risk is now in the risk registers of many organisations and is also one of the most commonly butchered risk descriptions. Here is an actual example:

"Increased asset maintenance costs due to climate change"

Wow, the risk bandit has got this risk off his desk and the asset manager is in the firing line. This description came out of a workshop and the risk matrix was used to assess it as "High" risk; but it's only a small part of the issue. Climate change may impact weather and hence asset maintenance but it may also have other physical impacts as well as regulatory impacts that may have consequences in not only costs but also safety and service delivery.

The risk matrix cannot handle multiple causal groups and a range of consequences so this organisation has ignored them. A much better risk description that will cause the risk manager a lot more analysis and work is:

"Revision of our climate change expectations/targets"

This description is an event that realises uncertainty relative to the organisation's objectives. Causes of change in the climate change targets may include not only increasing physical impacts, but also regulatory impacts as well as a decision to change maintenance regimes and other controls.

To help you spot the banditry here is an easy to read tabulation of some good and bad descriptions:

Confused Risk Descriptions		Risk Event Descriptions
Increased offshore sourcing leading to higher costs as the exchange rate falls	⟨1⟩	Foreign exchange gains / losses different from forecast
IT system failure resulting in loss of data	⟨1⟩	IT system non-availability
Increased asset maintenance costs due to climate change	⟨1⟩	Change in climate change expectations / targets
Poor operating performance due to failure to attract and retain key staff	⟨2⟩	Variation in organisation wide key staff capability
Stakeholder actions impacting operations and reputation	⟨3⟩	Change in stakeholder expectations or engagement demands
Safety procedures not followed in warehouse	⟨4⟩	Employee struck by falling object; Fork lift/vehicle collision*
Poor response to an environmental incident	⟨5⟩	Loss of containment of hazardous chemical*

Notes:

⟨1⟩ See earlier paragraphs

⟨2⟩ Ignores the many other problems of losing good people and ignores the possibility of improving key person standards

⟨3⟩ Presumably some actions were allowed for in budgets and plans, also assumes all stakeholder actions are detrimental and therefore closes the door on closer engagement

⟨4⟩ Focused on a behaviour, not an event and therefore far too wide to be manageable ... trying to boil the ocean

⟨5⟩ Focused on mitigation to the exclusion of preventing the incident. Also likely to be undertaken by a purely environmental team who will ignore safety and financial consequences. An integrity review of this critical control may be required, but not a risk assessment

*Incidents are events that usually only have negative consequences, the examples given are possible incidents that should be identified as risk events

Figure 6.14—Risk Event Descriptions

Including terms within risk descriptions such as "different from plan" (or forecast or budget) is a convenient way to relate risk events to organisational objectives. The use of "different" rather than "below" contemplates upside (positive consequences) as well as downside (negative consequences). For incidents with only negative consequences, such as injuries or IT system non-availability, the description is more accurate if it only contemplates downside.

Some organisations may include in their budgets an allowance for the financial impact of incidents. The question therefore arises as to whether the risk description of an event should contemplate the potential upside of incident impact costs being below budget. An example would be "IT system non-availability different from plan" rather than "IT system non-availability". We prefer the latter because the budget allowance is really a mitigating action to reduce the impact of incidents rather than a possible outcome of the risk event. The budget allowance, however, may well be deducted in the risk value calculation.

The Blueprint for Workshops

In Chapter 4 the risk workshop fad was exposed for its use as a primary tool of risk assessment. How can it be that the average "vote" from a group of people guessing at the severity of a poorly defined risk can be seen as a risk assessment? Democracy doesn't usually work well in organisations and is often only encouraged when dealing with a tokenistic process.

It won't surprise readers that we blame that pesky risk matrix! Sure risk bandits run the process and they should be held to account but they are usually allowed to get away with pleading that the risk matrix is almost universally accepted and demonstrating that a bunch of people agreed on an assessment is all that is needed to fulfil compliance obligations. Even the voting is kept anonymous much of the time to ensure it's a committee decision with no individual responsible for the nonsense output.

Do not misunderstand us here; workshops are clearly a valuable tool for brainstorming for risk identification and discussing the causes and consequences of risks amongst people of varying skills and experience. But it's the risk matrix that enables risk bandits to pretend a final answer is spat out before knock-off time. These workshops to go way beyond their design capacity.

But it Complies!

The most common retort when a risk bandit is challenged about the use of the risk matrix is 'but it complies with ISO 31000!' As discussed in Chapter 2, ISO 31000 is not a compliance standard. Think about what you might do when buying a new toy for your favourite baby niece, you no doubt would look at it carefully and if it was stamped as complying with an ISO or national standard you would take a lot of comfort. You would expect that it would comply with rules about toxic paint, pieces being able to be broken off, sharp edges and so on. The reason these standards are compliance standards is that they are very specific in design requirements, either the toy complies or it doesn't.

The reason that ISO 31000 is not compliance standard is because its design requirements are simply not as specific as for a baby's toy or a ball bearing; it's a guidance document. An organisation can't even volunteer for testing because passing a test would simply note its status at one moment in time but the guidance is for continually improving risk assessment capacity. If an organisation passes in one year, the same system may well be considered unsatisfactory the next year if it hasn't improved. Bear in mind the process intended for use by the local café and for NASA alike, which surely tells us that the compliance retort is simply rubbish. Nevertheless, the volumes of risk guidance material that are produced by organisations and governments for use in risk management are just as generic and usually bear a striking resemblance to the specific examples in the Standard.

But let's look at what ISO 31000 does say about the risk matrix. It is not mentioned in the body of the standard, which describes the alternatives of qualitative, quantitative and semi-quantitative risk analysis. Qualitative risk assessment is described in the supplementary handbook HB 436 as 'defines consequence, probability and level of risk by significance levels such as "high", "medium" and "low", may combine consequence and probability, and evaluates the resultant level of risk against qualitative criteria'. The risk matrix is not mentioned at this point in the handbook.

The handbook first mentions the risk matrix in an information table of 31 risk assessment tools that are rated for applicability. The "consequence/ probability matrix" is rated as follows:

Tools and Techniques	Risk Assessment Process
Risk identification	Strongly applicable
Risk analysis:	
• Consequence	Strongly applicable
• Probability	Strongly applicable
• Level of risk	Strongly applicable
Risk evaluation	Applicable

Figure 6.15—ISO 31000 Rating Of The Matrix

Can it possibly be true that what is strongly applicable to Luigi's Café around the corner is also strongly applicable to NASA?

The information table needs to read in conjunction with the referenced annex (B29), which makes two very good points about the matrix:

- 'It is commonly used as a screening tool when many risks have been identified, for example to define which risks need further or more detailed analysis ...'
- It '... may also be used to help communicate a common understanding for qualitative levels of risks across the organisation.'

To summarise, ISO 31000 does not prescribe qualitative risk assessment, the risk matrix is just one tool that is mentioned; if it is used it suggests that as a tool it's good for screening and perhaps presentation.

Lest we be misunderstood, let us make our views on ISO 31000 very clear. It has become the risk manager's holy book, it is a direct fledgling of that pioneering document AS/NZ 4360:2004 which was a world respected achievement and rightly so. However, Australian Standards Committee OB-007 made a material error in the original version that subsequent reshuffling could not redress, by including a simple matrix as the sole example of a risk assessment methodology in the entire Standard, and despite it being labelled "informative", this unintended showcase gave every lazy risk bandit in Australia and New Zealand the chance to jump aboard the train to Easy Street.

Professor Jean Cross (Dr. Cross in those days) chaired Committee OB-007 and she has been big enough to regret that error. In the 2004 edition of AS/NZ 4360, the matrix was finally taken out and combined with other risk assessment options in the supplementary handbook HB 436. When the 2004 version was replaced by ISO 31000, the matrix example was excluded from ISO 31000, but was one of the many assessment solutions covered in the sister standard IEC/ISO 31010.

Professor Cross is an impressive risk professional and we do not claim that we would have foreseen the ramifications of that early formatting decision. After all, who would have thought the readership could be so mindless, or so manipulating ... or both?

Bar Chart Versus the Heat Map

Having looked at the limitations of the risk matrix and how it is abused by risk bandits, this chapter concludes by returning to the story with which it started—the bar chart versus the risk matrix. As the unemployed policeman is hoping to see an "Alien versus Predator" type battle lets dress up the risk matrix to be a heat map, a risk matrix with lipstick.

In Chapter 4 the cuteness of risk bandits' heat map was highlighted as the reason for its survival. It was a masterpiece of marketing and a perfect example of totally useless risk junk. Why did so many smart people buy it then? It's probably true that many reasons were involved, but our guess is the next three were prevalent:

Reason 1—Visual Appeal

To a time-poor director or executive the heat map might just look cute or even clever—a kind of X-ray look at risk exposure. The shrewd masking of misleading scale graduations and huge ballpark ranges by smart colours and labels promotes visual appeal over substance.

Reason 2—Self Image

It was given a label that made it sound like it was specifically tailored for busy, important executives who needed to get straight to the crux of the matter, a type of diagrammatic executive summary. It was deliberately implied, and subsequently inferred, that executives and directors should not be bothered with the detail. If they were to ask a few insightful questions about the hot end of the spectrum; they will have performed their duty of oversight well. The originators of the beast knew their audience well, and a significant part of the audience repaid their knowledge with unquestioning acceptance.

Reason 3—Smart Enough not to Waste Time

The buyers had already concluded that risk management was a bit of a joke as far as business processes went (i.e. not serious like accounting, engineering, insurance, etc.) and were relieved that compliance could be achieved in such an easy way.

This is more than a discussion about qualitative versus quantitative risk analysis as the risk matrix or heat map is rarely presented by risk managers as qualitative risk analysis. In fact the pretence is usually that it has a quantitative foundation whereas the extent of analysis is no more than an average vote of impressions of workshop participants in a hurry to escape the room and get on with real work.

Let's compare the heat map to simple bar chart information for the following likelihood and consequence pairings:

Event	Likelihood (L)	Consequence (C)
1	Once every 10 years	1,000,000
2	Once every year	500,000
3	Once every 20 years	2,000,000
4	Twice every year	10,000
5	Once every 25 years	150,000
6	Once every 50 years	105,000

Figure 6.16—Example Likelihood And Consequence Pairings

The following are representations of these risks on a heat map after a matrix assessment (using Figure 6.16) and a bar chart that was developed by simply multiplying the likelihood and consequence pairings.

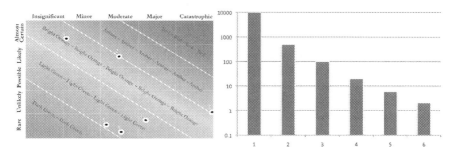

Figure 6.17—Heat Map Versus Bar Chart

The only area where both reports provide the same conclusion is that the biggest events are Risks 1 and 2. The heat map (left of diagram) sees these as amber ("High") and therefore more important than the lower rankings ("Medium") but not quite as high as the red area ("Extreme"). The heat map implies executive/board level should only be aware of Risks 1 and 2, as events to keep an eye on, all other events being in the zone for the care of line managers.

The heat map is in fact simply plotting likelihood and consequence on a matrix with the cell borders removed and the colours blurred. In Figure 6.17 the borders have been left in as dotted lines. The equivalent bar chart (right of diagram) shows risk value based on the matrix user guidelines for likelihood and consequence values. Have a look at the "Y" axis (vertical) on the bar chart; the spacing of the graduations between "0.1" and "1" are the same as that between "1,000" and "10,000". This is not a trick it's a legitimate use of a "log scale", as long as the user is aware that it is being used.

It is in a log scale so that all of the risks can be shown on one diagram within the limits of the size of a page. If the matrix in your organisation increases likelihood and consequence by factors of ten or thereabouts, that matrix would also be masking a log scale. In this example we have used small likelihood factors as often seen in ERM risk matrices.

The bar chart, even on a log scale, tells us much more than the heat map. For a start it has values and not colours. In fact it shows us that Risk 1 is clearly the biggest risk whereas one would be excused for concluding that

Risks 1 and 2 were of equal risk when using the heat map. Risk 1 tells us that the calculated risk is such that once every ten years we should expect a financial loss of $100 million. Of course, the risk event may not happen for a decade and we might not be too worried about that if we could be certain that would be the "hit" date—however, it is just as likely to happen this year as in 2025! More importantly, it tells us that this risk is far bigger than all of the other risks put together. Looked at a different way, if we could reduce the exposure from Risk 1 by 10% it would be the equivalent of completely wiping out the other five risks and reducing them to nothing.

To give a stark picture of how these six risks compare we can contemplate the bar chart without a log scale in Figure 6.18. Consider the risks not in thousands of dollars but in height. If Risk 6 is 50 centimetres (about the height of a couple of steps) then Risk 4 is 20 metres (the height of the Whitehouse), Risk 2 is 500 metres (approximately the height of the Petronas twin towers) and Risk 1 is 10,000 metres (where commercial planes fly). The heat map and its less colourful cousin, the risk matrix, provide little insight into this incredibly large value range, in fact it's downright misleading. For readers not used to interpreting log scales, the following diagram shows this real story, with Risk 1 dwarfing Risk 2 and with Risks 4 to 6 so small by comparison that they are less than the line thickness on the chart.

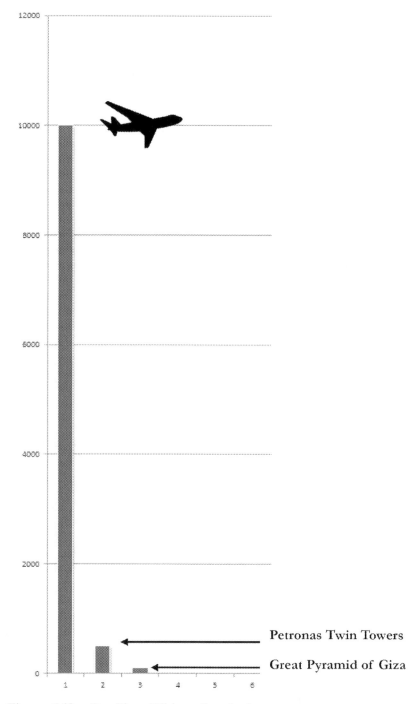

Figure 6.18—Bar Chart Without Log Scale

This analysis starts to give a genuine insight into how an organisation can greatly reduce the number of its risk assessments, critical control activities and risk reduction actions—and yet be right at the top of the risk management effectiveness league. These opportunities are covered in Chapter 8 and include turning risk management into a direct profit-making part of the business and playing a major part in how the rest of the business is planned and managed. The bar chart is a big improvement in reporting, but good risk assessment is also required to underpin the integrity of that report.

There are of course many other limitations to the heat map; how do you show risk appetite on a heat map? Is the red zone outlawed? Indeed, where does the red zone start and the orange end if you blur the lines? On a bar chart the targeted level of risk can be readily labelled. What about movements between reporting periods and demonstrating the impact of controls? It's so much easier on a bar chart. The bar chart can also be used to separately show financial and non-financial risk components of a single event; on the heat map it is impossible to know if financial or non-financial risk values are driving the position of the risk.

Perhaps the biggest limitations to the heat map relative to the bar chart are the obstacles it places in the way of good governance. Executive management and audit and risk committees are simply denied the opportunity to meaningfully approve a structured risk management approach and to monitor its progress.

Summing Up the Matrix

The only test that the matrix (or heat map) passes is simplicity, but picking a holiday destination by sticking a pin in an atlas passes that test. The matrix enables risk bandits to quickly produce large quantities of embarrassingly simple risk assessments. It appears to be easily understood but that's an illusion because it hides complexities with arbitrary and misleading scales and captions. The matrix also fails the most important test, effectiveness. It can't be used to prioritise treatment actions, assist in decision-making or in the governance of an organisation.

We will return to this critical aspect of governance in Chapter 8, but beforehand it's time to address the details of risk value that underpin the bar chart. We can hear the unconvinced matrix junkies screaming out their uninformed disapproval!

We will be right back to show you why you should ignore their screams— as you would a spoilt child—right after this intermission!

Intermission

Congratulations on reaching this far into "Risk Bandits". This is a landmark point, not just because it's past the halfway mark. Observant readers may have noticed to this juncture we have been a tad critical of the current state of organisation risk management. To some extent it's been like a confession as we are not free of blame. Whilst we never intentionally sold risk rubbish we can both recollect times where we provided it; subsequent experience, including compiling this book, has put risk rubbish into context. We were the kind of bandits that might say 'the client made us do it, we never really intended to deliver trash' had we been brought to justice, but we were guilty of aiding and abetting risk crime.

From this point forward we move into a constructive mode. Having explained what's wrong it's time to put forward some solutions that you can use in your own organisations. If we can't resist having an irreverent dig here and there, we do, however, promise to shift the main focus now to solutions.

This shift of course provides an opportunity for risk bandits in reader land to return fire. Bring it on! "Risk Bandits" is written for directors and executives but if some collateral reaction is generated from risk practitioners or regulators that would be a huge positive. Those returning fire should recognise that "Risk Bandits" has shown the risk management black box to be no more than a glass house, so stone throwing needs to be done with great care. We are trembling in our boots—NOT!

Thank you for staying with us. We hope you enjoy the second part of "Risk Bandits" but more importantly, we hope it helps you substantially improve the performance of your organisation.

7. Risk Estimation for Dummies; Steering the Ship

It Ain't Rocket Science

A distant memory of high school algebra will get you through this chapter. It's not the degree of difficulty of the maths that causes calculation of risk value to be less popular than the ballparkism of risk matrices and heat maps. Risk value calculations for most organisations are not complex mathematically but they do require detailed analysis and research and a strategic approach and these are the primary obstacles to its use.

The objective of this chapter is to provide executive managers and boards with an understanding of the risk value assessment process that can be applied in most organisations. The qualitative risk assessment process was compared with quantification of risk assessment in Chapter 4. This chapter describes a practical approach to risk value assessment that is suitable for organisations adopting most quantitative approaches to risk analysis.

Navigation Guidance

This chapter contains 12 Figures; they are designed for visual interpretation to illustrate the flow of logic in risk value assessment. It is not necessary to follow the calculations to stay with the plot for the remainder of "Risk Bandits". Alternatively, you may care to dwell on the detail in the Figures of greatest interest.

To Calculate Or Not to Calculate

Let's summarise some of the things we have discussed so far. Risk assessment in organisations today is largely based on heat maps using vague labelling of the level of risk based on a gut feeling of an outcome probably never experienced in terms of the more material risks. This is followed up by selecting risk improvement actions with little or no justification or transparency many of which are simply hobby horses of the assessors, which in turn result in the diffusion of precious risk resources across a great number of exposures. The resultant expenditure is not commensurate with the risk because there is inadequate granularity in the calculation of the risk value.

Wouldn't it be wonderful if we could quantify risk costs and benefits in the same way engineers quantify the cost and benefits of using a 100 mm structural beam over a 150 millimetre beam in a building? However, risk is about uncertainty and sometimes we don't have the clarity of information we desire, and the situation may not get any clearer no matter how long we procrastinate. In this respect, life hasn't changed much over the last couple of centuries.

> 'Life is the art of drawing sufficient conclusions from insufficient premises.'
>
> Samuel Butler, Victorian author

In many parts of the operations of our organisations we demonstrate our acceptance of this concept and set targets based on what we do know, understanding full well that we need to monitor and trim our route as more experience is gained. Profit forecasts, annual budgets and project cost estimates are all examples of where we often get it wrong but recognise we'd be a lot worse off if we didn't quantify our expected outcomes at all.

Picture a global corporation telling the market that its expected profit this year will be "Moderate" because their operating costs will be "High" but their capital costs will be "Low". We might even assist the investor by saying a "Moderate" profit is between $1 billion and $10 billion, operating costs between $10 billion and $100 billion and capital costs between $100 million and $1 billion. Can you imagine any stock exchange accepting this? Yet this is exactly what many global and major national organisations do with risk management.

Most of these arguments are based on the claim that calculation of risk value is often inaccurate because there is inadequate empirical/actuarial data available. This argument is made most forcibly by engineers and commercial professionals, but they are being a touch hypocritical in doing so. Whilst engineers' calculations are based on very well proven mathematical, physics and chemistry models for tangible products (bridges, refineries, power grids, etc.) their ability to predict costs and schedules is, put simply, embarrassing.

For example, 65% of megaprojects such as those in the Mining or Oil and Gas industries go more than 25% over budget and/or schedule or simply don't deliver the expected outcome[13] and for transportation infrastructure, 90% of projects overrun and 55% overrun by between 20% and 300%[14]. Economists shouldn't chuckle either. George Bernard Shaw once said 'If all the economists in the world were laid end to end, they wouldn't reach any conclusion' and John Kenneth Galbraith, an economist himself, said 'the only function of economic forecasting is to make astrology look respectable'.

The point is that both the engineering and accounting professions, and many others, realise that an intelligent guess and ongoing refinement of the original number is better than having no quantification at all. Guestimating becomes estimating and at its very best, estimating can be a meaningful projection. Cost, budget, profit estimation all have something in common with weather forecasting which, according to financial market author Patrick L Young, is 'right too often for us to ignore it and wrong too often for us to rely on it'. In this respect, risk assessment is no different.

Opponents of calculating risk value are really saying it's better to position ourselves in a huge ballpark than to be approximately right. But calculating risk value does much more than just place a number on a chart; it brings together all the analysis of the mechanics of the risk within an organisation. It provides checks and discipline in the analysis process as well as enabling a treetop view that hands the direction of the ship back to the captain. Risk value assessment requires an analysis of the mechanics of a risk way beyond the shallowness of the risk matrix to provide the basis for calculating risk value.

The ISO 31000 handbook rightly cautions in relation to risk value calculations, 'Care should be taken to ensure that they are not attributed a level of accuracy and precision inconsistent with the accuracy of the data and methods employed'. Astute risk value calculation users therefore work incrementally upwards with the degree of precision until a point is reached where the extra effort outweighs the additional benefits. In good risk management this is called "sensitivity analysis".

---

[13] Merrow, E., 2011, Industrial Megaprojects: Concepts, Strategies, and Practices for Success, John Wiley & Sons, New Jersey pp. xi

[14] Flyvbjerg, B., 2002, Underestimating Costs in Public Works Projects: Error or Lie? Journal of the American Planning Association, Vol. 68, No. 3, Chicago, IL. P283

Prior to looking at the details of risk value calculations it is important to review what the benefits are to understand why we are seeking their use.

Dealing with Uncertainty

A quick return to basics is needed to look at the main objective of organisation risk management. Given that organisational risk is 'the effect of uncertainty on its objectives' (or deviation from what it expected), what does it take to make risk management really useful in dealing with this uncertainty? We suggest a response using this simple formula, in keeping with this chapter:

> Useful risk management = Better decision-making + A rational defence if the Gods are against us

This response is consistent with the key principles of risk management set out in ISO 31000, 'risk management creates and protects value' and 'is part of decision-making'.

Hence risk management whether it is supported by heat maps or calculating risk value seeks to improve option taking and implement some karma protection. We contend that an organisation indulging in risk value calculations will get a much better result than it would from the heat map on both accounts due to the discipline the process provides in setting and delivering against organisational objectives.

Outrageous claim? Let's dig deeper.

It's about now that risk bandits armed with heat maps will say they know full well what is wanted, it's "no surprises", "no harm" and other popular albeit negatively expressed phrases. It is interesting that risk targets or objectives have a tendency to incorporate the word "no" or "zero" whereas corporate objectives usually lean the other way with "maximise" (shareholder value), "most efficient" (production), "largest" (market share), etc. It's hard to imagine Ferrari getting as excited about the team dietician helping their star driver to lose 1% of his weight as they do when an engineer creates an engine improvement that delivers 1% more horsepower. Whilst both are equally important, one provides greater enthusiasm in the team.

Negative phrases or not, if risk bandits armed with heat maps really could deliver no surprises and no harm that would certainly be useful to the organisation. Sadly, of course they can't because they are just aspirational targets, even if those quoting them often seem to have forgotten that fact. No realist expects to achieve them, at least not this decade, probably not this century, and maybe never. After all, what they are saying is the next slip-up is an infinite number of years away. They'll have the cure for eternal life soon. If you are with us on this one you will conclude that targeting zeros should be no more welcome in the New York Stock Exchange in 2015 than it was in Pearl Harbour in 1941.

The lack of discipline in establishing, using and monitoring the risk matrix and heat map allows these loose negative objectives to slip through without so much as a peep by executive management or the board. However, organisation objectives have to be properly defined to allow risk value calculations to take place. When calculating the frequency of project overruns it is necessary define the initiating event. Is it a change in scope, or a predicted overrun from the computer model? If the latter, is it a predicted overrun of one dollar or an overrun of 5% or more?

Better Decision-Making

Looking at the first part of our useful risk management formula, value creation is driven by sound decisions (option taking). So are decisions in an organisation better supported by heat maps or risk value assessment?

Consider this decision (using undiscounted cash flows for simplicity):

	Option A	Option B
Expenditure outlay on an asset	$5m	$20m
Income impact per year	$2.5m	$4m
Payback period	2 years	5 years

Which option is best noting that Option B has a longer payback but returns more after that period?

If the business is highly geared and is contemplating operating out of a different country with more competitive labour costs in five years, the first option might look pretty good, it provides a return of $7.5 million whilst the alternative solution will not have returned a cent. However, if the business intends to still be here for the next 20 years and it has low gearing, we might back the second option that gives us a $60 million return over 20 years whereas the first option would only return $45 million. The value creation decision becomes more significant when comparing investment in this asset over investment in other existing assets, or even comparing investment in production with investment in other parts of the value chain.

Organisations using heat maps simply can't make this type of decision within the risk management framework; it would need to be done quite separately. 'So what!', risk bandits say, 'the calculation can still be done outside of the matrix process and the right decision will be made'. But in most organisations multiple decisions like this are made every day so the heat map framework relies on good people consistently doing good things in accord with the objectives of the organisation. Good luck with that!

Is it not better to design the risk framework and processes so that these decisions are delegated to the appropriate person, applying defined tools and ensuring compliance with the process is subject to proper oversight? If risk management is a business tool then it should be looked at as a component of performance management across the organisation. In other words, it should be constructed with enough granularity to promote accountability and allow reporting and monitoring by executive management and the board. This design feature is key to risk value assessment but does not exist under the heat map.

Rational Defence if the Gods are Against Us

Moving to the second objective, tempting fate or as we prefer—a rational defence if the Gods are against us.

Great blackjack and poker players understand risk management (even though they might choke if asked to use the phrase). They do not focus on minimising losses; they invest with the expectation of winning. To this extent they put risk bandits to shame because they are great risk managers even though they have probably never heard of ISO 31000, SOX or COSO. They know that turning a profit is based on improving the odds in their favour and that if they get the odds (probabilities) right with good card counting, appropriate seating position at the table, etc. they will win more often than they lose. They also know they will lose big-time on occasions.

The world for businesses, politicians or any other organisation is just a casino … albeit an incredibly high stakes one (no $5 tables here). The size of the global stock market excluding bonds[15] is more than 3,000 times greater than the annual turnover of Las Vegas from gambling and entertainment[16] and the size of the winnings (and losses) at the stock exchange dwarfs those of even the highest of casino high rollers, many of whom play in both venue types. If gamblers put a massive personal effort into understanding and controlling risk isn't it a little embarrassing that CEOs and boards seem to only give it superficial effort in the formal risk management process?

As noted previously, gamblers know they will lose big-time occasionally. Sometimes this will be because they don't follow their own rules but more often they lose simply because the Gods (but not the odds) are against them. They didn't make a mistake, their cards were spectacularly good and effectively played, but another player's cards were simply, almost unbelievably, better.

Family responsibilities aside, gamblers have to account only to themselves, but for a CEO or a board it is a very public spectacle. They have to be able to demonstrate to their investors, possibly a government agency and increasingly the courts, that they played their hand well and were therefore diligent in their choice of actions.

We would not like to be in the shoes of any director or executive that said in their defence in court or at a shareholder meeting 'They told me it was an amber risk, and if they had told me it was a red one I would have handled it differently'. With risk value assessment it is possible to explain bad risk outcomes in the same way the gambler explains losing a poker game with a great hand. Even if the company has had a poor annual EBIT or a massive project overrun, there is still a strong chance that you can convince an investigator that the decision was made with appropriate data and questioning.

Of course people at the top of the organisation know very well that some things can derail operations and they spend a great deal of time making calls on risk issues. However, when it is done outside the risk management

---

[15]   Roxburgh, C, Lund, S, & Piotrowski, J, 2011, Mapping Global Capital Markets 2011, McKinsey Global Institute, August 2011, © McKinsey & Company, P2

[16]   Nagourney, 2013, Crowds return to Las Vegas but gamble less, New York Times, July 31, 2013, http://www.nytimes.com/2013/08/01/us/as-las-vegas-recovers-new-cause-for-concern.html?_r=0

system the supporting argument is not always recorded. It is often regarded as experience or judgement, but it's simply risk management, albeit informal, non-transparent and, usually incomplete. It is unlikely that management would accept it of anyone lower down the organisational hierarchy. Risk decisions should be treated like any other business decision; formalised within a process, on the record and with a clear cost/benefit case supporting the decision. If it is recorded, even if things go wrong, due diligence can usually be demonstrated.

The price that needs to be paid for this assurance in relation to risk management is that the organisation has to actually do what it says it is going to do—and do it in a bone fide manner. If the organisation says its operating units will have critical controls identified and key performance indicators (KPIs) established to determine that they are effective, then the executive will have to make sure that it is done—not mostly, or largely done but completely in accordance with the commitment. However, under most heat maps where a ridiculous number of actions have been promised by a vast range of people, many of which will have a negligible, or at least unknown impact on risk, it is delusional to believe 100% of commitments will be completed.

The trick, and the best tricks are often so very simple when uncovered, is to lower the number of risk scenarios, identify carefully the few critical controls that are really essential to avoid a material loss and only commit to measures where it can be calculated that a significant drop in risk can be achieved. Two-inch thick risk registers saturated with more promises than a rich widow gets from a gigolo, may make executives feel good right up to the moment they are clearly seen to be empty promises, at which time they will almost certainly be used as evidence of folly. A sound defence when the Gods are against you comes by making few definable promises and keeping them all.

The Specifications

To tabulate the specifications for risk value assessment that we should be seeking:

- Discipline in setting and defining measurable objectives
- Appropriate use of precision where decisions are sensitive to data accuracy

- Sufficient granularity to facilitate decision-making to create value

- Capacity to prioritise commitments to protect value

- Ability to delegate risk-taking across the organisation

- Enabling a treetop view with the ability to deep dive into detail if required

We return to these specifications later in this chapter and the design of the risk management framework to create and protect value is the subject of Chapter 8. Having understood what we seek from risk value assessment we can now review how it's done.

Calculating Risk Value, the Basics

The basic formula for risk value calculations, being likelihood x consequence, has been referred to in Chapters 4 and 6, and conceptually that's valid but it has been extensively simplified. It's like the saying 'success is 10% inspiration and 90% perspiration' in that both are constructed from truth but are distilled so much to make a point that it is unworkable in real life (try telling your boss you are not daydreaming for 48 minutes each workday, you are being inspirational). An unabridged formula for risk follows, but don't panic, we can simplify it somewhat for use within an organisation without turning our back on the fundamentals of risk and thereby negating its value in regard to decision-making.

To explain, and don't worry this is the total extent of fancy algebra in this book:

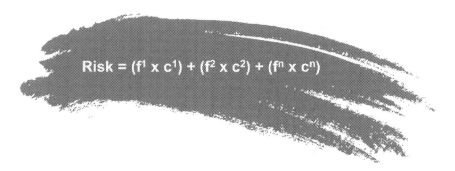

$$\text{Risk} = (f^1 \times c^1) + (f^2 \times c^2) + (f^n \times c^n)$$

Figure 7.1—Risk Formula

These f's and c's are not expletives; they mean the following:

- c^1 is the lowest loss outcome and f^1 is the frequency with which that outcome is expected to occur

- c^2 is the next, more severe outcome and f^2 is its associated frequency

- The value c^n is a cute way of saying etcetera meaning c^3, c^4 and so on which are increasingly severe levels of outcome

- The value f^n represents f^3, f^4 and so on, the frequency of the occurrences associated with c^3, c^4 etc.

When considering a scenario where there is potential for downside <u>and</u> upside, "c" values will be required for the range of loss consequences in which case "c" would be entered as negative values (e.g. c^1 is -$10,000; c^2 is -$100,000; etc.) plus the range of gain consequences in positive values (e.g. c^6 is $0; c^7 is $10,000; c^8 is $100,000 etc.). Examples of this upside and downside include most project, acquisition and hedging decisions.

To illustrate the calculation we return to the example from Chapter 6 of the middle tier company servicing a market prone to cyclones—the risk value calculation can be completed if we multiply each occurrence by the EBIT impact. Assume there are ten cyclones per year that do significant damage then the table below shows the consequence and frequency values:

Category	1	2	3	4	5	Total
% Spread of occurrences	90%	9%	0.9%	0.09%	0.01%	100%
Occurrences per annum (f)	9	0.9	0.09	0.009	0.001	10
EBIT impact per occurrence (c)	$10k	$100k	$1m	$10m	$100m	
Risk value (f^n x C^n)	$90k	$90k	$90k	$90k	$100k	$460k

Figure 7.2—Cyclone Statistics In Risk Value Terms

The monetary risk for each level of severity has been calculated and the total statistical risk value to the business is $460,000 per year. The expected value of the risk is determined by the probability-weighted average of the range of consequences. If the frequency of all categories of cyclones had been the same then the weighted average turns into the simple average. We now have an answer that the risk matrix in Chapter 6 could not deliver. We also have a basis for a strategic decision about whether the organisation can live with cyclone damage which over time is expected to cost nearly a half million dollars per annum or should it spend resources on reducing that impact.

Unlike the risk matrix, risk value calculations can aggregate the multiple frequency occurrences (likelihood)/outcome severity (consequence) couplings that occur in most risks. We can illustrate the mechanics of this risk using the high-level bowtie diagram from Figure 4.3 as a template:

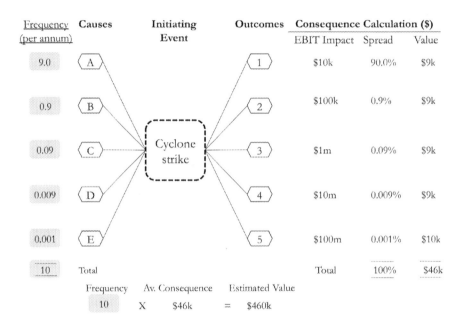

Frequency (per annum)	Causes	Initiating Event	Outcomes	Consequence Calculation ($)		
				EBIT Impact	Spread	Value
9.0	A		1	$10k	90.0%	$9k
0.9	B		2	$100k	0.9%	$9k
0.09	C	Cyclone strike	3	$1m	0.09%	$9k
0.009	D		4	$10m	0.009%	$9k
0.001	E		5	$100m	0.001%	$10k
10	Total			Total	100%	$46k

Frequency		Av. Consequence		Estimated Value
10	X	$46k	=	$460k

Figure 7.3—Cyclone Strike Bowtie

Armed with this knowledge of the basic risk value calculation let's also return to the "falling off a bike" example in Chapter 6 and Mr Punter's brush with colour blindness with the heat map. The two external risk bandits failed to deliver a useful answer from their beloved heat map—we can use the bowtie diagram format to illustrate why the two consultants were struggling with their analysis. The heat map and risk matrix can't cope with the multiple frequency/severity couplings that exist for almost every organisational risk. Their analysis was something like this:

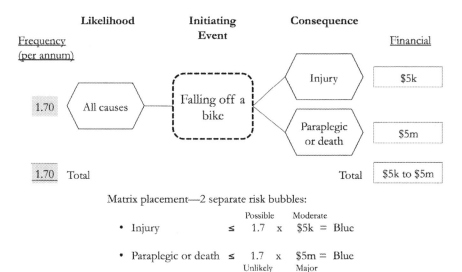

Figure 7.4—Ms Bandit's Falling Off A Bike Bowtie

This linear view of frequency and severity creates the need for the ballparkism of the risk matrix and heat map. Placing Noah's bubble within wide ranges hides the lack of analysis and precision in the estimation. No surprise that Mr Punter in Chapter 6 was left wondering, the quest for simplicity of the output drove simplicity in the analysis. Let's look at what the elegant Ms Bandit should have done.

A bit more analysis of Mr Punter's situation helps further explain the basics of calculating risk value starting with the objective, which we will assume is to have no serious injuries to employees commuting to and from work. Mr Punter's three-year experience of employee bike accidents can be supplemented with statistics from the state Ministry of Transport who publish cycling accident rates per kilometre travelled by frequency of cause and severity of outcome and, if he wants to be thorough, send a survey to all cycling staff asking how many kilometres they do each week. Care is needed in that past results are no guarantee of future performance, particularly with small datasets. However, for the purposes of this example it is assumed that this data provides the best available indication of the most likely outcomes.

If we again follow the mechanics of organisational risks set out in the high-level bowtie diagram in Figure 4.3, the risk description, describing the event noting that there is no upside for such an event, is "injury from falling off a bike". We can map the causes and consequences of this risk event as shown below in Figure 7.5. This bowtie diagram has an added feature from

Figures 7.3 and 7.4 in that "causal groups" and "outcome groups" are shown. When there are multiple causes and consequences these groupings are useful in preparing and presenting the analysis, as we will demonstrate shortly.

For the sake of simplicity of the example, Figure 7.5 only shows the financial consequences; the non-financial impacts are covered later in this chapter. The impact of controls will also be discussed later in this chapter.

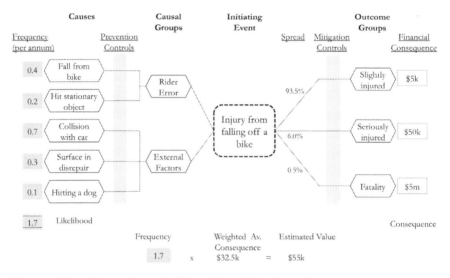

Figure 7.5—Injury From Falling Off A Bike Bowtie

The risk bandit linear view has been transformed into a view of the multiple likelihood frequency/consequence severity couplings existing in almost all organisational risks. The spread of possible outcomes is calculated by applying the probability that they will occur based on the Ministry of Transport statistics.

To look at the f^n and c^n formula in another way—risk value has been calculated as: the frequency of the initiating event (A) x probability of defined outcomes (B) x the estimated outcomes (C). For the pathway to success this means A x B x C and whilst it's not quite as simple as ABC, the maths is not difficult. The calculation is simply:

A	B		C	B x C	A x B x C
Frequency Of Initiating Event	Probability Of Defined Outcomes		Estimated Outcomes	Weighted Average	Risk Value ($ p.a.)
	Slight Injury	93.5%	$5,000	$4,675	$7,948
1.7	Serious Injury	6.0%	$50,000	$3,000	$5,100
	Fatality	0.5%	$5 million	$25,000	$42,500
	Total	100%		$32,675	$55,547

Figure 7.6—Injury From Falling Off A Bike Risk Value Calculation Summary

The "B" part of the above risk value calculation above includes all outcomes. Another option is to limit the calculation to individual outcomes beyond a defined level of severity. This option is used to focus analysis away from the rats and mice to the more material outcomes.

In organisations, the calculation of risk value requires data research, analysis and some estimation. Likelihood in an organisation is annualised to provide the likely deviation in a reporting period but is best calculated over a longer period so that an event that happens six times in ten years has a likelihood of 0.6 or 60%. Of course this would be adjusted to reflect any improvement or deterioration in the control system.

We now have a basic risk value calculation as a base for introducing the complexities of the organisational context to the calculation. This approach can be simplified further whilst still delivering significant cost benefit value and can also be refined to produce greater accuracy for scenarios involving great sensitivity over certain input data.

Behind this simple ABC calculation it is not an exaggeration to say only simple arithmetic is needed to cope with risk in regard to most methodologies. However, by oversimplifying the formula to just two parts (likelihood x consequence) in order to keep even the shallow end of the organisational gene pool in the risk game, risk bandits have gone a step too far. As a result, the already simple and genuine risk formula is made to appear complex by comparison[17]. This will bring out the "dog whistle" call from bandits that it needs to be kept simple to allow the workforce to understand it—primarily

---

[17] Cross, J. 2012, 'Risk' in HaSPA (Health and Safety Professionals Alliance)—The Core Body of Knowledge for Generalist OHS Professionals. Tullamarine, VIC. © Safety Institute of Australia, p11

for self-preservation purposes where a massive number of meaningless risk assessments are undertaken by engaging in the shallowest possible risk process. It is simply amazing that executive management allow this to occur.

Whilst risk value for each risk event is a convenient single number, care is needed in its interpretation. The probability-weighted average loss or gain from the possible range of outcomes is the most likely annual result over the medium term. Very low frequency events with unacceptable consequences still require critical controls in place irrespective of the risk value.

Calculating Risk Value, the Organisational Context

In Chapter 5 your domestic bill paying process was compared to that used by multiple location organisations with a high volume of bills to pay and many employees. Whilst the basics of both processes are the same, organisations have procedures to follow, controls in place and performance management budgets and reporting. This organisation context needs to be factored into the risk value calculation through estimating the impact of an organisation's control measures on the likelihood and consequences of risk events.

As described in the high-level bowtie diagram in Figure 4.3 when looking at risk mechanics, there are two types of controls:

- Prior to the risk event impacting likelihood—these pro-active "occurrence controls" seek to prevent negative causes (threats or hazards) or promote positive causes (opportunities)

- Post the risk event impacting consequence—these reactive "treatment controls" seek to mitigate negative outcomes or enhance positive outcomes

If the impact of management controls on consequence and likelihood is included in the risk value calculation, the cost/benefit of management introducing or removing controls can be systematically assessed. For example, with the risk of an IT failure event, a prevention control for a cyber attack cause would be a firewall. A mitigating control after the event would be back-up and disaster recovery procedures. The inclusion of the impact of both these controls in the risk value calculation helps determine the most cost effective combination of prevention and mitigations controls.

The impact of controls can be shown in a number of ways, we prefer to use for each control a simple percentage reduction in frequency (occurrence controls) or outcome severity (treatment controls). For Mr Punter's employees the risk event of injury from falling off a bike, the occurrence (prevention) controls can be shown on the bowtie diagram as follows:

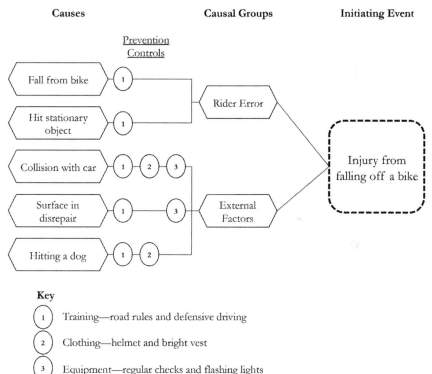

Figure 7.7—Injury From Falling Off A Bike Bowtie Occurrence Controls

Moving to the consequence side of the bowtie diagram, the treatment (mitigation) controls can be shown as follows:

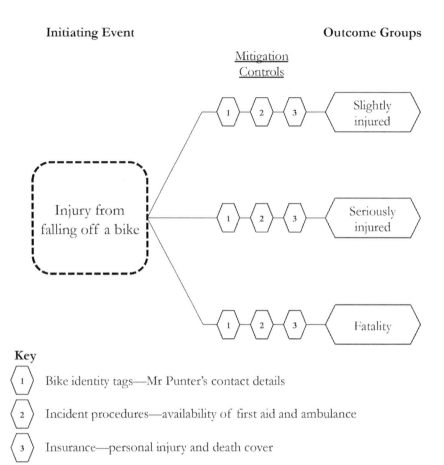

Initiating Event   **Outcome Groups**

Key

⟨1⟩ Bike identity tags—Mr Punter's contact details

⟨2⟩ Incident procedures—availability of first aid and ambulance

⟨3⟩ Insurance—personal injury and death cover

Figure 7.8—Injury From Falling Off A Bike Bowtie Treatment Controls

Having identified the occurrence and treatment controls, illustrated in Figures 7.7 and 7.8, their impact on the calculation of risk value can be shown by extending Figure 7.6 using the same ABC formula. Figure 7.9 reflects:

- The "base case position"—before identified control improvements
- The "action reduction"—being the percentage reduction in frequency (for occurrence controls) and outcome severity (for treatment controls)
- The "post action position"—for frequency and outcome severity

Event

Injury from falling off a bike

Likelihood			**A**
Occurrences	Frequency (base case)	Action Reduction	Frequency (post actions)
Fall from a bike	0.40		
Hit stationary object	0.20		
Rider error total	0.60	25%	0.45
Collision with car	0.70		
Surface disrepair	0.30		
Hitting a dog	0.10		
External factors total	1.10	10%	0.99
Total	1.70		1.44

Consequence	**B**			**C**	**B x C**
Distribution	Probability (spread)	Outcome (base case)	Action Reduction	Outcome (post action)	Weighted Average
Slight injury	93.5%	$5k	0%	$5k	$4,675
Serious injury	6.0%	$50k	10%	$45k	$2,700
Fatality	0.5%	$5m	50%	$2.5m	$12,500
Total					$19,875

Risk Value Calculation	**A**	**B x C**	**A x B x C**
	Likelihood	Consequence	Risk Value
	1.44	$19,875	$28,620

Figure 7.9—Injury From Falling Off A Bike Risk Value Calculation

The base case position needs some explanation; it's a useful concept and is not complex. It is simply frequency, on the likelihood side, and outcome, on the consequence side, before identified actions. For risk events that are incidents, the identified actions reduce the frequency of causes (threats) or the severity of negative outcomes. For risk events with opportunities and positive consequences the identified actions can enhance the frequency of causes and the extent of outcomes.

The tricky bit is what is meant by "identified actions". These actions are identified in the risk value assessment when it is practical and useful to do so. They are shown as a percentage change in frequency (occurrence controls) or outcome severity (treatment controls). If they are in place but are not separately identified then they remain in the base case and post action positions. The analysis of the impact of existing and proposed identified actions enables the cost/benefit of their existence to be assessed.

The base case position on the likelihood side is the frequency of each cause before identified occurrence controls. In Figure 7.9 the impact of each identified action is estimated at the causal group level rather than for each cause, in most cases this level of precision will be sufficient. As the frequency data is based on experience, care is needed not to double count the impact of identified actions in the base case and then again in the action reduction calculation. For example, if the Ministry of Transport's published cycling accident rates include riders wearing helmets, then this control is in the base case and should not be included in the action reduction calculation.

The base case position on the consequence side is the severity of each outcome group before the identification of treatment controls. As with frequency data, care is needed not to double count the impact of identified actions in the base case and then again in the action reduction calculation. For example, if the base case cost of injuries is net of personal insurance then it should not be included in the action reduction calculation.

In Figure 7.9 the risk value from the base case position has been reduced by about 50% by the impact of identified actions and Mr Punter can now assess the cost component of the cost/benefit case for the identified controls and whether there is any need to introduce more controls to render the risk as low as reasonably practicable.

Calculating Risk Value, a bit More Complexity

The ABC risk formula doesn't hide critical parts of the equation from us and can be readily applied in most organisations. Of course more sophistication and complexity can be added where the greater precision is worth the extra resources needed to obtain the underlying data. An overview of this fine-tuning identifies some key points underlying risk value.

We have established that f^n and c^n are actually not a threatened species in risk registers, the little buggers are thriving, they're just a bit too swift to be spotted by the lumbering nature of bandits. Most risks have multiple frequencies both for the occurrence of individual causes and the multiple severities of outcomes, and they will range from tolerable to disastrous. If we are to use risk to create value (better decision-making) and protect value (a rational defence if the Gods are against us) then we have to get a reasonable handle on the range of frequency occurrences (likelihood) and outcome severities (consequences).

The importance of the probability part of the risk value calculation ("B" in the "A x B x C" formula) comes down to the level of certainty in the predicted risk value. Probability theory books could fill a library, an approach is needed for organisations that is practical enough to be readily implemented but also scalable so that sophistication can be added when needed.

Frequency

Looking firstly at the frequency of occurrence (the f^n bit) we have seen that for independent or unrelated causes of risk events the frequency of each cause can be simply added together as long as there are no dependent causes (where one cause couldn't trigger the incident without the help of another cause). In such cases the resulting total frequency, is the total likelihood part of the basic risk value formula. Of course many causes occur concurrently and have complex inter-dependencies. As these causes are inputs/outputs to each other, their occurrences can't be simply added and fault tree analysis may be needed to analyse the relationships.

So if a risk event could occur if four sequential failures occur and they each have a 90% certainty of occurring then the frequency is 90% x 90% x 90% x 90% = 66%. If each of the sequential causes has differing frequencies and impacts of controls these calculations may need to be included for each cause if an appropriate value cannot be defined for an entire group of causes. Complexity is also increased when the dependency relationships between causes vary according to differing circumstances. It is not necessary to go any further with this maths, the point is that once the causal inter-relationships are understood the complexities can be well handled in a spreadsheet by a competent risk manager and the subject matter expert (e.g. line manager) as needed in most cases.

There are a number of risk analysis tools that can be used to assist in analysing frequency ("A") and probability ("B"), the most common are the fault tree (for frequency of the occurrence) and the event tree (for the probability of each outcome severity). For those that enjoy their maths more than we do, they are Boolean logic diagrams (like "IF" functions in a spreadsheet). The fault tree tracks failures back from the "risk event" (a release of a toxic gas from a chemical plant or radiation from a nuclear plant for example) and the event tree is a simpler diagram to assess the range of outcomes and their probability after the release has occurred.

Whilst the event tree is simpler in terms of its design, it is often supported by very complex consequence modelling such as gas dispersion, explosion pressure waves and radiation impacts. The fault tree was originally developed in the US in the 1960s to predict the reliability of the original minutemen missile launch system. This is not unlike what police detectives try to do in their heads except they apply their approach after the event has occurred and risk assessors look to prevent or facilitate an event occurring.

Probability forecasting can be done by either simply throwing the dice a few thousand times and counting up the times each number is thrown[18] using Monte Carlo modelling or a range of other tools can be used to suit the degree of precision required. Such tools are essential for the risk profession's most advanced probabilistic assessment tool, Quantitative Risk Assessment (QRA), that is used primarily outside of the finance industry for the avoidance of safety disasters and also in equipment reliability prediction. Whilst QRA can be used to calculate the risk of any type of business or moral value-based event, it is seldom used outside the safety arena because that is the only area where detailed failure frequency data has been kept on an international scale for many decades. It is also rare for organisations of any size to have in-house resources capable of undertaking QRA risk modelling, as the number of qualified practitioners in the world is extremely limited.

Where the probability has so many variables that it is simply too complex to make the probability calculations, Monte Carlo modelling is sometimes used provided a model can be built to closely reflect real life. One of the trickiest parts of the modelling is in inputting to the computer software which kind of distribution can be expected on each of the variables. Monte Carlo modelling adds great value in the right hands and can be used to integrate a very high number of variables. The challenge of course, is to be able to recognise what you don't know and not to assume the software will mystically conjure up the right answer if we throw in enough crude guesses. As we all know, computers are blindingly quick and tireless. They are also extremely dumb and will not therefore correct the modeller when a mistake is made.

---

[18]   Bernstein, P, Against the Gods: The Remarkable Story of Risk, 1998, Wiley Online, ISBN: 978-0-471-29563-1

Proprietary software such as "@ Risk" and "Crystal Ball" will undertake thousands of runs, randomly selecting a new value from the defined possibilities for each uncertain variable and recalculate the outcome. Such software, with appropriate data and modelling can produce a level of confidence in the outcomes of a decision that poses substantial opportunities and downside to the organisation. Examples include a "late/early or over-run/below project budget", "the purchase of a new super airliner and its potential commercial outcomes", or a "hedging contract with a price far below the current value of your product".

Those new to the use of risk value assessment should keep it simple to start with and only add complexity where greater precision is needed. The first cut of estimating the frequency of a risk event can be simply done by adding the estimated annualised occurrences of each of the causes, this provides a starting point that still represents much greater precision than the risk matrix. If dependencies are identified between causes then the benefit of greater precision should be assessed before adding complexity.

Outcome Severity

Moving to outcome severity (the c^n bit) we have seen that all possible outcomes within the range of severity are alternatives so the spread, or probability percentages, need to add to 100% when all outcomes are being analysed. If the range of outcomes are analysed only beyond a defined level of materiality then the total of the spread will not add to 100%. The resulting probability-weighted average outcome, is the total consequence part of the basic risk value calculation summarised above as A x B x C.

There are a number of methods used to determine the probabilities of different severities of outcomes depending on the degree of precision required. The simplest method is to take a probability-weighted average of the two ends of the total range of possibilities, whilst the most sophisticated involves complex graphing with ISO bars, contours, risk planes and other methods to relate the variables impacting probability across the range of possible outcomes.

In most cases the middle ground will do which is assessing the probability of intervals within the spread of say at 20%, 40%, 60% and 100% of maximum value. An advantage of this approach is that whilst the predicted value is the weighted average, the intervals help assess the range from tolerable to disastrous.

Non-Financial Outcomes

The Price for Life Argument

To this point the consequences or outcomes of risk events have been expressed in financial terms such as EBIT. Is it possible to calculate and bar chart non-financial outcomes such as health and safety, reputation and for the public sector, service effectiveness or "public value"? The answer is yes.

When talking of a single risk framework and integrated reporting of risk across an organisation, this is one area guaranteed to send even the most senior of executive managers and directors scurrying into the land of political correctness. It arises whenever the integration of financial and ethical risk is discussed. Whilst stakeholder focus on environment and social issues are in enthusiastic cacophony with their workplace health and safety pals on the issue of not mixing the two, no phrase has quite the passionate— yet unfounded—resonance as "price for life!" when any suggestion of introducing a clearly defined method of determining ALARP is discussed. Just as the environmentalists assumed righteousness for themselves when they borrowed the word "pollution" from the clergy who had used the Latin verb "polluere" for centuries. It meant to dishonour, defile, degrade or violate people through illicit or immoral actions.

During a company event after-dinner speech on risk management about a decade ago, the topic of providing financial bands to guide an organisation on when to implement safety measures and when not to, was raised. It was unwise of the speaker, who had noted that much red wine had been consumed prior to his walk to the lectern, to push on with his planned message. That message was, if there is no measurable form of determining what is practicable, how can a persuasive case for funding be made? In those days the sum of $10 million was the most common number used, as the amount an organisation should spend to save a statistical life without further deliberation. If the risk assessment suggested that a measure would save one life in 1,000 years and the company would be operating for another 20 years, then up to $200,000 ($10 million x 20 ÷ 1,000) should be sanctioned to implement the measure. In other words, one fiftieth (2%) of a life would be saved (20 years ÷ 1,000 years) so prima facie 2% of $10 million or $200,000 is justified expenditure.

In QRA, such numbers are called the "Implied Cost to Avert a Fatality" or ICAF and they form part of national guidelines for safety in the nuclear, petroleum and chemical industries in many countries including the UK and Australia. The ICAF number does not address the potential inconvenience cost to the organisation, or regulator fines or family compensation; it is simply a representation of the organisation's shock and emotional loss at the concept of an employee fatality. Note that these are commitments based on theoretical projections and not known direct threats. If an organisation is certain of impending fatalities, as in the infamous Ford Pinto case[19], there is no sum of money that can be considered acceptable to an ethical organisation—the practice must be changed or the activity ceased.

Returning to the after-dinner speech, fortunately for our unintended hero, the CEO of the organisation politely asked if he might say something to the audience. The speaker readily accepted, fearing things might actually boil over into fighting as some guests were calling for the objectors to be silent, and the bulging veins in the neck of the objector currently shouting 'there is no price for life!' could be seen from 30 metres away. The CEO walked slowly to the lectern and asked his employees to raise their hand if they had life insurance. A little less than half raised their hands. The CEO pushed for more hands, but no more were raised. He then issued a second instruction, for individuals to lower their hand if they had insurance for less than $10 million. Almost all of the hands were slowly lowered with only five left in the air and the noisiest objector was not one of the five. The CEO then said ...

'It seems to me that Mr Pooley values your lives more than the great majority of you do!'

The CEO realised that a sound logical argument has no automatic rite of passage past people defending their principles unless accompanied by an equally principle-driven argument to support it. No protester had valued himself or herself as highly as they expected the company would. The revolt was over. Yet midway through the second decade of the 21ˢᵗ century this remains a contentious issue, despite the fact that wherever it is actually used it most often draws nil attention. Like drugs and alcohol testing and vehicle tracking devices, for those brave enough to introduce them, the upside dramatically outweighs the downside and cases of reverting back are almost unknown.

---

[19]   Dowie, M., Pinto Madness, Mother Jones 18 (Sept./Oct. 1977)

The irony is that most large organisations show an inferred "price for life" value in their risk matrix consequence table. The following extract is from tables proudly displayed on the internet and one just like it probably exists in your organisation. Just input 'risk consequence table' in your search engine if your organisation doesn't follow the norm. They infer values for life of between $100,000 to $5,000,000.

	Consequence Level	Safety Metric	Financial Metric
Example 1	Major	Single death and / or multiple injuries	Loss / destruction of assets of $100,000 to $5m
Example 2	Catastrophic	Multiple fatalities	Asset / equipment loss > $500,000
	Major	Single fatality / extensive injuries	Asset / equipment loss $100,000 to $500,000
Example 3	Major	Single death and / or multiple injuries	Financial loss not covered by insurance $2.5m to $5m

Figure 7.10—Risk Consequence Table Metric Extracts

The Organisational Trauma Concept

Risk bandits extol the virtues of the risk matrix, as being better able to deal with non-financial risk outcomes than quantitative methods but Figure 7.10 shows the matrix does not do this. Apart from the conflict between metrics previously mentioned, there are two key problems.

Firstly, the metrics cannot be integrated into a single risk reporting system for the entire organisation when the risk matrix is used. The safety measures in the matrix criteria are independent of the organisation's safety management system. Safety metrics (LTIFR, TRIFR etc.) measured and used in the operations and reported to management and often a board health and safety sub-committee are inevitably completely separate. The result is that the audit and risk committee use different metrics than the board health and safety sub-committee, wow! The matrix descriptions don't matter too much because this is the only place they are used!

The second problem with the non-financial metrics used in the risk matrix lies in the clarity of the metrics. The non-financial metrics for the risk matrix are expressed in terms of an outcome but not the outcome impacting the organisation. A loss of EBIT is clearly an organisational outcome but is the non-financial outcome for an organisation of a fatality having one less person available or is it the resulting organisational trauma that a colleague that was laughing with you yesterday will never laugh again? Clearly it's the trauma; why not express it that way? Similarly, the metrics behind the risk matrix for reputation often involve the extent of unfavourable media coverage, this is just an influence on reputation it is not the outcome for the organisation.

It is the "organisational trauma" concept that is best used for risk value calculation of non-financial outcomes. The objective is to define a level of trauma of a financial loss equivalent to the level of trauma for the organisation of a non-financial outcome. A $10 million loss for a small organisation would be a significant trauma; is this about equivalent to the trauma the organisation would suffer if one of its employees were seriously injured? Is this level of trauma equivalent to that if the national rag ran headlines for three days about the poor quality of the organisation's production processes? Some organisations will be able to define trauma very precisely if they have mature well-being and culture programs. Other organisations will need to make the best assessment they can of the impact on well-being and culture focused on the short-term impacts plus structural adjustments that may need to be made. There may be a need to refine initial estimates of trauma equivalent over time based on experience.

Care is needed not to duplicate or omit any of the outcomes of a risk event. A risk event causing national media coverage may have direct financial consequences such as additional costs, lost sales and possibly contract penalties—they are readily measurable in financial terms. The reputation impact may be able to be estimated by the decline in future sales due to a loss in brand value. The non-financial organisational trauma is however a quite distinct element and whilst the mechanism may be to express it in equivalent financial terms, the estimate is first determined by assessing the level of sadness or loss felt by the organisation through failing to deliver on its core values.

The bar charts from Chapter 6, which were simply showing financial outcomes, can now also include non-financial outcomes. Also the risk value calculations for "injury from falling of a bike" earlier in this chapter can include organisational trauma as well as financial impacts with an aggregated value that is larger than either value alone. Now, a single event can be shown in a single bar on a bar chart with different colours for the safety, reputation and direct financial losses if required.

Treetop View Calculations

To avoid not seeing the wood for the trees, let's move out of the detailed risk value calculations to the treetop view of risk within an organisation. When an organisation has risk values for its major risks it can prioritise, compare, aggregate and perhaps disaggregate risk values. Provided there are no dependencies between different calculations it is valid to undertake all this high-level analysis.

Most organisations have performance management systems into which this treetop analysis can neatly fit. But imagine if your organisation prepared a set of accounts for each operating unit that showed the performance of all of the operating units and they couldn't be aggregated to show the total net profit or loss? It's unimaginable isn't it? But that's what happens with risk matrix users. How do you add two ballparks? Does that result in a bigger ballpark or two ballparks? Do two "High" risks from different operating units added together result in an "Extreme" risk? Treetop view calculations simply can't be done under the risk matrix.

Throughout this book risk bandits have been described as lacking in many ways—guile and cunning have not been mentioned because that is possessed in spades. Risk bandits have invented "qualitative numbers" to overcome this treetop view calculation problem. The best-known example is of course the risk matrix itself; by putting percentages and dollars on the axes it's dressed up to look numeric. It's been an unqualified sales success, almost universally accepted despite the fact that it can't be used to prioritise risks. As we saw in Chapter 6, the risk matrix v bar chart match is no contest but the risk matrix survives and flourishes.

Unfortunately there are other prominent examples of "qualitative numbers" used by risk bandits. How do risk bandits compare risk profiles between operating units of an organisation? With risk value this can be done neatly with bar charts comparing operating units. Risk bandits simply tabulate the break-up of the number of "Extreme", "High", "Medium" and "Low" risks add a bit of salt and stick them in a pie chart. Now you can compare one operating unit against another; because it's a pie chart it's accepted by audit and risk committees as a measure of which unit is carrying more risk, ignoring the inherent ballparks. Unbelievable but true!

How do risk bandits show the movement of risks over time? With risk value this can be done neatly with bar charts comparing this year and last year. Risk bandits just stick arrows on the positioning of the risk on the matrix or heat map—going south means likelihood has reduced, going west means consequence has reduced and going southwest means both have reduced. The positioning of the arrow is of course vague and only ever goes across a row or column in the matrix if there is a noticeable change that can be identified.

Finally, how do risk bandits aggregate risks to get a group risk profile if the matrices have been compiled by each operating unit? Alternatively if the matrix was compiled for the group, how do risk bandits disaggregate the group risk profile back to the operating units where accountability lies? Risk bandits of course have a "qualitative number" approach for this challenge. They categorise risks by function or source and we all know that strategic risks are always more important than operating risks—right? Wrong! A simple question such as what is the break-up of our total foreign exchange risk across operating units cannot be answered but the internal risk bandit knows that it's all right because the total risk has been allocated to the finance guys.

The "It's Too Complicated" Objection

Heat map junkies trying to dodge some challenging work offer the objection that risk value assessment is too complicated for the intended audience to comprehend because of the level of detail. This is both insulting and untrue. We have seen at the treetop level how much more powerful the analysis and reporting can be with risk value assessment, this ain't an "Alien Versus Predator" type battle! It's more James Bond versus Maxwell Smart.

But what if the executive management team and the audit and risk committee ask to see the detail? Let's look at the response from a risk bandit peddling a heat map; there is not much to show about the risk assessment. If they kept a record of the voting at the workshop they could produce some bar charts showing the distribution of participant votes and the use of the average. Alternatively, they can produce the dreaded risk register with 18 columns, in size seven font and reduced to fit the page requiring the Hubble telescope to read it!

To be fair some risk registers, usually driven by sensible software, are well set out and contain copious amounts of data. It's just not information, as it has not been processed for interpretation. In many ways it's a brain dump, although in some cases the source is a different part of the human anatomy! Risk value assessment is the process that transforms the raw data into useful information.

Risk value assessment information can be readily presented in summary form requiring minimal explanation. Let's take an example of the risk of IT system disruption, or to put it in neutral risk event terms, "IT system non-availability". Eleven causes such as cyber attack have been identified and assessed and so have the preventative controls such as firewalls. The spread of outcomes has also been identified and assessed and so have the mitigation controls such as back-up and data recovery processes. Here is the summary for executive management:

Event

IT System Non Availability

Likelihood			**A**
Occurrences	Frequency (base case)	Action Reduction	Frequency (post actions)
Fire	0.20		
Flood	0.10		
Physical damage total	0.30	25%	0.23
Storage failure	1.00		
Other failure	0.10		
Equipment failure total	1.10	50%	0.55
Blackouts	0.10		
Supplier loss	0.33		
Software bugs	0.20		
Supplier failure total	0.63	29%	0.45
Laptop lost	0.33		
Cyber attack	0.20		
Server access	0.20		
Security breach total	0.73	15%	0.62
Total	2.76		1.85

Consequence	**B**		**C**		**B x C**
Distribution	Probability (spread)	Outcome (base case)	Action Reduction	Outcome (post action)	Weighted Average
Tolerable	30%	$20k	50%	$10k	$3,000
Disruptive	30%	$40k	50%	$20k	$6,000
Recoverable	20%	$140k	50%	$70K	$14,000
Unrecoverable	20%	$840k	50%	$420k	$84,000
Total					$107,000

Risk Value Calculation	**A**	**B x C**	**A x B x C**
	Likelihood	Consequence	Risk Value
	1.85	$107,000	$197,415

Figure 7.11—IT System Risk Calculations

Is this too complicated for executive management to understand? Within two minutes they can see it is estimated that there will be 1.85 unplanned disruptions per year and 20% of those will result in unrecoverable data. They can review the controls in place and work with the organisation's risk appetite to make decisions around creating and protecting value. The cost/benefit of introducing new controls and the most effective mix can be assessed. Internal audit have clear guidance for their work on critical controls.

We can summarise Figure 7.11 a little more for the audit and risk committee by using "causal groups" and "outcome groups", as they may prefer to see less detail:

Event

IT System Non Availability

Likelihood — A

Occurrences	Frequency (base case)	Action Reduction	Frequency (post actions)
Physical damage	0.30	25%	0.23
Equipment failure	1.10	50%	0.55
Supplier failure	0.63	29%	0.45
Security breach	0.73	15%	0.62
Total	2.76		1.85

Consequence — B, C, B x C

Distribution	Probability (spread)	Outcome (base case)	Action Reduction	Outcome (post action)	Weighted Average
Tolerable	30%	$20k	50%	$10k	$3k
Disruptive	30%	$40k	50%	$20k	$6k
Recoverable	20%	$140k	50%	$70K	$14k
Unrecoverable	20%	$840k	50%	$420k	$84k
Total					$107k

Risk Value Calculation

A	B x C	A x B x C
Likelihood	Consequence	Risk Value
1.85	$107k	$197k

Figure 7.12—IT System Risk Calculation Summary

It's not complicated, it just takes time to prepare and present it meaningfully and perhaps one minute for an explanation.

Managing the Outliers

The key output from risk value assessment is a monetary value that can be aggregated, disaggregated and compared across time and operating units. Because risk value is the probability-weighted average of the range of consequences, the outliers within the spread of consequences need to also be considered.

Whilst risk value is the predicted annual gain or loss over the medium term, these outliers can still occur in the short term. Figures 7.11 and 7.12 illustrate the example of 20% of unplanned IT system disruptions resulting in unrecoverable data. If this is unacceptable then further treatment (mitigation) action is needed regardless of risk value.

The masking of extremely high-impact low-frequency events inherent in the matrix was explained in Chapter 6. Risk value assessment estimates the spread or distribution of outcomes so the analysis shown in Figures 7.11 and 7.12 is needed in addition to the estimated risk value.

A Recheck on the Specifications

To conclude this chapter let's relook at the specifications from risk value assessment that we said we should be seeking:

- Discipline in setting and defining measurable objectives
- Appropriate use of precision
- Sufficient granularity to facilitate decision-making to create value
- Capacity to prioritise commitments to protect value
- Ability to delegate risk-taking across the organisation
- Enabling a treetop view and oversight of detail

Risk value assessment supports the design of the risk management framework to create and protect value, which is the subject of Chapter 8.

8. Performance Management of Risk

Discontent Can be Good

To quote Thomas Edison, 'discontent is the first necessity of progress'. If you are a director or executive manager reading this book then you are most likely already a little discontented with your organisation's risk management. Hopefully you are now inclined to make some changes and guide your risk managers.

What are the reasons for your discontent with risk management? It probably originates from the reports that tell you little more than how busy the risk manager has been; heat maps and endless action lists are not that helpful to boards and executives in governing an organisation. You probably feel like you are being presented with thousands of jigsaw pieces with no idea of how to put them together. You're unlikely to be alone—probably no one in your organisation does, least of all the risk professionals. But don't think the source of your discontent is these reports; they are merely a symptom of the underlying problem.

No matter how user friendly the reports are, their content is unlikely to result in your contentment! Would knowing that risk registers are 100% complete comfort you any more than knowing your favourite niece has completed her final-year exams but you have an uneasy feeling that she hasn't done enough study? Without seeing the results you remain concerned but are unable to shape the outcome. Anyway, what the hell does "complete" mean? Risk management isn't a chore that can be completed, it's continuous monitoring and responding to deliver value just as are revenue generation, cost control and social performance.

Most risk management reports are about the activity within the risk process not an account of what has been achieved in the operations of the organisation. It has to be this way because of its disconnect with what actually happens in the operations of the organisation. Have you seen a risk management report that measures the impact risk management is having?

Sure you may have seen some southerly pointing arrows on a risk matrix to indicate the risk has reduced. Is this "achievement" supported by hard data, and if so, was the cost of doing so worthwhile? Could that risk treatment effort have been better directed elsewhere?

Discontent with organisation risk management usually comes from the lack of linkage to performance. Performance in this sense relates to two aspects discussed in Chapter 7:

- Changes in the levels of risk to which the organisation is exposed (protecting value)
- The operating metrics across the organisation (creating value)

You may ask—is it possible for risk management to link to performance in these ways? The answer is yes—a small number of organisations are doing just this. These organisations are able to reasonably accurately measure and monitor their level of risk and impact of risk management on operational metrics. After all, the purpose of risk management is to deal with the uncertainty in achieving organisational objectives being the threat of not achieving them and the opportunity of exceeding them. This means managing deviations from expected performance, both minimising underperformance and looking to stretch targets when there is a strong business case to do so.

Producing a single quantitative value or qualitative caption for the likelihood and consequence of each risk in a pod does not automatically link to management of organisational performance. This chapter describes how the risk management process can be incorporated into an organisational framework to drive performance. This linkage is possible for risk value assessment but qualitative risk assessment is simply too shallow to move down this path.

Navigation Guidance

This chapter contains 12 Figures; they are designed for a high-level overview without losing the plot for the remainder of "Risk Bandits". Alternatively, you may care to dwell on the detail in the Figures of greatest interest.

Why Do It?

Boards and executive management teams need to be honest as to why the organisation has a risk management function in place. The commonplace response is of course to limit risk exposures (protect value) but many organisations go further and say to enhance performance (create value). The problem is that most of these organisations do not then make it happen and the risk management function falls back to simply supporting compliance sign-offs.

If compliance is the objective, why not be upfront about it, keep spending on the risk management function to a minimum and monitor the risk taking across the organisation as best you can? Sound dangerous? It is, but your organisation is probably doing it right now anyway. Better to accept it and minimise the waste than to pretend, and in so doing, make risk management compliance more cost effective.

Set out below is a summary of risk management approaches that have been mentioned in this book organised in a continuum of options:

Documentation Focus   **Organisation Goal Focus**

	Compliance	Protect Value	Performance Management	Value Management
	Pacify	Defend	Win battles	Win the war
Objective	Documentation of identified risks and actions for external reporting	Minimising negative consequences from threats	Management of risk and return linkages	Management of risk value including: capital, assets, cash flow, social licence and long term performance
Driver	External standards and regulations	Negative consequence limitation	Board approved performance parameters	Computed cost benefit analysis of loss and opportunity decisions
Tools	Qualitative positioning of a single consequence and likelihood on a descriptive scale after arguing controls are good	Qualitative positioning of a single consequence and likelihood on a descriptive scale after subjective improvement of some controls	Quantification of the risk supported by available data and bowtie or fault tree development with transparent cost benefit ranking of proposed control improvements	Quantification of risk based on increased data collection whilst assessing risk events within a prescribed value chain framework

Figure 8.1—Risk Management Continuum Options

This continuum is not to be confused with the "maturity benchmarking" model described in Chapter 4 that focuses on process adherence and not business outcome. Maturity assessment is a point reached on a journey of progression to the nirvana of embedded integration, even though the tools and processes in place are self-defeating. The continuum in Figure 8.1 involves a decision—it's the strategic positioning that should be proposed by executive management and approved by the board. This decision on "why do it" should not be left to the risk manager, their role is simply to implement.

Options 3 and 4 above involve extensive preparatory work, analysis and strategic choices so there is a journey to reach increasing levels of sophistication. This progression involves jettisoning Options 1 and 2—they are a different pathway that was probably started because most organisations were led astray at the outset of the risk management juggernaut. It's not like a upgrading a computer rather it's more like a deciding between computer options; a laptop or a tablet. In both cases there can be hybrids. For example, the risk matrix from Option 1 or 2 or a rapid quantification tool might be used as an initial screen of risks to decide in which order material risks should be subject to more detailed quantitative analysis in Options 3 and 4.

If you are in any doubt as to which option your organisation has adopted, here are some litmus tests. Risk appetite is a good indicator—generic statements across all risks fit Option 1, statements by risk type fit Option 2 and detailed calculated risk/return metrics fit Options 3 and 4. Reporting of success to executive management and the audit and risk committee is another good indicator—a focus on risk register completion and flimsy graphics fits Options 1 and 2 whilst performance and at-risk metrics fit Options 3 and 4.

The best test is, who is in charge? The risk manager largely develops and runs Options 1 and 2 and executive management and the board run Options 3 and 4. Option 1 is defensive against stakeholder criticism and Option 2 is defensive against exposures. Options 3 and 4 hand strategic risk management to the board and better control of the organisation to executive management to improve shareholder return and "social performance" and better governance is a by-product.

However Beautiful the Strategy

The "why do it decision" should be supported in a documented risk management strategy for the organisation developed by executive management and approved by the board. The strategy should recognise the Sir Winston inspired observation about risk management documents from Chapter 2—so much has been written, for the guidance of so many that has benefited so few.

The strategy need only be a few pages and should be a standards and guidance free zone—keep it strategic and closely monitor whether it is delivering the expectations of executive management and the board. Take heed of an actual quote from the British bulldog, 'However beautiful the strategy, you should occasionally look at the results'.

It's this focus on results from the risk management function that needs to be developed and then driven by executive management and the board. In Chapter 2 we saw that regulators varied in their views about the role of the board in risk management, so if regulators don't require it why should the board approve the risk management strategy? It gets to the heart of governance as an integral part of the board overseeing the organisation achieving its objectives rather than just sating regulators or avoiding negatives.

The intent of a risk management strategy is to develop around three or four complementary game plans for the functioning of risk management in the organisation. They should be high level, not at the implementation level, and supported by explanatory analysis and reasoning. Once the strategy is approved by the board then executive management can get on with implementation. There are usually a variety of views amongst board members and executives on how risk management should work; formulating the strategy is a way of bringing on and resolving that discussion—it's then push forward or push off!

Structuring a Functional Strategy

Here is a suggested structure for a risk management strategy:

Topic	Themes
Desired end state	• How risk management is to inform the organisation's decisions
	• How operating functions benefit if changes were delivered effectively
Situation analysis	• Where the organisation is at with risk management today
	• The organisation's business needs
	• A summary of strategies to get to the desired end state
Strategic positioning	Proposed positioning on the continuum described in Figure 8.1
Functional strategies	Two or three game plans for the functioning of risk management in the organisation
Governance	• The overall responsibility for driving and facilitating risk management
	• The delegation of risk management responsibilities to executives and personnel
	• The risk management reporting framework
	• Targeted internal audit

Figure 8.2—Risk Management Strategy Structure

The definition of the desired end state should be short and sharp without using clichés like "best practice", "fully embedded" and "integrated framework"; if these are objectives then describe what it will look like. The objective row in Figure 8.1 is a good guide—honesty is needed in laying out how risk management is to be used.

The situation analysis should carefully consider the nature of the organisation, for example, a multi-location decentralised organisation with a relaxed conformance culture will be quite different from a single location organisation with a very disciplined conformance culture. Cognisance should also be taken of "risk management fatigue". Have the previous attempts at rearranging the risk deck chairs turned key people in the organisation away from the formal risk management function and what needs to be done to ensure change isn't just seen as the next fad?

The proposed strategic positioning should reference the continuum described in Figure 8.1 to inform the debate. A potentially glib statement that the organisation is to use risk management to enhance performance needs to be supported by processes and tools that are capable of doing so.

The strategies for the functioning of risk management in the organisation should not be confused with the approach to managing individual threats or opportunities; these are better dealt with in detailed plans. Functional strategies are about implementation of risk management.

Functional Strategies to Match

Have you ever walked around your home dressed in pyjamas where the pants and top don't match? Maybe your family noticed and chuckled or more likely no one cared, it's a bit different to wearing a formal outfit with sneakers to a wedding. This matching dress sense applies to the functional risk management strategies in that these strategies need to match the desired end state, and if that involves the organisation's situation and strategic positioning for risk management, it had better be Armani or Jimmy Choo shoes, not whatever floated to the top of the "let's not throw them away yet" level of the shoe rack!

Remembering that we are looking at functional strategies about implementation of risk management, not strategies to manage threats or opportunities, let's consider what these matching strategies might cover. The starting point should be the target impact of risk management, sure financial impacts are the most obvious and easiest to measure but also consider the importance of other impacts such as health, safety and environment (HSE); reputation; community and for public sector organisations, service levels or "public value".

A second consideration for setting the strategy is how it will be driven. Will risk management be driven by the executive management team and the process facilitated by the risk manager? Most organisations would probably say they already do this but in practice few do so. As demonstrated throughout this book, commonly the risk manager is left to drive the risk process by incessant use of the shepherd's crook or whip, rather than demonstration of value. If the executive is simply not up to the task then something has to change, and if the organisation is so widespread and management decentralised then a common functional risk management strategy is needed.

A final consideration for setting the functional strategy is the focus or scale of risk management. Is the objective to analyse the most important risks or as many risks as can be identified? The 80/20 rule normally applies—80% of the risk value in an organisation is likely to reside in say the top ten risks. The organisation should start with the biggest risks and then move down— but how far is appropriate before quantity impacts quality?

Example Strategies

Three example designer label strategies are provided below.

Consider the example from Chapter 3 of the company that owns multiple large processing plants located in remote areas near agricultural land. The formal risk management system to date has been driven from head office by the group risk manager for reporting back to the audit and risk committee. The risk register exists but looks obese and is hardly used by those that make the decisions on site. Let's assume that management of each plant is quite decentralised with strict budgets overseen by head office because cost pressure is intense.

The following functional risk management strategies might be appropriate where the board and the executive have decided that the strategic positioning on the risk continuum is "performance management":

- Top-down guidance driven—group risk metrics are set by the executive and applied consistently at all locations by site management assisted by the group risk manager

- Performance impact focus—risk management is focused on having a performance impact on EBIT (revenue and costs), HSE and community

- Quality rather than quantity—initial priority is deep analysis of the top ten strategic and operating risks

The second example is a not-for-profit that is funded by public donations and funds received from government to manage skilled volunteers working in developing countries on short to medium term assignments to improve the well-being of impoverished communities. There has been no formal risk management framework in place but the risk management procedures in place are strong because of the high in-country safety and security exposures facing volunteers.

The following strategies might be appropriate where the board and the executive have decided that the strategic positioning on the risk continuum is "protect value":

- Consultation driven—group risk metrics are established after consultation with management and staff, volunteers, donor government agencies, host governments and security specialists

- Administrative control focus—these controls provide the most effective method of reducing exposures to hazards for volunteers. Control assumptions must be tested for every new venture and whenever change occurs in existing ventures

- Wide-ranging scope—initial priority is breadth rather than depth in order to have some processes in place for local control of as many safety and security hazards as possible

The third example is a gaming regulator for a specific jurisdiction whose objective is to effectively and efficiently foster integrity in the gaming environment with honest and competitive gaming that is free of corruptive elements. The formal risk management system has been driven by a cat drover who has managed to document 488 risks in the risk registers, paper cuts et al! Let's assume that problem gambling is a key community issue but the government under budget pressure is regularly reducing funding to the regulator.

The following strategies might be appropriate where the board and the executive have decided that the strategic positioning on the risk continuum is "performance management":

- Top-down control driven—risk metrics are aligned with the allocation of decision-making responsibility between the Minister, the board and the CEO and the delegation of control procedures for compliance and enforcement activities by officers. These metrics encourage economic activity and only intervene where clearly necessary

- Performance impact focus—risk management is focused on promoting efficiency and effectiveness. Resources are concentrated in the areas of the potential greatest harm to society whilst maintaining accountability and independence from regulated parties and government

- Quality rather than quantity—initial priority is deep analysis of the top ten strategic, operating and public value impacted risks

Start at the Top

Reference has been made in this chapter to a top-down approach, the term has widespread use in risk management but it is applied in a variety of ways, usually unsuccessfully. For bandit-infested organisations, top-down means a statement written for the CEO at the front of the risk policy and a mention in the annual CEO message of the importance of risk management. The CEO and executive management don't get involved in formal risk management because the process has very little to do with managing the organisation. On the other hand, for organisations at the right hand end of the continuum in Figure 8.1, risk management is fundamental if performance management is to be effectively driven by executive management and appropriate governance provided by the board.

Debate exists as to whether it is best to approach risk management from the bottom-up or top-down. Proponents of bottom-up argue that risk is best understood at the operating level—operating people deal with risk every day and so they are best to identify and assess risk. Proponents of top-down argue that a high-level view of risk is needed to understand the organisational context to identify and assess risk.

Of course both points of view have merit but when risk management is part of the performance management of an organisation it must start at the top whilst capturing the knowledge and experience of people at the operating level. The top-down approach seldom leads anywhere unless the tools to deliver it exist because qualitative captions of risk levels cannot be aggregated, disaggregated or compared over time or between operating units. When risk bandits are asked how heat map based risk management systems contribute to the performance of the organisation, the responses are usually in the form of "the dog ate my homework" excuses like:

- There is no one size fits all solution, which translates to 'It's all far too difficult'

- We embed a risk culture applying the tone at the top, which translates to 'I got the board to sign off on what I put in front of them'

- We apply focus to the sources of greatest value creation and destruction, which translates to 'The Standard says we have to include "opportunity" in addition to "risk" nowadays—I hope the board doesn't ask me how you actually do it'

It's not only risk managers and boards that struggle with the challenge of how risk management systems contribute to the performance of an organisation. Academic literature and consultant white papers expand on the shortcomings and excuses but provide few clues on solutions. In the spirit of the promised constructive mode post the Intermission; we make an effort to fill this gap below.

In summary, a top-down risk management approach used for performance management has three key aspects:

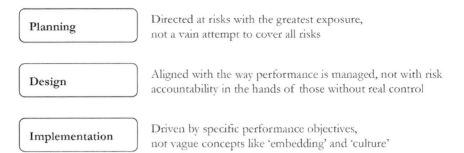

Planning	Directed at risks with the greatest exposure, not a vain attempt to cover all risks
Design	Aligned with the way performance is managed, not with risk accountability in the hands of those without real control
Implementation	Driven by specific performance objectives, not vague concepts like 'embedding' and 'culture'

Figure 8.3—Risk Management Approach To Manage Performance

The remainder of this chapter explains these three aspects, not surprisingly they are achievable with risk value assessment but not by pinning the tail on the risk matrix donkey.

Material Risks and the 80/20 Rule (the Planning)

The first aspect of the top-down approach—planning the approach so it is directed at the greatest exposures—sounds logical but as we saw in Chapter 4 a common approach is to go for quantity rather than quality of risk management. Risk analysis then becomes broad and shallow rather than focused and deep. It is no accident that in academia deep learning has proven dramatically more successful than surface learning when developing future leaders. When the fear is whether all risks have been identified and assessed, filling in a risk register with 488 risks is the primary objective. Broad, shallow coverage provides a false sense of security, is an inefficient use of resources, and the risks that really matter don't get the attention they require.

Risk value assessment as described in Chapter 7 enables priority decisions to be made about the risks with the greatest exposure. These are usually few in number and probably contribute most (usually at least 80%) of the total aggregated value of key risks in an organisation (risk value-based criteria) and all risks that threaten the organisation's existence (consequence-based criteria). The strategy of "fewer assessments better directed" is key to a top-down approach designed for performance management.

This approach is often referred to as a focus on "material risks" but organisations usually struggle with an explanation as to what that means. The notion behind this positioning is really a planning level of materiality and is the "threshold" of exposure (upside or downside against objectives) the organisation is seeking to identify. To implement this approach a screening process is needed to determine which risks have the greatest credible consequences (i.e. forget the probability of it occurring for this step). This involves establishing an initial threshold that can be moved down over time as more risks are analysed to a point where it is agreed further analysis is not warranted but continued vigilance on control integrity and management of change continues.

The starting point is the meaning of risk, within the context of an organisation, 'uncertainty in the achievement of objectives'. This requires an organisation to define those objectives, both financial and non-financial, and then establish the threshold for the level of uncertainty beyond which it is seeking to identify risk events and make decisions about their treatment. The initial threshold can be set using the risk value assessment methodology described in Chapter 7 that estimates the probability-weighted average of the range of consequences.

The threshold for an organisation is best expressed in terms of predicted consequences of risk events rather than at the individual cause level because of the complex interfaces between causes and the range of severity of outcomes. For example, the potential for an IT system disruption from any one cause might be dismissed easily, but looking at a bowtie diagram full of pathways to the "non-availability of the IT system" risk event will have a very different impact on the risk assessor's thoughts as to the credibility of the event. The threshold is set as an approximate level of the deviation from financial and non-financial objectives from an individual risk event. It could be set as in the following example:

- Financial outcomes (such as EBIT) at $10 million
- Non-financial outcomes (such as Safety, Environment, Reputation and Service levels) at internal trauma equivalent $5 million

The safety trauma threshold issue often invokes the "price for life" discussion illustrated in Chapter 7. As the threshold is a materiality-planning concept, a $5 million threshold might be appropriate for an organisation that genuinely considers safety as paramount. If an organisation's operating philosophy is that 'no task will be undertaken unless it meets the reasonable expectations of investors, employees and the community', then it might even be appropriate to use a $10 million trauma equivalent threshold for all outcomes.

The use of the threshold in the initial screening of risks may be shown as follows:

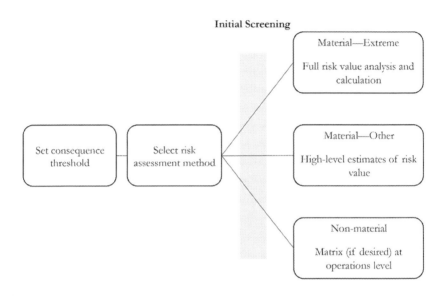

Figure 8.4—Initial Risk Screening

The risk matrix can be a tool used for this initial screening but as the process is only considering the consequence at the time, no risk assessment is really required at all. It is simply a matter of answering the question, what is the maximum credible outcome?

However, the matrix may be used to establish a crude priority list for genuine assessment of those events that exceed the threshold.

Alternatively, broad-based risk value calculations can be done. The process involves:

• From the list of identified risk events, screen out those where the maximum credible consequence is clearly below the thresholds. Losing the entire board in a plane crash is both possible and credible without a suitable control in place, but losing the entire management team in a pandemic is possible but not credible in risk terms. A non-credible event usually takes into account the extreme rarity of such events and the small degree of control the organisation has over it

- For the remaining risk events an estimate of the maximum risk value can be calculated using the ABC formula from Chapter 7. As the estimates are not based on precise data they will only provide orders of magnitude of the frequency of the initiating event ("A") x probability of defined outcomes ("B") x the estimated outcomes ("C"). However the resulting estimated probability-weighted average of the range of consequences should be sufficient to screen out those clearly below the thresholds

- For the remaining risk events using the risk value assessment process to the point where they are clearly above the threshold before completing the analysis

Executive management and the board are in the best position to set the planning level of materiality and promote the efficient use of the organisation's resources.

Performance Metric Alignment (the Design)

The second aspect of the top-down approach used for performance management is designing the approach so that is aligned with the way the organisation manages performance rather than with the way risk accountability or ownership is assigned. As we saw in Chapter 6, risk bandits are adept at designing risk descriptions to help them herd the cats. Risks are also often categorised as financial, operating, environment and so on because the risk manager designs the approach to make life easy. Often professional groups within organisations also like it that way. For example, safety and environmental people love to keep their "exclusive clubs" separated even though that makes life harder for the overall business. A top-down approach takes the responsibility away from the risk manager and hands it to executive management by aligning the design of the approach with the way the organisation manages performance.

Risk Taxonomy

This top-down approach to the description and categorisation of risks is best referred to as the "taxonomy" and provides the basis for reporting and monitoring risks. If risk management is to be used for performance management then the risk taxonomy should align with the way executive management and the board monitor performance across the organisation. Performance monitoring in an organisation is usually focused both on recent performance and the outlook and linked to organisational objectives at three levels:

- Strategic intent—such as market share
- High-level performance metrics—such as total revenue
- Operating metrics—such as individual product revenue

The best place to base the design of the risk taxonomy is the high-level performance metrics that are most likely already in place in most organisations. These metrics are usually focused on value creation based on the organisation's "value chain". This concept, first introduced 30 years ago by Michael Porter[20], is very useful in risk management.

The Value Chain

The value chain is the series of activities that an organisation undertakes to satisfy a customer value proposition. Sometimes referred to as "core processes" they are at the coalface involving interaction with customers and suppliers. Support processes or back office functions/services feed into the value chain but usually do not create value for the organisation. Such internal services may well involve critical control owners (IT security systems, key personnel retention schemes, etc.) and may be the recipient of the material damage. Here are some value chain examples for different organisations:

---

[20] Competitive Advantage (1985); Michael Porter page 87

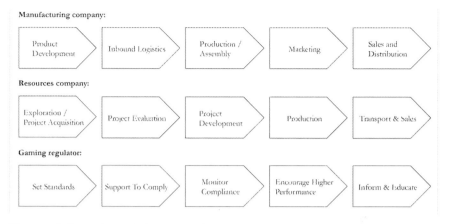

Figure 8.5—Value Chain Examples

The risk taxonomy (description and categorisation) should therefore be built from the top-down, using the highest-level risk exposures and based on each value chain component (VCC). Some examples of the alignment to a VCC and therefore performance management include:

- Production output, costs and sales different from forecast (for both the manufacturing company and the resources company)
- Commodity reserves less than forecast (for the resources company)
- Percentage market share different to forecast (for the manufacturing company)
- Compliance monitoring different from plan (for the gaming regulator)

The risk taxonomy is pitched at the level that executive management and the board want to monitor because the focus is on value creation and it aligns with the overall monitoring of performance. Sales objectives are subject to the impact of uncertainties and risk reporting can complement reporting of recent sales performance and outlook. The point is that there are not many "top risk events" from a board perspective, which facilitates the treetop view referred to in Chapter 7. Executive management and VCC managers will of course require more granularity and this is provided within the mechanics of each risk event as they are analysed.

If we use the example of the gaming regulator, the key risk events to the VCCs may be something like this:

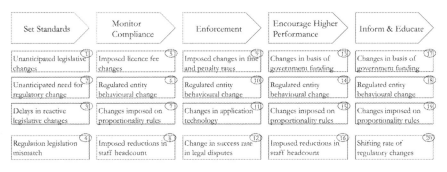

Figure 8.6—Value Chain Risk Examples

Don't worry too much about the accuracy of the detail in Figure 8.6, the stock exchange is the only casino we really understand, but the point is that behind each VCC there are a number of risk events that the VCC manager needs to manage but the CEO and the board don't need this level of granularity. The taxonomy enables those lower level risks to be aggregated into the treetop view for the CEO and the board in a logical manner aligned with the way performance is managed. Each lower level risk is likely to be a cause at the higher level in the taxonomy. Executive management or the board can always dig deeper if the big picture looks bleak.

If we continue with the example, let's assume the regulator has one set of financial objectives and three non-financial objectives shown below:

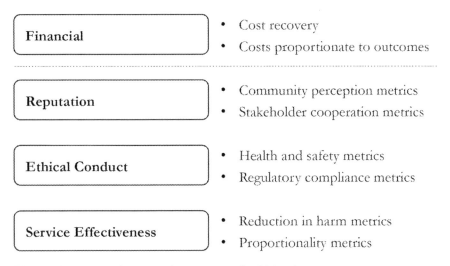

Figure 8.7—Gaming Regulator Example Objectives

If we take just the financial performance objectives as an example the VCC level risk events can be tracked to the "top risk events" on which the CEO and the board want to focus as follows:

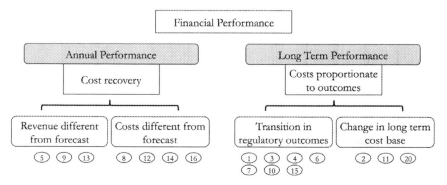

Figure 8.8—Gaming Regulator Risk Reporting Architecture

Avoiding Causes and Risk Event Confusion

This approach to the risk taxonomy not only focuses on performance management but also helps reduce confusion between risk events and causes and tightens the resulting risk profile. Many organisations include a bubble on their risk matrix for scenarios such as "Loss of key person" or "World recession" amongst hundreds of loosely worded risks. This taxonomy takes the focus away from performance management and adds unnecessary bulk to the risk profile because each entry is but a single cause, albeit of many events. "Loss of key person" or "World recession" might be a cause of poor sales but they also might be a cause of costs being over or even under forecast, whilst the loss of a key person may also impact the strength of competency-based controls across the organisation.

The impacts of these causes, and possible improvements to controls can be assessed by applying the cause → event → outcome concept of risk mechanics summarised in the high-level bowtie diagram in Figure 4.3. When reviewing causes, occurrence controls, outcomes and treatment controls; care is needed to avoid double counting of the impacts of the same cause across different risk events in the aggregated risk value calculation. A clear distinction between what constitutes a risk, what causes it and which controls manage that risk is therefore a major contributor to a smaller, better risk register brought about through fewer, but better risk assessments. When this is combined with a taxonomy that is aligned with the value chain, the top-down approach is designed for performance management.

The risk events arising in support processes to the value chain processes, such as HR, IT, Legal, Finance and Safety, generally, but not always, drive a focus on value protection rather than value creation. IT system disruption or a safety incident are good examples of such risk events where value protection effort is needed. The design of the taxonomy for value protection risk events also starts at the top with a focus on the greatest exposure but is more directed at responsibility for preventative and mitigation action than value creation. This allocation of responsibility can be to a risk owner in their own right or to the owner of a critical control that manages a risk event in one of the VCCs. Let us explain.

Most organisations will concern themselves about the loss of key people and HR (as a support process) will have a large impact on how well this is controlled. The loss of a key person in "Sales" will have a direct impact on EBIT; however, there will also be losses in other VCCs if key people are lost there. As a result, the HR department must focus on appropriate organisation attraction and retention strategies but it will not be in a position to calculate and manage individual situations as effectively as the relevant VCC manager. As long as the combined risk value across all VCCs from a loss of a key individual can be aggregated, it will be possible to calculate risk value. For performance management it will also be possible to undertake cost/benefit analysis of potential changes to the HR attraction and retention program both at individual VCC and organisation levels. The VCC manager will be able to compare any retention control improvements with the cost/benefit of alternative measures that are more within their direct control (e.g. promotion, development, etc.).

In such cases, the individual VCC managers will own the risk relating to their part of the value chain within their performance parameters (e.g. cost control) but HR would be the critical control owner for the wider attraction and retention program for the organisation. Alternatively, the HR manager can be the risk owner for a "Loss of key person" assessment and the VCC manager can report on their elements of the overall risk mechanics to the HR manager as the risk owner. Each executive team needs to make these decisions around their own circumstances whilst recognising the need to avoid double counting of risk value, the second option requires the VCC managers to extract "key person loss" from their "cost overrun" risk value calculation otherwise double dipping occurs.

In addition to the risk events lying below the value chain in the support processes, there are also some risk events lying above the value chain, they are commonly called "strategic risks" and loose examples include "sovereign risk", "political risk" and even "world recession". This concept is abused by many risk bandits to refer to risk events that they can't pin on an individual VCC manager. The result is that the responsibility is allocated to the CEO or the executive team but is not really demanding of their attention (e.g. "Collapse in commodity prices", "Removal of government funding", etc). This is not to say the executive wouldn't lead a crisis management response if such an event occurred, but it is not their responsibility to prevent it occurring.

The design of the taxonomy for the so-called strategic risks follows the same approach—top-down focus on the greatest exposures. Fortunately most strategic risks can be absorbed into other risk events by applying the cause → event outcome concept of risk mechanics in Figure 4.3. Sovereign risk is a category of causes not a risk event. Examples of causes of risk events include: "Expropriation of assets" or "Increased restriction on foreign investment". Just because a problem is designated a "cause" and not a "risk event" does not lessen its importance. It simply means that the right tool for the job is a control integrity review and not a risk assessment. Applying the right analysis tool saves time, frustration and releases precious resources to support more value creation.

There are however a small number of strategic risks to be owned by the board, CEO or executives team, an example is: "Takeover at value different from fair value". They are so few in number that they can be directly assessed and monitored at the CEO or board level.

Driving Value Objectives (the Implementation)

Having planned for the risks with greatest exposure and designed the risk taxonomy to align with performance management we can now move on to implementation. This is the third aspect of the top-down approach designed for performance management to ensure risk management is driven by specific value objectives. A risk matrix-based approach cannot be driven in this way because value is just a ballpark punt that may give a smidgeon of comfort to some but is really far too broad to provide any meaningful guidance on performance. Statements like 'we consider risk in everything we do' illustrate the limitation, it's like throwing a handful of darts at a dartboard and hoping one hits the bullseye and none hit a spectator. The fallback is to have faith that the "tone at the top" and "organisational culture" will "embed risk management" and "integrate risk" into the "way we work". It's pod of clichés as well as a forlorn hope!

Risk value assessment enables the implementation of a top-down approach designed for performance management with three specific value objectives. These three objectives arise from targeted actions along pathways as summarised below:

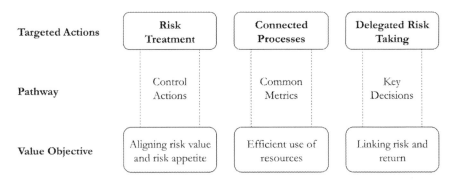

Figure 8.9—Risk Management Value-Focused Implementation

Aligning Risk Value and Risk Appetite

The first targeted action for the performance management of risk is the treatment of estimated risk value that has been identified as requiring action using risk value assessment. The pathway to the objective of aligning risk value and risk appetite is the refinement of control actions—both promotion/prevention and enhancement/mitigation—identified as requiring action from the risk value assessment.

Most risk managers say they do this already but their tools limit their potential solution to deciding who approves which colour on the matrix or heat map. This is somewhat amusing in that any risk can be broken down by causal groups, and if necessary by individual causes to get to the colour the risk assessor desires. Indeed, the result is bigger registers—a bonus for all risk bandits.

Decisions on control actions can be taken with a much greater degree of confidence when the results of risks value assessment are reviewed by executive management and the proposed target risk values are transparent and open for debate. Where the target is below the current estimated risk value level the necessary adjustments to controls or prevention and mitigation actions can be identified as requiring action and timelines and responsibilities allocated. On the upside there is the potential to promote the likelihood of opportunities leading to a risk event and enhance positive consequences from the risk event. There is also the possibility to redirect or even remove unnecessary costly controls leading to better use of resources.

The alignment of risk value with risk appetite should not be considered just on an individual risk basis. As described in Chapter 7, treetop view calculations enable risk value and risk appetite for individual risks to be aggregated to estimate a meaningful risk positioning for an organisation. At an aggregated level the value of individual risks becomes less important and a portfolio management approach can be adopted in looking at adding or removing controls across the risk portfolio to produce the optimal cost/benefit result.

In Chapter 2 reference was made to the "forest versus tree contradiction" where an organisation's risk forest is managed on a tree-by-tree basis rather than at the forest level. Most organisations have no idea whether their risk position is improving or declining because their risk management process is aimed at individual risks with no capacity to aggregate them. This process provides a vague idea of priorities for treatment within huge ballparks but no indication as to the movement in the total level of risk the organisation is facing? The likely range of total upside and downside in variation from organisational objectives is simply unknown to executive management and the board. The risk bandit response of "qualitative numbers" such as pie charts of red and orange bubbles, described in Chapter 7, provides no clues.

By way of a simple but fairly realistic example, imagine an organisation where there is a 5% chance of a $100 million loss and a 75% chance of a $20 million gain on a development project like a new shopping centre, mine site or skyscraper, and assume the remaining possible credible outcomes are no big deal either way. The oversight for the board of an organisation that undertakes 20 such projects per year is very different to that of an organisation undertaking one per year. Both would gain an average of $10 million on each project undertaken but the former would expect to gain $200 million every year from 15 successful projects at $20 million minus one loss at $100 million. The latter however would expect to gain $15 million each year they had a successful project, but expect to lose $100 million once in six years—probably wrecking the organisation's annual performance for an entire year. Even if the board comprised exactly the same members for both organisations, the risk appetite should differ markedly at the portfolio level.

Efficient Use of Resources

The second targeted actions column, for the performance management of risk covers the other processes or activities within an organisation having links to the risk management process, referred to as "connected processes". The objective of more efficient use of resources is the common metric used in the risk management process and the connected processes. The rationale here is to make use of the beneficial impacts flowing through to activities outside of the risk management process.

These linkages identified in risk matrix-based approaches are sometimes attempted but the metrics are too nebulous to be meaningful. You may have seen condensed versions of the risk matrix in internal audit or insurance cover reports. The linkage is in risk never-never land, where ballparkism ensures there can be no objective arguments presented to assist in the efficient use of resources.

Use of risk value assessment enables these linkages to be made to connected processes because the metrics are numeric not just descriptive captions. Numeric metrics enable specific value objectives to flow through to connected processes to assist in the efficient in the use of resources. Some examples of processes that can be connected to risk management with specific value objectives include:

Connected Process	Resource Efficiency Value Objectives
Governance	Prioritisation and tracking of: • Risk / opportunity commitment completion • Operation of critical controls • Effectiveness of the risk framework
Annual and long-term budgeting	• Approving investment costs to avert future losses or deliver future gains • Critical control maintenance and monitoring costs
HR (Employee performance reviews / competency issues)	Performance review focus on KPIs on: • Risk-based business case commitments • Individual performance by risk and control owners Competency review focus on: • Critical control adequacy assessments
Incident investigation and reporting	Focus on: • Incidents material to risk value • Critical control failures or breaches of risk appetite • Identification of missing critical controls
Insurance coverage	• Acceptance of tolerable risk value outcomes • Cost / benefit analysis of transfer of intolerable risk value outcomes • Use of the organisation risk management process to negotiate lower premiums
Business continuity, emergency and crisis management plans	Before event focus on: • Scenarios with greatest exposure • Effectiveness of critical controls • Pre-definition of the most effective recovery options During event focus on: • Existing bowtie / fault tree analysis and risk assessment to accelerate understanding of what has occurred
Internal audit and specific process audits	• Prioritise work in higher risk value areas • Focus on critical control testing

Figure 8.10—Risk Management Connected Processes

In case you are wondering why the above examples exclude reference to strategic planning and risk-based decisions, don't worry. These linkages could be included above but they deserve the separate focus below.

Linking Risk and Return

The third targeted actions column for the performance management of risk in an organisation is delegated risk taking which is the process used to link organisational risk and return. The pathway from delegated risk taking to the value objective of linking organisational risk and return is the basis of the "key decisions" taken in the organisation.

Key decisions are the major source of significant variation from organisational objectives; this is where the rubber hits the road and so provides the primary pathway or implementation link between identified risks and performance management. Risk considerations lead decision makers to better-informed choices about an uncertain future and prioritise actions amongst alternatives in accordance with the acceptable level of risk set by executive management and the board.

Risk matrix junkies rarely claim this third aspect of the link to performance management—it's a bridge too far—and perhaps even a hint of honesty within bandit circles. Is the risk matrix used to assess a merger or acquisition? How about cost/benefit analysis? It can't even be used in annual planning and budgeting. All these decisions require some numeric metrics.

The widespread use of the risk matrix across organisations has created a large black hole in the development of methodologies to apply the organisation risk management framework in key decision situations. As this aspect is so poorly implemented in practice it is worthy of detailed explanation.

Delegated Risk Taking;
the Secret Ingredient

In the operations of an organisation, uncertainty about the future means choices between options have to be made. These decisions in an organisation are not always made by executive management or the board. A process is needed to delegate risk taking, as illustrated when the family owned lamp-importing business in Chapter 4 moved into public shareholding. Whilst the experience and risk appetite of the decision makers is relevant, it is the organisational metrics that should be applied in these decisions.

Linking risk and return through delegated risk taking enables the right people to apply agreed parameters to make decisions when considering and acting on information about what could happen. Whether this leads to better performance than would be the case if personal metrics were applied is pretty much irrelevant. In an organisation, performance management is about the board and executive management making the big calls and monitoring implementation of all the smaller calls.

Decision Points in Organisations

There are many ways to analyse the decision points and related activities in an organisation that might drive the most significant variation from organisational objectives. The most relevant basis for analysis of risk taking is "line of sight" of the board (sometimes called "proximity to power") because in an organisation the board delegates authority for different types of decisions and how they are to be made. Decision points in most organisations can be categorised as follows in decreasing order of line of sight of the board and increasing order of incidence:

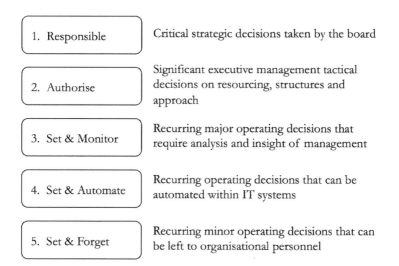

1. Responsible	Critical strategic decisions taken by the board
2. Authorise	Significant executive management tactical decisions on resourcing, structures and approach
3. Set & Monitor	Recurring major operating decisions that require analysis and insight of management
4. Set & Automate	Recurring operating decisions that can be automated within IT systems
5. Set & Forget	Recurring minor operating decisions that can be left to organisational personnel

Figure 8.11—Organisational Decision Point Analysis

The board of an organisation is directly involved in Levels 1 and 2 and so it can decide how risk is to be assessed for these decisions. As the decision-making moves further away from executive management and board line of sight to Levels 3, 4 and 5, the number of decisions increases but the significance of each decision probably declines. Executive management and the board manage this expansive decision-making process by:

- Setting policies and procedures, delegations of authority and performance metrics, and

- Monitoring results of the more significant delegated decisions

Sources of Significant Variation from Objectives

The above analysis can be used to systematically identify the decision points and related activities in an organisation that might drive the most significant variation from organisational objectives. The intention is to consolidate down to a manageable size, perhaps initially around 20 to 30 decision points and related activities, which can be managed as follows:

- Level 1 and 2 decisions—as many of these decisions do not lie within the day-to-day business processes subject to regular risk analysis, separate risk value assessment can be applied to those decisions deemed necessary by the board and CEO and subject to KPI measurement and monitoring

- Level 3, 4 and 5 decisions—the decisions within key controls or prevention/mitigation actions that most influence the organisation's risk events can be sourced from the risk value assessment of the impact on controls on the level of risk. They should be rechecked for adequacy of "Delegations" and "Policies and Procedures" and subject to KPI measurement and monitoring

The initial list of say 20 decision points and related activities subject to KPI measurement and monitoring may be extended over time as the benefits of the approach are realised. The selection of the initial list of key decisions is based on the extent of impact on the estimated risk value and should be readily identified, as they should align with existing performance metrics in operation.

Do not confuse this approach with the odorous SOX process described in Chapter 2; this is not a review of the design and operation of controls. It is simply identifying performance metrics for decisions that lie within controls that have the greatest impact.

Executive management and the board may require the annual planning and budgets process to be substantially built around risk and opportunity assessment findings based on cost/benefit analysis when there is a need to have various risk/return improvement proposals compete for available organisational resources. Risk management then becomes a fundamental part of planning, not just a line item in the budget. Equally the approval by the board of a major decision such as an acquisition might be dependent on the outcome of a risk weighted cost/benefit analysis.

Performance measures in the form of KPIs can be related to the key performance metrics established as the organisation's objectives using the taxonomy or reporting architecture as described in Figures 8.6, 8.7 and 8.8. These performance metrics should be extracted by the risk manager from the operational metrics already in use in operations. The result is:

- Critical controls, being those assessed as having the greatest reduction in the frequency and/or severity of consequence of events, have direct linkages to executive management and the board

- Key and strategic decision outcomes optimise the utilisation of resources enhancing performance

Risk reporting for boards and executive management should encompass these performance linkages. Chapter 9 illustrates how this can be done.

Performance Metrics, a Quick Word

The use of operating performance metrics in risk management analysis and reporting is not an attempt to hijack what VCC managers are already doing in managing performance. In fact the objective is to utilise what they are already doing well, with the expectation of further improvement knowing the process is now transparent to executive management. The spare parts example in Chapter 3 illustrates that VCC managers often already adequately monitor these performance metrics.

For risk analysis and reporting the challenge for the risk manager is to use the operating performance metrics that provide the best insight into the decisions being made regarding controls. A good example is injury metrics for safety incidents. Two common metrics are "LTIFR" (Lost Time Injury Frequency Rate being the number of lost-time injuries relative to the total number of hours worked) and "TRIFR" (Total Recordable Injury Frequency Rate being the number of recordable injuries relative to the total number of hours worked).

LTIFR provides insight into the financial impact of injuries as it is impacted by mitigation controls such as injury management processes whereas TRIFR provides better insight into safety hazards and the impact of preventative controls. Both metrics are useful albeit lagging (i.e. after the horse has bolted), but the point is to decide which metric best suits the objective of the analysis.

Setting Risk Appetite; it's a Cinch

Setting of risk appetite or target levels of risk and their approval is one of the most fundamental aspects of performance management of risk by an organisation. Yet as we saw in Chapter 5, most organisations struggle with it and end up with meaningless generic statements based on risk type or risk level captions because qualitative targets go with qualitative assessments. There is no point in trying the "qualitative numbers" approach described in Chapter 7 to setting risk appetite it won't work. If an organisation wants to use a quantitative target it needs some form of quantitative risk assessment meaning values with units of loss or gain per annum.

Risk value assessment not only enables quantitative targets to be set for risk appetite, it also enables the same treetop analysis of risk targets that is applied to risk value as described in Chapter 7. These targets can be disaggregated into tolerance levels for particular controls, aggregated and compared across operating units and compared across time periods. Sound useful? Properly set risk appetite targets provide enormous power to executive management for the performance management of risk as well as ready means of setting approval limits by the board.

Setting risk appetite targets is an iterative process, involving setting limits from a top-down viewpoint and aggregating tolerance levels from individual control points. There is no right or wrong answer; judgement as to what is acceptable will be built up over time and experience. Whilst the risk manager may do the detailed work, the executive management team should closely manage the process. The resulting targets should be aggregated, analysed and presented to the board for approval. The analysis could include comparisons of targets with metrics such as EBIT or net asset loss or gain per annum or similar.

Risk appetite targets will generally remain reasonably constant over time, but are likely to vary when circumstances change such as new exposures to product lines, geographies, operating processes and also investment in improved controls. Some organisations may use declining targets over time to encourage better controls, alternatively too restrictive targets reduce return and they may be eased over time with experience.

Some directors may feel uncomfortable with setting quantitative risk appetite targets because they are concerned they may have to defend the approved levels after a discovery process in the event of litigation. This particularly applies to safety and environmental harm and the "price for life" argument discussed in Chapter 7. The fallback position to attempt to avoid this issue is to continue with an inferred "price for life" inherent in a risk matrix table as illustrated in Figure 7.10 and also continue with the audit and risk committee using different safety risk metrics than the board health and safety committee. Any risk expert engaged by the prosecution can produce numbers from most organisations' qualitative guidance documents ("less than once in ten years", "more than $10 million", etc.) and when they do there will be nothing but red faces all around the board and executive meeting rooms.

It is much easier to defend a properly constructed, carefully deliberated risk value trauma target that links in with how safety is managed every day. There is a clear demonstration that the board has diligently implemented a process to manage health and safety, that safety performance is not abandoned for a few dollars more, and that it is very well managed and monitored.

The outlier discussion in Chapter 7 is also relevant when considering risk appetite or targets in monetary terms. Whilst the risk value of an individual risk or pod of risks might be acceptable to executive management and the board, the underlying weighted average may include extremely high-impact low-frequency outcomes that are unacceptable. Accordingly, the setting of risk appetite or targets in monetary terms should be after action has been taken to mitigate unacceptable outcomes.

That's a Framework!

To summarise how organisation risk management is linked to performance, we revisit the organisational framework for risk management. In Chapter 2 we pointed out that topping and tailing of the basic risk management process adopted by ISO 31000 and COSO, is organisational lipstick rather than transformation to a framework. The adoption by ISO 31000 and COSO of the four steps in the basic risk management process as the core of the framework illustrated in Figures 5.1 and 5.2 places the focus on tools and compliance rather than performance management. The tools in risk management should be seen as supporting infrastructure not the energy source.

In Chapter 5 we looked at how a simple cash payments system can be adapted to an organisational framework, bringing into play issues around governance such as delegations, implementation across multiple sites and the need for cost management and reporting. The same principles apply to an organisation risk management framework as shown below:

Governance

Mandate & Commitment	Performance Criteria	Structure & Accountability
Policy and Procedures	Taxonomy / Reporting Architecture	Audit and Risk Committee
Guidelines	Appetite Limits	Executive Team
Strategy	Key Decision KPIs	Risk Manager
Plan	Risk Management Function KPIs	Risk and Control Owners

Implementation

Infrastructure

Tools and Processes	Knowledge Management	Socialisation
Establish The Context	Risk Registers	Communication Plan
Risk Identification	Treatment Plan	Training Program
Risk Value Analysis		Reporting Plan
Risk Value Calculation		
Evaluation		

Figure 8.12—Risk Management Framework Revisited

Performance based organisation risk management is an energised framework with three elements:

- "Implementation" is the energy source
- "Infrastructure" transmits that energy
- "Governance" ensures it's effective use.

The organisation risk management framework is an integral part of corporate governance interacting with the organisation's strategy and performance in order to achieve its objectives as part of the overall risk/return decision framework.

The reporting to executive management and the board to enable oversight of this framework is the subject of Chapter 9.

9. Risk Dashboards for Boards

Black Box Reporting; the Bandit Mask Removed

The quality of risk reporting within organisations has a direct correlation with the quality of the underlying process that produces the content of the reports. Risk matrix-based reports are shallow because the risk matrix process is shallow, the reports don't focus on impact because the process has very little reportable impact. These reports are not used by executive management and the board in governing the organisation because the process runs parallel (never touching) with how the organisation is actually managed. To top it all off, risk matrix-based reports flagrantly insult the audience's intelligence by focusing reporting on the underlying process because risk bandits are convinced that they have their audience fooled that this process is sound.

If you are scratching your head and asking how can this be, then join the queue. Many users of risk reports ask the same question but not too loudly in case they are shown up, just like the Emperor's adult subjects. Risk bandits have done an incredible job in not only getting widespread acceptance of the risk matrix as a reporting tool but also in creating the perception that it shouldn't be challenged. Like a guilty parent explaining to their partner how missing the kid's soccer game or school concert 'is all very complicated', but it seldom is complicated, it's just a diversion. Risk bandits suggest the matrix is needed for ISO 31000, even though the standard itself does not even mention the matrix. It's universally accepted as best practice, largely because acceptance for most executives and directors is more about a strategic withdrawal from regulatory and political correctness minefields than a statement of confidence in the process.

In looking at risk reporting to the board in this chapter, we won't revisit the discussion in Chapter 3 about whether risk is a whole of board matter and the role of the audit and risk committee. For convenience, we will assume risk reporting is for the whole board via the audit and risk committee.

Audit and risk committees in most organisations seem to just accept the status quo with risk reporting almost without question. Yet these same committees in the last decade have taken on a much stronger role with internal audit reporting which has generally improved with a quantum leap over that period. The old style thick internal audit reports full of text and process analysis have been replaced with focused, easy to read, value adding reports allocating remedial actions, accountabilities and time frames. Status reports track these actions and overview completion of detailed internal audit plans. So why has risk reporting not had the same attention from audit and risk committees?

Again, hats off to the risk bandits lurking in the bowels of various organisations. They have successfully engaged with the risk management profession to ensure that risk matrices and heat maps have become the standard report. Risk management conference presentations, consultant white papers and academic literature usually follow the same line. Even regulators have been convinced. The last hope is the directors overseeing these organisations, and perhaps there is reason for optimism.

Directors in most countries have almost universally strongly resisted attempts by regulators and corporate governance advocates to disclose the organisation's risk profile. As we saw in Chapter 3, there are a variety of approaches around the world to this divergence in view but the result is limited external reporting of organisational risks. Directors have realised the poor quality of what they get internally and are most uncomfortable with lifting the veil externally. Perhaps as directors get more comfortable with internal risk reporting they may become more comfortable with more external reporting.

In the same way that many charming bandits like Dick Turpin, Ned Kelly and Jesse James became folk heroes it is tempting to almost admire this black box banditry for its audacity and persuasiveness if nothing else. Perhaps it is only jealousy based on our lack of charm that led us to write this book, armed only with experience, logic, simple mathematical competence and common sense. No matter how attractive the banditry there are victims, shareholders in this case, whose return is not being maximised. Call it ethics, jealousy or an intolerance of stupidity on our part, but we encourage leaders of organisations to challenge these unprofessional board reports, and to start the process. We've taken a shot at something better in the rest of this chapter.

This chapter contains 25 Figures; they are designed for a high-level overview to illustrate the power of risk reporting using risk value assessment. Alternatively, you may care to dwell on the detail in the Figures of greatest interest.

The Usual Matrix-Based Offerings

Before looking at better risk reporting, it's helpful to analyse the limitations of the suite of risk reports that usually accompany the risk matrix or the heat map. There are plenty of pitfalls to avoid. The three matrix-based offerings are generally; the matrix or heat map, risk treatment action status and some attempt at treetop analysis.

The risk matrix or heat map is the core of the reports to boards; it purports to be a risk profile, a sort of balance sheet or snapshot of the risk position at a point in time. In Chapter 6 we looked at its limitations as a tool for risk analysis but how does it perform as tool for reporting to directors? Some directors express the view that they like the matrix for its simplicity and because it gives them an idea of high-frequency/low-consequence versus low-frequency/high-consequence risks. They don't know why but they want to see this break-up—they just feel a risk with a consequence of $100,000 occurring ten times per annum is different from a risk that occurs every ten years with a consequence of $10 million.

These risks have the same financial risk value so why would a director feel they are different? In this reaction, directors are like the public en masse who react mildly to homicides, a couple here and a couple there every hour of the day (over 16,000 per year in the US alone), but will watch 24-hour news coverage of cyclones that kill on average 25 people per year in the US. Humans are far more emotional in their assessment of risk than we would like to admit and we need to feel disasters aren't going to happen to us and unconsciously play them down in our mind. This is why, when a big disaster does occur and we realise we are not as secure as we thought we were (from physical harm or lifestyle change) we react strongly. We want it never to happen again so that we can resume our level of comfort. In risk management we need to create that discomfort before the event ever occurs and try to prevent it occurring and mitigate its consequences if it does occur.

This may explain the connection that some directors feel with the risk matrix, even though they are probably not sure of the reasons. The matrix can only handle a risk with a range of causal groups by breaking it down into several assessments which results in lower risk rankings that cannot be summed up to get the overall risk. It can't handle risks with ranges of consequences that can land in multiple matrix columns either because they also are not possible to summate. Very few risks have a single consequence used in the examples above and will involve many "Moderate" or "Major" consequences for every "Catastrophic" one. Which end of the consequence spectrum represents the greatest loss or gain will vary with every assessment so taking them all into account is the only professional way to go.

Nevertheless some will continue to argue that organisations should manage risk in line with the way they expect shareholders will react. If shareholder reaction to one annual result that is $10 million below forecast in a decade is expected to be greater than that for ten years straight at $1 million below forecast, then organisations are right to worry more about the former than the latter. However, second-guessing stakeholder reaction to chronic versus acute failures would surely be best left to social scientists whilst the executive and board focus their proven talents on maximising the organisation's profits across the performance spectrum.

The biggest issue with risk matrix reports, however, is the ballparkism. The scale within the matrix can mean that some risks sitting side-by-side are many thousands of times larger than other risks. Most organisations use risk matrix reports with a likelihood scale where "Rare" is ten years or greater. This means that catastrophic events such as the risk of having the board members hijacked whilst flying (less than one in 1,000,000 flights) will get the same rating as the risk of a catastrophic project loss (one in 20 years if one project is carried out per year).

Reporting to boards usually prioritises "Extreme" and "Very High" risks but even within those captions the relative size of the risks can be a factor of hundreds within a single colour/ranking or even within a single cell in some cases. The matrix as a reporting tool just can't deal with the need of directors to focus on the most important issues, it gives that feeling but when we look closer it's only a hologram, form without substance.

What happens if a director asks to the see the analysis of a particular risk? There is no analysis behind the matrix that summarises the decisions made as to where to pin the tail on the donkey. The response to such a request is likely to be the relevant page of the dreaded risk register which faithfully records all sorts of details about what the assessor and the workshop decided but is of little use to a director because there is no substantive basis for these decisions.

The report to directors that usually accompanies the assessment is the risk treatment action status. It's usually a spreadsheet of many rows listing everything from the workshops that participants came up with that might reduce risks. Sometimes attempts are made to tier these reports and just show the actions for "Extreme" and "Very High" risks but we already know these are just ballparks. These reports can't prioritise actions that most reduce risk value because the assessment has not been done to identify critical controls so again directors are fed information that does not allow them to focus on what really matters. In short, "gut feel" assessments only allow the board to undertake "gut feel" oversight.

Often in risk reporting to directors, accompanying the risk matrix (or risk profile) and the risk treatment action status (or to-do list) is some form of treetop analysis. These are the "qualitative numbers" described in Chapter 7, examples include:

- Comparison of risk profiles over time or function—pie charts of the break-up of "Extreme", "High", "Medium" and "Low" risks

- Movement of specific risks over time—almost always south and west pointing arrows on the risk matrix

- Aggregation of common risks across operating units—the risk matrices side by side

These qualitative numbers reports may look pretty but then lipstick often does.

The Three Ps; Performance, Position and Process

The above analysis of risk matrix-based board reporting does in fact provide some valuable lessons for proposing a better basis. Firstly, start with the big picture of what the board needs for the role it sets itself. As this varies between countries and organisations we will assume the board approves the approach and monitors performance.

The second lesson is the reporting strategy should be documented and approved as part the risk management strategy and plan described in Chapter 8. Executive management should drive the development of the strategy; it should not be left to the risk manager, who will probably not have the strategic understanding necessary to make a good job of this critical step. The reporting strategy should cover all risk management reporting to risk owners, management, executive management and the board. Any reports that are prepared specifically for the board should be looked at with suspicion— why would the board get reports that are not used by management? Any customising of management reports for the board should be to summarise content not to provide additional content that is not used by management.

The final broad lesson is that board reporting needs to focus on what really matters, not a "cover-your-ass" approach of reporting everything. This means defining what is reported and when, whether it is for approval or for information and whether all aspects are reported or if it's reporting by exception. This will drive the content of reporting towards "Performance" with a secondary emphasis on "Position" and an almost incidental emphasis on "Process". This approach is in stark contrast with risk matrix-based reporting that is almost all about, the least important "P", "Process" and not enough about the most important "P", "Performance".

A good model for board risk management reporting is the approach used in financial reporting because it's well developed, universally used and it's done the rounds with most boards that are pretty interested in the topic. It also involves reporting of numerical data as a basis for board information for monitoring and approval as necessary.

Financial reporting is well focused on "Performance" with say monthly profit and loss and cash flow information against budget, variance analysis and forecast updates. "Position" reporting is perhaps less regular for most organisations, say quarterly, and provides a more detailed window into performance by reporting of the balance sheet and analysis of key assets and initiatives over a given period. The third "P", "Process", probably gets a look once or twice a year when reporting controls, accounting issues and standards are looked at by the board. We can tabulate a typical financial reporting strategy as follows:

Reporting Details	Executive Management	Board / Audit and Risk Committee
Performance [results]:		
• Profit & loss / cash flow	Monthly	Monthly
• Key operating metrics	Monthly	Monthly
• Variance analysis and incidents	Monthly	Monthly
• Management analysis	Monthly	Monthly
Position [snapshot]:		
• Balance sheet	Monthly	Quarterly
• Key asset analysis	Monthly	Quarterly
• Key initiative status	Monthly	Quarterly
Process [the means]:		
• Controls over financial reporting	Quarterly	Six-monthly
	Quarterly	Six-monthly
• Accounting issues	Six-monthly	Six-monthly
• Accounting standards	Annually	Annually
• Budgets and metrics		

Figure 9.1—Typical Financial Reporting Strategy

Although the details of the financial reporting strategy will vary greatly between organisations, by summarising the overall picture in this way we can get a treetop view and determine if it is appropriate for the role of the board in that particular organisation. If we apply the earlier lessons using Figure 9.1 as a model, we can then tabulate a typical a sound risk management reporting strategy as follows:

Reporting Details	Executive Management	Board / Audit and Risk Committee
Performance [results]:		
• Movement in risk value		
• Key operating metrics	Monthly	Quarterly
• Variance analysis and incidents		
• Management analysis		
Position [snapshot]:		
• Risk value profile		
• Key risk analysis	Quarterly	Six-monthly
• Key initiative status		
Process [the means]:		
• Risk appetite targets		
• Risk performance metric architecture	Annually	Annually
• Risk management strategy		
• Risk management plans and policies		

Figure 9.2—Better Risk Management Reporting Strategy

This reporting strategy provides the basis of the development of the content of risk reporting to the board, which we are referring to as a dashboard.

Performance Reporting; Results not Activities

The temptation with risk "Performance Reports" to boards is to detail activities (what's been done) rather than summarise results (what's been achieved). Risk matrix-based reporting inevitably falls into this mode because the results are not measurable, so what's been achieved cannot be demonstrated. The content of Performance Reports as summarised in Figure 9.2 is derived from the performance metrics described in Chapter 8. Let's look at them and illustrate some dashboards using simplified performance curves such as continuous arcs and straight lines.

Movement in Risk Value

Movement in risk value is the first facet of Performance Reports listed in Figure 9.2. This information should be provided to the board for information on a regular basis, say quarterly.

Here are some examples of the way the movement in the total risk value of say the top ten risks could be presented to executive management and the board. This aggregated value was used to demonstrate the treetop view calculation referred to in Chapters 7 and 8.

The first example is an annotated chart of total risk value movements:

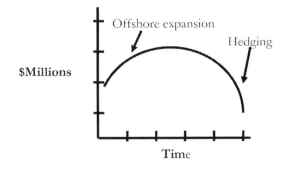

Figure 9.3—Example Total Risk Value Movement Report

The report shows that the total value of the top ten risks initially increased when the organisation expanded offshore but reduced as knowledge of the offshore market increased. A further significant reduction occurred when hedging controls were put in place. Major occurrences like this will usually be foreseen in the budget and planning process, but are not always reflected in risk reports.

The board may want more information behind this summary so risk value may be reported in waterfall diagram form to allow tracking of the impact of risk treatment actions that have been approved. The following chart illustrates the benefits in terms of overall risk value reduction:

Tracking of Risk Value of top 10 risks

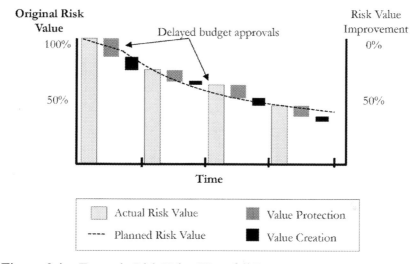

Figure 9.4—Example Risk Value Waterfall Report

The report illustrates the benefits in terms of overall risk value reduction. It should be noted that this chart represents the most mature level of reporting and can be only undertaken by an organisation adept in all of the other enhancements discussed in this book because it requires that comparative risk assessments are consistent in accuracy, the risk value reduction estimated is realistic and appropriate measurement of progress has been established.

The following report complements Figure 9.4 in that it tells the board that the risk treatment program is behind schedule and has achieved only 74% improvement for 81% of the expenditure:

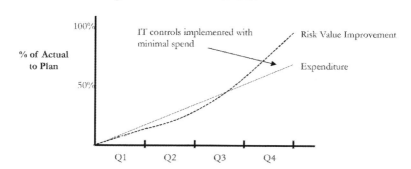

Figure 9.5—Example Annual Risk Management Performance Report

Further information could be reported, if required by the board to track individual decisions and circumstances.

The next example is an annotated chart of financial and non-financial risk movements:

Movement in Risk Value of top 10 risks

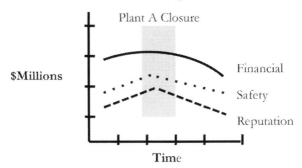

Figure 9.6—Example Financial and Non-financial Risk Value Movement

The report shows the reduction in the components of the total value of the top ten risks due to a plant closure.

The final example is an annotated chart including a comparison with aggregated risk appetite:

Movement in Risk Value of top 10 risks

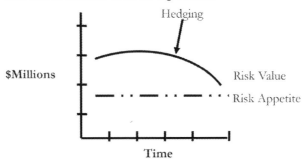

Figure 9.7—Example Total Risk Value Movement v Risk Appetite

The report shows a comparison of total risk value to total risk appetite, which is a mathematically valid treetop view for all risks where risk value exceeds risk appetite. The gap represents the task ahead in terms of risk treatment actions. A separate total comparison report could also be presented for risks where risk value is below risk appetite as the "surplus" risk appetite may indicate unnecessary controls.

Some boards may wish to see more detail on a regular basis than these examples. Additional information could include breakdown by operating units, support functions or risk owners.

Key Operating Metrics

Key operating metrics are the second facet of Performance Reports listed in Figure 9.2. This information should be provided to the board for information on a regular basis, say quarterly.

Key operating metrics for risk management, as explained in Chapter 8, can be either organisational performance metrics for value creation and protection or metrics for the performance of the risk management function.

Metrics for the first aspect, value creation and protection, relate primarily to the Level 3 decisions in Figure 8.11, 'Set & monitor'. These metrics can be either input or output KPIs that help the board monitor the most important decisions within the critical controls. Some examples are below.

The first example is for the gaming regulator (using an input KPI):

Critical Control	Control Impact
Licencing Approval Process (LAP) decisions	$5m

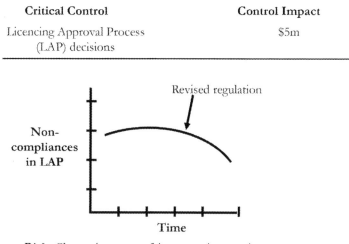

Risk: Change in extent of inappropriate gaming in licenced operators within territory

Figure 9.8—Example Critical Control Decision, Gaming Regulator

The report shows that instances of non-compliance by the regulator with its license application process have reduced with the introduction of the revised regulations that the regulator had recommended.

The second example is for the spare parts in the agricultural product processing company:

Critical Control	Control Impact
Work Maintenance Scheduling Process decisions	$5m

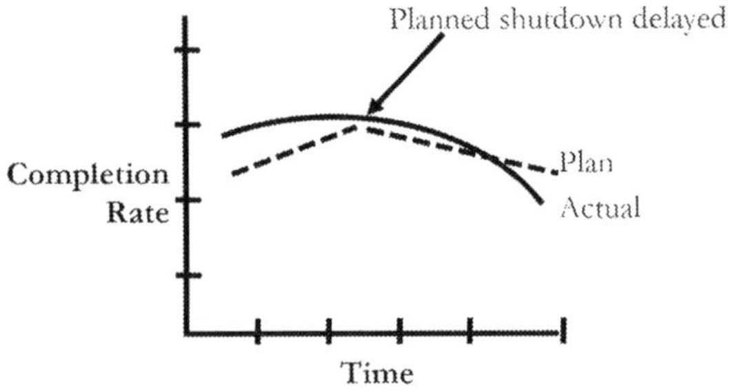

Risk: Non-availability of spare parts

Figure 9.9—Example Critical Control Decision, Agricultural Product Processor

The report shows the impact of a poorly considered decision to delay a planned shutdown on the maintenance completion rate (i.e. backlog) that is a critical part of the management strategy for the risk event relating to "non-availability of spare parts".

The final example is for safety in the mining company:

Critical Control	Control Impact
Contractor review process	$5m (Trauma equivalent)

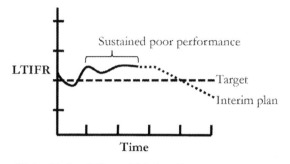

Risk: (Various) Potential Injury Events

Figure 9.10—Example Critical Control Decision, Selection of Contractors

The report shows that halfway through the year the LTIFR is not trending well. Contactors were the injured party in all but one of the actual injury cases and a review of incidents and near misses uncovered eight different risk events that had occurred in six months with no event having occurred more than twice. Risk assessment bowtie diagrams and calculations showed that the "Contractor Review Process" had been identified as a critical control in five of the eight events but also appeared in the other three bowties too. Critical control integrity analysis had recognised on multiple occasions that the hiring of short term local contractors was a primary weakness in the "Contractor Review Process" but planned work in this area was not undertaken by sites because a whole-of-company solution was being planned for later in the year. An interim plan is being introduced to bring LTIFR performance into line with the target by the end of the year.

These KPIs provide executive management and the board with clear insight as to how decisions within critical controls are impacting the realisation of the greatest sources of uncertainty. There is little such insight in long to-do lists of control remedial actions. The choice of using input or output KPIs is often driven by what is reasonably available to the VCC managers without creating a measurement task beyond the value derived for the effort. Input KPIs provide insight into the factors influencing decisions whereas output KPIs provide insight into the results of the decision.

Value protection KPIs can also be reported to the board where 'Set & monitor' decisions (Level 3 from Figure 8.11) lie within critical controls, here is an example:

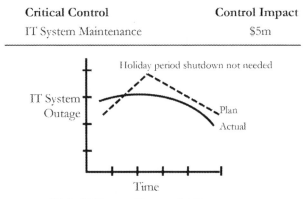

Critical Control   **Control Impact**

IT System Maintenance $5m

Risk: IT System Non-availability

Figure 9.11—Example Critical Control Decision, IT System Maintenance

The report shows the impact of the cancellation of the planned shutdown on the planned outage rate that is a critical control for the risk event relating to non-availability of the IT system. Whilst the actual outage is below plan, perhaps it could have been even lower if the planned outage had occurred.

The second category of key operating metrics for risk management is metrics for the performance of the risk management function itself. The best measure is whether the planned alignment of risk value and risk appetite was achieved:

Alignment of Risk Value to Risk Appetite of top 10 risks

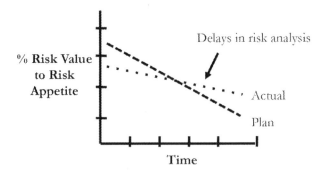

Figure 9.12—Example Risk Management Function Performance Metric

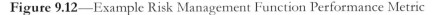

The report shows the impact of delays in risk analysis and the relationship between risk value and risk appetite.

Sophisticated risk management functions may also aim to identify performance in relation to linking of risk and return. Such measures may include savings identified and that could even be extended to a rate of return calculation for the risk management function. Care is needed in moving down this path due to the challenges of measuring such metrics and the delineation of performance recognition amongst executive management.

Variance Analysis and Incidents

Variance analysis and incidents are the third facet of Performance Reports listed in Figure 9.2. This information should be provided to the board for information on an exception basis, say quarterly.

The basis for reporting variances is the annual plan prepared for implementation of the high-level risk strategy as outlined in Chapter 8. As the subject matter is more about activities than results, the report should focus on variances from plan as leading indicators of future performance. Here is an example:

Planned Activities	Operating Units			Projected Impact
	Unit 1	Unit 2	Unit 3	
Risk value assessment	✔	✔	✖	Complete by year end
Risk treatment actions	?	✔	✔	Unit 1 may miss target
Control audits	✖	✖	✖	Deferred due to staff availability
Major decision application	✔	✖	✔	Unit 2 not applying methodology

Figure 9.13—Example Risk Management Variance Analysis

This exception report allows the board to focus on what planned activities have not taken place based on the projected impact.

Material incidents are likely to be reported to the board within their functional discipline such as "Health and Safety", "Environment" or even "Finance". To avoid duplication of reporting the same information, risk management reporting of incidents should focus on the risk value implications. An incident for risk management reporting should therefore be an occurrence impacting estimated risk value such as the identification of a hazard not previously in the risk value assessment, control failures and breaches of policies or appetite limits. Sometimes an incident can be a near miss where the occurrence was prevented by sheer luck but the learning can be as valuable as if the incident had actually occurred.

Board reporting summaries should focus on incidents "material" to risk value such as critical control omissions or failures or material breaches of risk appetite. The basis for reportable incidents should be set out in the strategy. Here is an example of board reporting:

Incident Details	Risk Context	Risk Value Impact
Waste water discharge	Over-estimate of prevention control impact (flow meter)	Increase by $1m
Community backlash over new plant	Cause not identified—risk value assessment updated	Increase by $1m
IT failure during peak usage period	Dependence between causes not understood by IT—risk value assessment updated	Increase by $1m

Figure 9.14—Example Risk Management Incident Analysis

Management Analysis

Management analysis is the final facet of Performance Reports listed in Figure 9.2. This information should be provided to the board for information on a regular basis, say quarterly. The analysis should be a brief commentary on results if the context and implications are not clear from the individual reporting templates.

Position Reporting; Snapshots (not To-Do Lists)

Risk "Position Reports" provide boards with a periodic snapshot of the status of risk management across the organisation relative to the target metrics approved by the board. Risk matrix-based reporting struggles to do this because the target and actual metrics are not measurable. The content of Position Reports as summarised in Figure 9.2 is derived from the performance metrics described in Chapter 8. Let's look at them and illustrate some dashboards.

Risk Value Profile

The risk value profile is the first facet of Position Reports listed in Figure 9.2. This information should be provided to the board for information on a periodic basis, say six-monthly.

This report is like the balance sheet of risks; being the calculated exposure relative to the approved risk appetite. Here are some examples of the way the risk value profile of say the top ten risks could be presented to executive management and the board:

As a chart of total risk value:

Risk Value Profile—top 10 risks

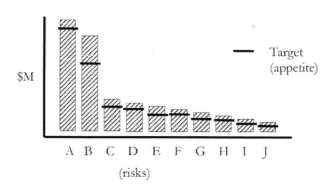

Figure 9.15—Example Total Risk Value Bar Chart

As a chart of total risk value broken down between financial and non-financial risk value:

Risk Value Profile—top 10 risks

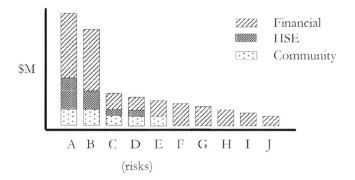

Figure 9.16—Example Financial and Non-Financial Risk Value Bar Chart

This chart can be used in many ways; another example is a chart of total risk value by operating units:

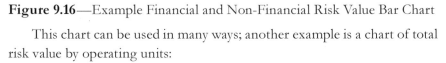

Risk Value Profile—top 10 risks

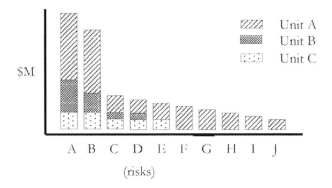
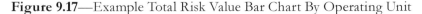

Figure 9.17—Example Total Risk Value Bar Chart By Operating Unit

The above three reports show the break down of risk value by risk event through three different lenses. They follow the usual pattern that aggregate risk value is concentrated in a small number of high value risks.

As we saw in Chapter 6, the corresponding report to the above bar charts under risk matrix-based systems is the risk matrix or heat map plus a long unprioritised to-do list of risk treatment action promises. The comparison is a no-contest; executive management and boards can clearly see the risk profile of the organisation relative to target in the above three reports.

Risk treatment actions should normally only be reported to a board on an exception basis, when important planned actions have not taken place. There should be no need to report the tiresome and endless details of the promised actions when the resulting risk value summarises their impact. Boards don't normally receive a list of unreconciled general ledger accounts when they see a balance sheet during the year, it should be no different for lists of treatment actions behind a calculated risk profile.

Key Risk Analysis

Key risk analysis is the second facet of Position Reports listed in Figure 9.2. This information should be provided to the board for information on a request basis, or otherwise a periodic basis, say six-monthly.

A board or an audit committee may make requests to see details of the analysis of key risks on an adhoc basis or it may decide to look at one key risk every six months, for example. Risk matrix-based systems struggle to provide a meaningful high-level analysis of an individual risk so what is sent to the board/audit committee in response to these requests? You guessed it, a copy or extract of the page from the risk register!

Using risk value assessment a possible format for a report was provided in Figure 7.10. Some directors may prefer a graph; here is the same information in a graph:

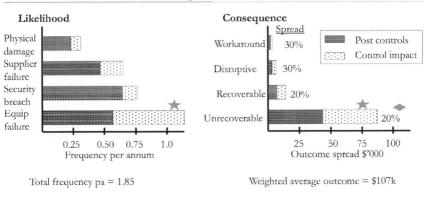

Event
IT System Non-Availability
Likelihood x Consequence = 1.85 x $107k = $198k

Total frequency pa = 1.85 ㅤ Weighted average outcome = $107k

⭐ Critical control

◈ Key action—reduction of probability of Unrecoverable outcome

Figure 9.18—Example Specific Risk Analysis

The report shows the break-up of the elements of the risk value calculation and their relative importance after controls and the control impact. On the frequency side, equipment failure would be the largest single cause of the risk event if it were not for the critical prevention controls. On the consequence side, the catastrophic outcome eventuates 20% of the occasions that the risk event occurs. The critical mitigation controls reduce this outcome by 50%. The power of risk value assessment for executive management in making decisions and for directors in oversight is clearly demonstrated by this analysis.

Key Initiative Status

Key initiative status is the final facet of Position Reports listed in Figure 9.2. This information should be provided to the board for information on a periodic basis, say six-monthly.

In the same way that the board receives financial reports on the status of key initiatives, such as major projects or key operating decisions, the board should also receive risk reports on these initiatives. Risk matrix-based systems normally add little value to board monitoring of such initiatives but useful data is readily available when using risk value assessment. Here is an example of a chart that might assist the board in the deliberation of setting the annual plan and budget; it uses the risk taxonomy set out in Figure 8.8:

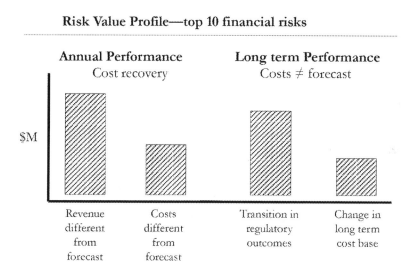

Figure 9.19—Example Risk Analysis For Planning and Budgeting

This report illustrates to the executive and the board of the gaming regulator that in setting the annual budget and long term plans, the key risk exposure is not costs. Of greater significance are the falling revenue base and the transition that is occurring in regulatory outcomes.

Position Reports to boards on the status of major projects can be greatly enhanced through powerful data that is readily available using risk value assessment. The power of this information is enhanced because projects, be they large internally focused expenditures or externally focused acquisitions, usually have defined and measurable metrics that can be readily related to risk value. The key metrics are usually cost (are we doing the project right) or NPV (are we doing the right project).

The bar chart in Figure 9.15 could be used for project risks with the target risk value set by allocating the project contingency reserve across the key risks. This could be summarised as follows:

Project A—Risk Value Profile

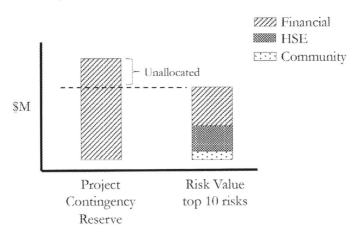

Figure 9.20—Example Risk Analysis For A Major Project

This report shows that the predicted value of top ten risks for the project account for about 70% of the project contingency reserve.

A worked example of risk value assessment for an acquisition is included in Chapter 10.

Process Reporting; the Means not the End

Risk "Process Reports" provide boards with information on how the risk management processes operate. Whilst the main purpose of these reports is background information for directors, there may be some aspects that need to be approved by directors and this information needs to be presented in a form that facilitates board analysis and approval. Aspects that should be approved by executive management and the board, such as risk matrix criteria, rarely see the light of day at board meetings. There is almost an unwritten truce between the risk manager, executive management and the board—don't question these metrics too deeply because they won't stand scrutiny and then we can get on to the important parts of the agenda.

The content of Process Reports as summarised in Figure 9.2 is derived from the performance metrics described in Chapter 8. Let's look at them and illustrate some dashboards.

Risk Appetite Targets

Risk appetite targets are the first facet of Process Reports listed in Figure 9.2. This information should be provided to the board for approval on an infrequent basis, say annually.

In Chapter 8 we saw how risk appetite can be set using risk value assessment. Unlike risk matrix-based systems, where appetite is a coloured area on a heat map, a series of matrix cell numbers or high-level generic statements; risk target levels can be set at a specific risk value in total and can also be scaled down to tolerance levels for specific control points, decisions and performance metrics if required. For most organisations this is too much detail for a board, it needs to be approved in detail by executive management and presented at a high level to the board for approval.

Risk target information could be presented by risk in bar chart form as illustrated in Figure 9.15, in approving these limits the board would be saying that they can live with the actual risk profile coming in at these target levels. Alternatively, the risk targets could be presented using the risk taxonomy as per Figure 9.19. Here is an example of how the risk appetite information may be presented to the board for approval at total level:

Figure 9.21—Example Risk Appetite Board Report

This report shows that the appetite for risk this year in millions of dollars per annum has tightened in comparison to last year and has been restored to the value of two years ago before offshore expansion caused an increase. Target risk value as a percentage of total assets and EBIT has increased in the current year due to the fall in total assets and EBIT following the site closures.

Risk Performance Metric Architecture

The risk performance metric architecture is the second facet of Process Reports listed in Figure 9.2. This information should be provided to the board for information on an infrequent basis, say annually.

In Chapter 8 we saw how a top-down approach to the description and categorisation of risks (risk taxonomy) provides the basis for reporting and monitoring risks as illustrated in Figure 8.8. We also explored the linkages to performance management through the identification of key decision points and related activities subject to KPI measurement and monitoring as illustrated in Figures 9.8 to 9.11. The risk taxonomy and risk related KPIs can be referred to as "risk performance architecture".

This risk performance architecture needs to be approved perhaps on an annual basis to ensure it is relevant and providing useful information. For most organisations this is too much detail for a board, it needs to be approved in detail by executive management and presented at a high level to the board for approval. Here is an example of how the risk performance architecture may be presented to the board for information at a high level:

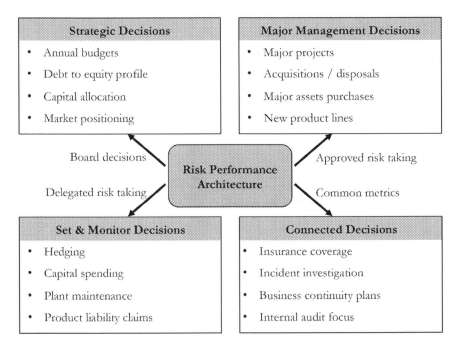

Figure 9.22—Example Risk Performance Architecture Board Report

Risk Management Strategy

The risk management strategy is the third facet of Process Reports listed in Figure 9.2. This information should be provided to the board for approval on an infrequent basis, say annually.

The risk management strategy should not vary much from year to year, perhaps with some refinements as circumstances vary. As described in Chapter 8, it should only be two or three pages, with suggested content set out in Figure 8.2. The key aspects for approval of the board are:

- Positioning on the risk continuum as set out in Figure 8.1
- The issue of depth versus breadth of risk analysis
- The extent of board involvement

Risk Management Plans and Policies

Risk management plans and policies are the final facet of Process Reports listed in Figure 9.2. This information should be provided to the board for information on an infrequent basis, say annually. Approval of the plans and policies is the domain of executive management and strong resistance is needed against attempts to delegate their preparation upwards by risk managers looking to offload responsibility.

I'll Have What She's Having

If you, as an executive manager or board member, are contemplating referring this book to your risk manager, point to the next three Figures and use the wonderful line from the movie 'When Harry Met Sally'—'I'll have what she's having'.

Below is a summary of the risk performance dashboards for boards set out in this chapter, the size is cramped to fit the page but you can still see the power that is handed to the board when risk management is properly designed and implemented:

Here is an example quarterly report:

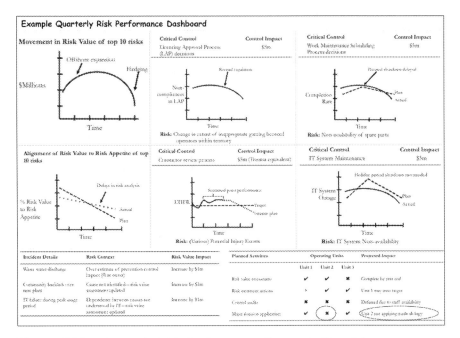

Figure 9.23—Example Risk Performance Quarterly Board Report

On one or two pages the board (perhaps via an audit and risk committee) can readily see:

- The movement in risk value for the quarter relative to appetite
- The metrics around the key operating decisions involving uncertainty
- The impact of the risk management function
- The likely impact of incidents and variances from plan

The board receives this Performance Report for information; there is no need for approval. The board has the opportunity to ask meaningful questions, request more information and ask for action to be taken. The report is focused on performance not on the risk management process.

Here is an example six-monthly report:

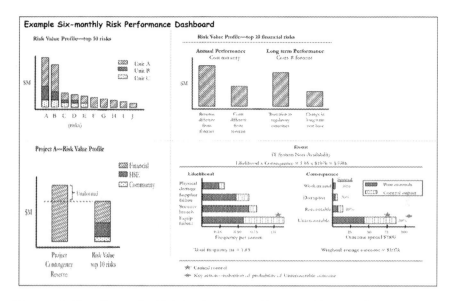

Figure 9.24—Example Risk Performance Six-Monthly Board Report

Again just one or two pages for the board and/or the audit and risk committee to see:

- The risk value profile as at the end of the period
- The impact of risk value on the key metrics from the annual plan
- The impact of risk on key initiatives

There is no need for approval but the board has the opportunity to ask meaningful questions, request more information and ask for action to be taken. The Performance Report is focused on positioning but still not the risk management process.

Here is an example twelve monthly report:

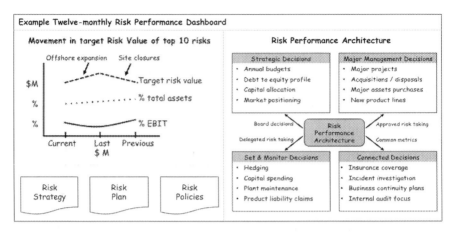

Figure 9.25—Example Risk Performance Twelve-Monthly Board Report

On this occasion the board on one or two pages can readily see:

- The movement in target risk value (appetite) for the period
- The risk performance architecture

Also provided to the board is the risk strategy, risk plan and risk policies.

The board receives this Performance Report only once a year. The only aspects requiring approval are the risk appetite targets and the risk strategy. The board still has the opportunity to ask meaningful questions, request more information and ask for action to be taken. Whilst the report is necessarily directed at process the focus is on board needs to overview performance not on the risk manager's tools and processes.

Defence Against Being Read

We are again inspired by a Sir Winston Churchill quote in concluding that risk reporting in most organisations, by its content and length, is a great self-defence mechanism used by risk bandits against the threat of the reports being read by executive management or the board. Board reports need to focus on the board's role in oversight of risk management, which means:

- Performance reports on results not activities, perhaps on a quarterly basis
- Position reports on status not to-do lists, perhaps on a six-monthly basis
- Process reports on the means not the end, perhaps on an annual basis

The change from the currently widely accepted process reporting is significant and the catalyst for change is demands from the board not reliance on risk managers.

To conclude "Risk Bandits", Chapter 10 looks at two case studies.

10. Practice Beats Theory

Making it Useful

To complete the account of the strategy for dealing with risk bandits and extracting value from organisation risk management, two applications of risk value assessment are worked through in detail in this chapter. They are based on real examples, simplified for publication.

The first worked example relates to an organisational risk event, being the "non-availability of spare parts" at an agricultural product processing company. This example has been referred to throughout this book.

The second worked example relates to a major business decision, being the cost/benefit analysis of a major acquisition. This application was referred to in Chapter 8 as part of the process of delegated risk taking.

Navigation Guidance

If your enthusiasm remains high for understanding the detail behind risk value assessment then this chapter can be used as a detailed step-by-step guide. The detail in the Figures is sufficient for this purpose. Alternatively you may choose to follow the flow of logic in the Figures and focus on the outcomes of the examples. The design of the Figures also enables a high-level overview of this logical flow.

Non-Availability of Spare Parts

The Risk Bandit's View

You may remember the example from Chapter 3 of a large agricultural product processing plant located in a remote area, near agricultural land. The soon to be replaced risk manager, in true risk bandit style applied a quick and dirty risk assessment using the risk matrix. He concluded that on average the most expensive part fails every two years because this has occurred twice in the last four years and the lost revenue for three days production would be

$12 million based on the average lost production last time it occurred. The bubble placement in the likelihood/consequence matrix shown in Figure 3.2 was "Extreme".

The Production Department effectively ignored the risk bandit's analysis because they've fixed the problem that caused the previous two events. The formal risk management process run by the risk bandit, who has since been appointed as the new Sales Manager, is not linked with the underlying spare parts risk management process and the "Extreme" rating reported to executive management and the board lacks credibility.

Context of the Risk

The risk event that has been referred to is "non-availability of critical spare parts". If the parts are not available then production of up to about $4 million a day may be disrupted until a replacement can be delivered but the cost of carrying multiple spares on site can be prohibitive. The risk/return decision of the holding of spare parts is likely to be significant to the plant.

The Production Department has substantial data about the failure rate of parts based on maintenance regimes and works with suppliers for emergency back-up to determine the appropriate holding on site. These teams have a sophisticated decision-making process that is largely effective in practice but it is not linked into the organisation's formal risk management governance framework set up by the former resident risk bandit. The new risk manager— let's call him Ralph—won't tolerate any of this and rolls up his sleeves and starts work.

Ralph uses a high-level bowtie diagram as set out in Figure 4.3 to understand the mechanics of the risk:

- The causes (threats) are circumstances such as part failures, parts reaching their useful lives and other destructive forces

- The occurrence control framework over these causes would include regular inspections, a replacement and maintenance regime and fire protection measures

- The middle of the bowtie (initiating event) is the "non-availability of critical spare parts". Whilst it would take days of lost production to result in a material financial loss, any unplanned shutdown due to non-availability of critical spare parts indicates a significant breakdown of occurrence controls and an uncomfortable degree of dependency on treatment controls

- The outcomes of the event would be lost production ranging from a few hours to many days plus any flow on costs, such as contract penalties, and perhaps even some safety and reputation issues

- The treatment control framework over these outcomes includes spare part repair strategies, back-up arrangements with sister plants and loss of profits insurance

Describing the Risk Event

In Chapter 6 we looked at how, and how not, to describe risk events. The description should be an event such as a happening or incident that realises or initiates uncertainty in achieving the organisation's objectives; it is not a state or a circumstance. The place to start is the organisation objective, which in our example is to maximise shareholder value, and its strategy involves being a low cost and reliable supplier of processed agricultural product.

As the cost of production is a key competitive driver there is pressure on the Production Department from the executive to make "risk-based decisions" on cost control. Non-availability of critical spare parts (which are prohibitively expensive) is a key part of the uncertainty that needs to be managed by the Production Department. The initiating event description does not allow for upside because it is an incident with only negative consequences as described in Chapter 6. The description should fit in with the risk taxonomy similar to that set out in Figure 8.8 under "Annual Performance". It may sit in a sub-category such as "Production different from forecast".

Defining the risk event up-front in clear terms as the "non-availability of critical spare parts" enables the causes, consequences and controls to be readily identified during the detailed risk analysis. If the risk description is confused with causes, consequences or controls the rest of the analysis becomes difficult.

Ralph now has the centre point of the bowtie diagram as set out below:

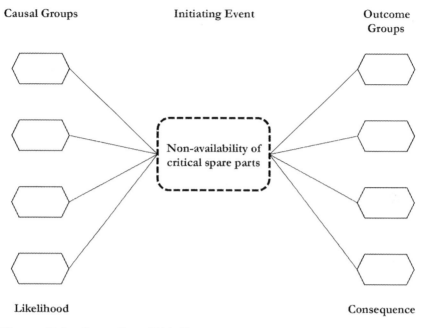

Causal Groups   Initiating Event   Outcome Groups

Non-availability of critical spare parts

Likelihood   Consequence

Figure 10.1—Spare Parts Risk Event

Approach to the Analysis

The simplified bowtie diagram in Figure 10.1 guides the risk analysis, which can move to the right to consequences (range of outcomes) or to the left to likelihood (multiple causes). Ralph decides that as the risk mechanics are being analysed for the first time, rather than reviewing a previous analysis, it's better to start on the likelihood side of this diagram. Analysing the causes first provides strong insight into how the underlying processes work and the potential range of outcomes. The use of causal groups helps drive a top-down view before getting immersed in the detail and is useful for summarising the risk value calculation later on.

Ralph in approaching this analysis collects as much information as possible before interviewing Production Department personnel or running workshops. The information reviewed includes spare parts reviews completed by the Production Department and by external consultants involving asset criticality, supplier spare part availability and the maintenance strategy and program.

Ralph is not second-guessing the strategy adopted by the Production Department; he is simply assessing the risk from an organisation point of view. In understanding the risk and collecting information Ralph becomes focused on the interaction between causes of unplanned spare parts usage and the levels of spare parts held. As the Production Department budget is too tight to carry all spare parts, decisions are necessary to optimise the cost effectiveness of spare parts inventories. The decision is a balance of the exposure to lost production versus the cost of holding the spare parts that includes acquisition costs, carrying costs (interest), storage costs and obsolescence, damage and shrinkage.

Collecting the Data

Armed with some useful background information Ralph starts discussions and runs a workshop with Production Department personnel. He learns that a formal maintenance strategy is in place; it involves planned maintenance in accordance with plant manufacturer specifications and predictive maintenance based on recording instrumentation and weekly inspections. Further a prioritised availability strategy exists for all critical spares that involves in-house repairs, approved temporary substitutes and original equipment manufacturer replacements.

Ralph summarises the spare parts inventory-holding decision as a series of well-considered and deliberate steps undertaken by the Production Department:

- Materiality has been defined and spare parts have been categorised by value

- Criticality has been assessed and spare parts have been categorised by impact on individual production lines and the whole plant. Non-financial impacts have also been assessed around safety and environment

- Detailed data on "mean time between failure" is maintained for all critical spares

- The probability of equipment failure where critical spare parts are needed is estimated and ranked

- The impact is estimated of each of these possible equipment failures on production and safety and the environment. These estimates involve an assessment of supplier delivery lead times, the value of production disrupted and the flow on impact to customer deliveries

The end result is a well designed and documented process for prioritising the critical spare parts holdings for on-site demand and agreements with suppliers to minimise lead times and arranging back-up supplies. It achieves a balance between carrying too many spare parts and incurring the extra cost and carrying too few and disrupting production.

Ralph reviews the circumstances of the two critical part failures that have occurred in the last four years that resulted in lost revenue for three days production on both occasions. The first occurrence was due to planned maintenance not being carried out and the weekly inspection not being sufficiently robust to detect the faulty part. Both these activities have been strengthened and the Production Manager now receives regular detailed reports on both processes.

The second occurrence was the failure of a part close to the end of its scheduled life but the part supplier, with whom there is a contractual obligation to provide back-up within 12 hours, could not supply the part for three days. This supplier has since been replaced and regular updates of relevant stock levels held, form part of the new supplier's contract.

Analysis of Causes and Occurrence (Preventative) Controls

Ralph is now in a position to start filling out the likelihood side of Figure 10.1 starting with the causal groups. He uses the information he has collected but broadens his analysis beyond the specific part failure focus of the Production Department. He notes the bowtie diagram needs to reflect three key failure aspects:

- Part failure
- Supplier failure
- Stock-outs

Ralph now undertakes a detailed analysis over the last five years of the production, maintenance and critical spare parts plans and records. He looks at how often critical part failures occur and finds that it is multiple times each year with the parts planned to be replaced from stock about 20% of the time and from suppliers about 80% of the time. His analysis of the causes of critical spare parts not being available is as follows:

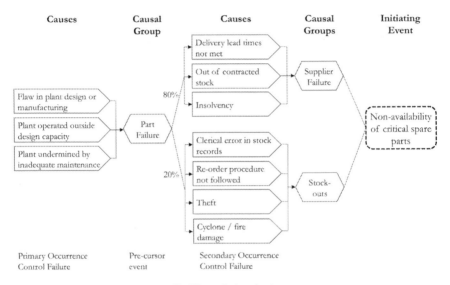

Figure 10.2—Spare Parts Likelihood Analysis

The analysis shows three causes of parts failure, three causes of supplier failure and four causes of the stock of parts not being available. The two phases of the causal groups are shown in sequence rather than in parallel because for the risk event to occur there has to be a parts failure plus either a supplier failure or a stock-out. This sequence is important when Ralph applies the risk value calculation metrics.

He decides not to map the planned parts replacements because they occur during the scheduled shutdowns in June and January and have a record of 100% availability from suppliers or stock for over five years.

Ralph then looks at the "occurrence" or "preventative" controls that impact these causes. Some of the controls identified are:

- Original design and fabrication standards
- Contractor selection procedures

- Competency-based training program
- Safe operating parameters
- Plant instrumentation alarms and trips
- Computer-based monitoring and maintenance program
- Failure modes, effects and criticality analysis
- Inspection and breakdown reports
- Supplier qualification process
- Supplier compliance confirmations
- Supplier audits
- Post-award supplier financial assessments
- Cyclical stock-takes
- Stock record approvals and audits
- Secure storage protocols
- Plant design and fire protection measures

Ralph maps these controls against the causes that have been identified:

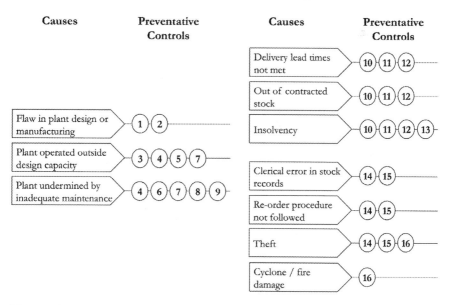

Figure 10.3—Spare Parts Likelihood Preventative Controls

Analysis of Consequences and Treatment (Mitigation) Controls

Ralph is now in a position to start filling out the consequence side of Figure 10.1 starting with the outcome groups. He uses the information he has collected from the Production Department but broadens his analysis beyond the specific financial impact on individual production lines and the whole plant focus of the Production Department. He considers other costs such as emergency transport costs, contract penalties and legal costs. He also broadens the non-financial impacts assessed by the Production Department around safety, involving injuries from releases from the high-pressure air system, to include reputation.

He decides the outcome groups are:

- Temporary workarounds—involving no loss of production as the in-house engineers are able to immediately repair parts or use temporary substitutes

- Single production line disruption—involving no loss of total plant production as some production can be maintained on other production lines as repairs are made or substitutes used

- Total plant production disruption—involving more than one production line but a loss of total plant production of less than two shifts as production across the whole plant is reorganised whilst repairs are made or substitutes used

- Prolonged shutdown—involving the loss of two or more shifts of full plant production

Ralph now undertakes a detailed analysis over the last five years of the production and costing records. There have only been two major part failures in the last four years that have had significant consequences. However, he discovers that there are many minor impact critical spare part failures that are either repaired or substituted by the Engineering Department or the resulting disruptions are handled by the Production Department changing the production scheduling. His analysis of the range of outcomes of critical spare parts not being available is as follows:

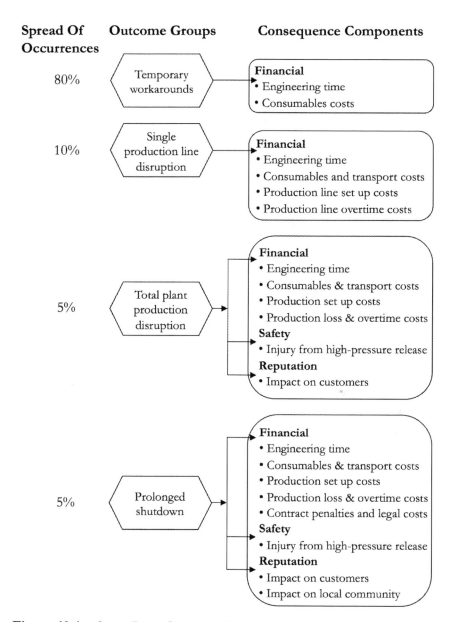

Figure 10.4—Spare Parts Outcome Range Analysis

This analysis shows that 80% of the occurrences of critical spare part failures where a replacement is not available from stock or within agreed lead times from suppliers can be resolved by temporary workarounds (repair or substitute) until the part is available. The more severe outcomes occur much less frequently with lost production of two or more shifts only resulting from 5% of occurrences.

Ralph then looks at the "treatment" or "mitigation" controls that impact these consequences. He identifies the following controls:

- Production continuity plans
- Engineering repair strategies
- Supplier warranties
- Back-up arrangements with sister plant
- Cyclone, fire and business disruption insurance coverage
- On-site rescue facilities
- Emergency medical evacuation contract
- Workers compensation insurance
- Customer delivery variation arrangements
- Contract lawyer arrangements
- Public relations protocols

Ralph maps these controls against the consequences that have been identified:

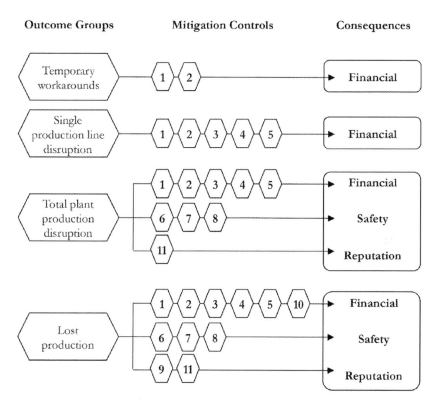

Outcome Groups   **Mitigation Controls**   **Consequences**

Figure 10.5—Spare Parts Consequence Mitigation Controls

Summarising the Analysis

Ralph has now completed his analysis of the risk mechanics. In the interest of readers, the summary below maps the flow of the analysis using the shapes from the Figures 10.1 to 10.5. Any attempt to include the descriptions within the space limitations inherent in a book would reduce the font size to levels dangerous to your eyesight:

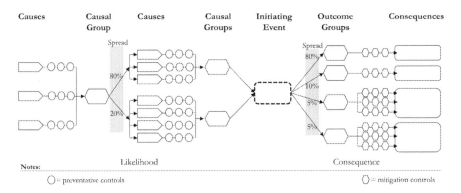

Figure 10.6—Spare Parts Risk Analysis Summary

Doing the Calculations

Ralph has now done the risk analysis (risk comprehension in ISO 31000) part of the risk value assessment (i.e. he has made sure he understands the entire picture); it's time to move onto the risk value calculations to complete the risk value assessment. He has already collected most of the monetary data he needs to do the base calculation; the systematic application of the bowtie analysis provides this discipline. The challenge is now to fill in the gaps in data through a little more research and some extrapolation, apply the monetary values and review and test the results.

He starts on the likelihood side with the causes and tabulates the frequency data he has extracted from the spare parts records over the last five years. It's worth noting that data on the frequency of risk events is often surprisingly good because events (but usually not the very bad outcomes) occur relatively frequently. In populating the frequency data on the left hand (likelihood) side of the bowtie diagram, Ralph recognises that the two phases of the causal groups are in sequence rather than in parallel. For the risk event to occur there has to be a parts failure plus either a supplier failure or a stock-out.

This sequence of causes means that a frequency rate per annum can only be applied to the first causal group (part failure). For the downstream causal groups (supplier failure and stock-out) a frequency rate is calculated based on the frequency of the first causal group and the probability of a control failure in the downstream causal groups.

Ralph decides to plot the bowtie diagram to show the flow of causes and a separate fault tree diagram to calculate the frequency. The bowtie diagram is as follows:

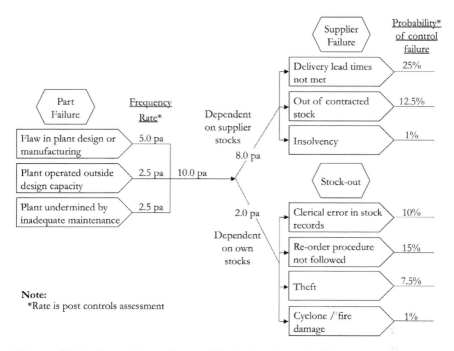

Figure 10.7—Spare Parts Causes Tabulation, Bowtie Diagram

Ralph now moves to the fault tree diagram, shown below in Figure 10.8, to calculate the frequency of causes using the information shown in Figure 10.7. He is careful to deal with the sequencing of causes and their dependencies. Independent causes (described as "OR" in Figure 10.8) are added whereas dependent causes (described as "AND" in Figure 10.8) calculate inputs from dependent causes and apply the probability of control failure to determine their frequency[21].

---

[21] To keep the mathematics simple, the "Supplier Failure" and "Stock-out" causal groups are assumed to be independent and therefore added. In reality there is likely to be some degree of dependence in that a stock-out following a part failure may result in approaches to suppliers to cover the non-availability.

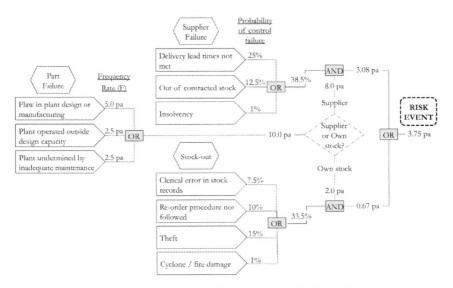

Figure 10.8—Spare Parts Causes Tabulation, Fault Tree Diagram

The above calculations are net of the impact of preventative controls in the calculation of likelihood. They are assumed to reduce the causes by 50% in the summary of the likelihood calculation below:

	Failure Rate	Frequency Rate	Frequency (base case)	Action Reduction	A Frequency (post actions)
Event					
Non-availability of critical spare parts					
Likelihood					
Occurrences					
Causal group 1					
Design/ plant flaws			10.00		
Outside design capacity			5.00		
Inadequate maintenance			5.00		
Plant failure total			20.00	50%	10.00
Causal groups 2 and 3		80%	20%		
Lead time					
Out of stock	38.5%	16.00	6.16		
Insolvency					
Supplier failure total			6.16	50%	3.08
Clerical error					
No re-order	33.5%	4.00	1.34		
Theft					
Cyclone					
Stock-outs total			1.34	50%	0.67
Total frequency					3.75

Figure 10.9—Spare Parts Likelihood Calculation

Moving to the consequence aspect of the risk value calculation Ralph applies recent Production Department experience to the consequence components analysed in Figure 10.4. He includes the non-financial parameters using the "trauma to the organisation" concept outlined in Chapter 7. His analysis shows a wide range of severity within the four outcomes shown in Figure 10.4 so Ralph prepares a summary analysis for the financial consequences as follows:

Outcome Groups	Severity ($'000)		Severity (%)		Average ($'000)
	Low	High	Low	High	
Workarounds	10 ↔	50	60% ↔	40%	26
Single prod. line disruption	200 ↔	1,000	50% ↔	50%	600
Production disruption	1,200 ↔	2,000	20% ↔	80%	1,840
Lost production	2,200 ↔	5,000	20% ↔	80%	4,400
Total					6,906

Figure 10.10—Spare Parts Financial Outcome Severity Range

Ralph does a similar calculation for safety and reputation. He now moves to the impact of probability and controls in his calculation of consequences.

The spread of outcomes between the four groups extracted from the Production Department records shown in Figure 10.4 provides the probability impact. Ralph decides the impact of the identified mitigation controls needs to be included because most of the five-year history he is using was before the controls were strengthened after the last major unplanned shutdown. He is able to extract useful control impact data from the sister plant. His consequence calculation is now complete and he can now combine it with the likelihood calculation:

Event					
Non-availability of critical spare parts					

Likelihood					A
Occurrences	Failure Rate	Frequency Rate	Frequency (base case)	Action Reduction	Frequency (post actions)
Causal group 1					
Design/ plant flaws			10.00		
Outside design capacity			5.00		
Inadequate maintenance			5.00		
Plant failure total			20.00	50%	10.00
Causal groups 2 and 3		80%	20%		
Lead time					
Out of stock	38.5%	16.00	6.16		
Insolvency					
Supplier failure total			6.16	50%	3.08
Clerical error					
No re-order	33.5%	4.00	1.34		
Theft					
Cyclone					
Stock-outs total			1.34	50%	0.67
Total frequency					3.75

Consequence	B		C		B x C
Distribution	Probability (spread)	Outcome (base case)	Action Reduction	Outcome (post action)	Weighted Average
Workaround	30%	$26k	50%	$13k	$3,900
Single production	30%	$600k	50%	$300k	$90,000
Production disruption	20%	$1.84m	50%	$920k	$184,000
Lost production	20%	$4.44m	25%	$2.22m	$666,000
Total					$943,900

Risk Value Calculation	A	B x C	A x B x C
	Likelihood	Consequence	Risk Value
	3.75	$943,900	$3,539,625

Figure 10.11—Spare Parts Financial Risk Value Assessment

Reporting, Analysis and Treatment

Ralph now considers how to report the results of his work. The former risk manager has reported that the risk is "Extreme" at $12 million every two years but the actual risk value is half that at $3.5 million per annum which approximates one day's production each year. Because Ralph is dealing with numeric values rather than qualitative captions, he is able to do some treetop calculations on the mechanics of the risk for his report which are shown below:

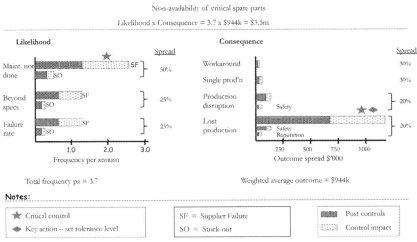

Figure 10.12—Spare Parts Risk Value Report

Ralph in presenting this report has four recommendations. Firstly, the holding costs versus risk calculation needs to be revisited, as the risk level is now more precisely determined. The tolerance level for non-availability of critical spare parts needs to be reconsidered by the executive as part of this rethink. Secondly, if adjustments are to be made then they should be primarily directed at the failure to meet planned maintenance and the arrangements with suppliers. Thirdly, the executive should be receiving monthly KPI reports on the progress of planned maintenance and supplier compliance audits. Finally, any internal audit work in this area should be focused on the identified critical controls.

Cost/Benefit Analysis of a Major Acquisition

Ralph's next assignment relates to the cost/benefit analysis of a major business decision. The former risk manager, who is the new Sales Manager of the agricultural product processing company, has presented the executive with a business case for the acquisition of another processing plant. Ralph has been asked by the CEO to review the cost/benefit analysis within the business case. This is a Level 1 decision described in Figure 8.11 because it will be taken by the board on the recommendation of executive management.

The Risk Bandit's View

The business case has concluded that the risk of the acquisition is "Moderate" because the rate of return in the business case is well above the company hurdle rate and the company has extensive experience in the industry. Ralph is already feeling a little anxious based on his experience with the spare parts risk assessment but counsels himself to make sure his neutral risk assessment hat is firmly in place before starting.

The business case summary presented to Ralph is as follows:

Base Case Summary		Commentary On Risks
Investment cost—year 1	$240m	No risk—agreements locked-in, subject to Board approval
Cash return—years 1 to 20:		Moderate risk—key variables are:
• Stand alone operations	$500m	• Sales volume in units
• Synergies and savings	$100m	• Unit sales price
• New strategies	$40m	• Unit production cost
Total cash return	$640m	All key variables are expected to vary within a range of +/- 10% and the sensitivity
Net cash return	$400m	analysis shows a return above (or marginally below) hurdle rate for all sensitivities.
Rates of return:		
• NPV	$74m	Applied at the company Cost of Capital of 8%
• IRR	11.9%	Well above the company Hurdle Rate of 10%
• Hurdle rate cash return	$560m	Well below the expected net cash return

Figure 10.13—Plant Acquisition Business Case Summary

The business case summary shows that for an investment of $240 million the total cash return over 20 years is $640 million yielding a net cash return of $400 million, a healthy Net Present Value (NPV) and an Internal Rate of Return (IRR) above the company's cost of capital.

Context of the Risk

Whilst the company is very experienced in agricultural product processing, it has not been involved in a major acquisition for many years. Ralph's concern is not so much with company's capacity to run the plant but more with the management of the integration and the expanded sales and marketing challenge. It took him little time to find that most research concludes that acquisitions are successful only 50%[22] of the time and he intends making sure that the business case properly supports the conclusion that this acquisition bucks that trend before giving it his endorsement.

In thinking through his approach, Ralph decides to use the same methodology as the spare parts risk value assessment in considering events that realise uncertainty around the NPV calculations in the business case. The methodology has been well accepted and understood by the executive and whilst a more detailed quantitative approach (such as Monte Carlo modelling) may allow more precise probability distribution analysis, it will not be readily understood by the executive. He also doesn't want to cloud the results of his work by being accused of setting up a peeing contest with the Sales Manager.

Ralph recognises that he needs to consider upside as well as downside and to ensure that he does not follow the common practice of a sole focus on threats/hazards and negative consequences. He knows that because he is dealing with numeric values rather than the qualitative captions in the business case risk assessment, he will be able to add the risk values of the different risk events to determine the impact on estimated NPV and IRR, provided he accounts for dependencies.

Valuation Model and Dependencies

Ralph tabulates from the business case two key sets of data. The first is a summary of the value build in the business case in cash flow terms before discounting to NPV and calculating IRR:

---

[22] http://www.forbes.com/sites/forbesleadershipforum/2012/03/19/why-half-of-all-ma-deals-fail-and-what-you-can-do-about-it/

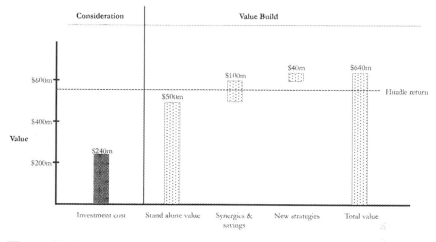

Figure 10.14—Plant Acquisition Business Case Value Build

Ralph notes that the value of the business without enhancements, referred to as the "stand alone value", will not achieve the required rate of return. The business case does however include cash flow projections for synergies and savings as well as new strategies that take the return over the hurdle rate.

The second tabulation Ralph extracts from the business case is the sensitivity analysis, prepared by the Sales Manager, of the impact on cash return, NPV and IRR of a +/-10% movement in the key variables:

Variable	-10%			Base Case			+10%		
	Cash	NPV	IRR	Cash	NPV	IRR	Cash	NPV	IRR
Sales volume in units	$360m	$55m	10.9%	$400m	$74m	11.9%	$440m	$94m	12.9%
Unit sales price	$340m	$45m	10.4%	$400m	$74m	11.9%	$460m	$104m	13.4%
Unit production cost	$320m	$35m	9.9%	$400m	$74m	11.9%	$480m	$113m	13.9%

Figure 10.15—Plant Acquisition Business Case Sensitivity Analysis

This table summarises the impact on net cash flow (before discounting), NPV and IRR of the three most significant variables in the business case. The Sales Manager has strongly pointed out that the company hurdle rate is only marginally threatened in one scenario. Ralph notices that the impact of each of the three variables is shown independently, and that if they all variables are down by 10% then the net cash return may well be below the hurdle rate.

It is also clear to Ralph that the business case is heavily dependent on the achievement of synergies and savings, new strategies and a smooth integration. So Ralph, apart from noting the real stakes of the game, decides the risk events that he will analyse further are not the variables in the sensitivity analysis but the components in the valuation build. These variables will be some of the causes of the risk events but Ralph wants to focus on the value build rather than concentrate on sensitivities alone. Ralph decides that the risk events to be analysed are:

- "Synergies and savings impacts are different from the business case"
- "New strategy impacts are different from the business case"
- "Stand alone value is different from the business case"

Ralph's intention is to analyse these three risks and calculate the net risk value for each risk in terms of annual undiscounted cash flows, taking account of both upside and downside. The net risk value as the predicted most likely variation from the business case can then be input into the business case valuation model to determine the impact on NPV and IRR.

Risk Value Assessment

Ralph's analysis of synergies and savings identifies six key elements as follows:

- Increase in sales volumes to existing customers
- New sales to new customers
- Increase in unit sales prices
- Production efficiencies from plant product specialisation
- Reduction in marketing cost per sales unit
- Reduction in labour costs per unit

He first looks at the causes of the first risk event, "synergies and savings impacts are different from the business case". His analysis identifies three causal groups with the following estimated frequency per annum:

Identified issues are not implemented	20 per annum
Unidentified existing issues	12 per annum
Unforeseen future issues	11 per annum

Ralph then looks at the outcome groups and identifies four groups with the following spread:

Incidental operational differences (variances from forecasts)   80%

Specific circumstantial differences (isolated situational changes)   17%

Widespread differences (pervasive situational changes)   2%

Fundamental differences (inaccurate critical assumptions)   1%

Ralph then calculates the upside and downside differences for each of the outcome groups as follows:

Causal Groups	Initiating Event	Outcome Groups	Upside	Downside	Net	Spread	Value
20.0 (A)		1	200	(300)	(100)	80%	(80)
12.0 (B)	Synergies and savings are different from the business case	2	500	(700)	(200)	17%	(34)
		3	1,000	(1,200)	(200)	2%	(4)
11.0 (C)		4	4,000	(1,500)	2,500	1%	25
43.0			Total			100%	(93)

Consequence Calculation ($'000)

Frequency Av. Consequence Predicted Value
43.0 x ($93k) = ($4m)

Figure 10.16—Plant Acquisition Business Case Risk Analysis

In looking at the range of outcomes he discovers that the Sales Manager has included in the business case large synergies and savings upsides even though they have a low probability of occurring. For example, the reduction in labour costs per unit assumes retention of the best people despite the need for relocation and renegotiation of wages of union members. The downsides are smaller (e.g. improved systems required for support services, dissatisfaction over revised management team, etc.) but have a much higher probability of occurring and outweigh the less probable upsides. Ralph's calculations show a predicted downside of $4 million per annum.

Ralph looks at the other two risks in a similar fashion, in the interests of readers' attention span, the details of this analysis are not provided but they result in upside of $2 million and downside of $3 million per annum respectively. He summarises his analysis of the three risks in undiscounted cash flow terms:

Risk	Annual			20 Years
	Upside	Downside	Net	
Synergies and savings		$4m	-$4m	-$80m
New strategies	$2m		$2m	$40m
Stand alone value		$3m	-$3m	-$60m
Total	$2m	$7m	-$5m	-$100m

Figure 10.17—Plant Acquisition Business Case Risk Analysis Summary

Ralph is able now to input the annual undiscounted cash flow risk value adjustments into the 20-year business case valuation model (which is not shown)—the result is:

	Net Cash	NPV	IRR
Base case	$400m	$74m	11.9%
Hurdle rate	$324m	$37m	10.0%
Predicted	$300m	$25m	9.4%

Figure 10.18—Plant Acquisition Business Case Return Analysis

Ralph's report to the CEO notes that whilst the predicted (risk assessed) return is below the hurdle rate, it is still above cost of capital and contributes shareholder value. The level of precision in Ralph's risk value assessment is not sufficient to categorically rule out the acquisition but his work does illustrate the need to analyse the probabilities of the range of outcomes with a focus on the areas highlighted by the quantitative assessment. With the support of a well-constructed Monte Carlo model using distributions based on Ralph's insights, it may well be possible to enhance the statistical level of return by adjusting the occurrence and treatment controls inherent in Ralph's calculation.

Epilogue

Excitement in Risk Management; Really!

The concepts, methodologies and tools in "Risk Bandits" have been tried and tested over many years across a diverse range of organisations by ourselves and other like-minded risk management professionals. What is new is that all the elements of risk value assessment have now been brought together, further developed and explained for use by directors and executive management rather than for risk managers.

During the book preparation period we have separately guided the implementation of risk value assessment, as set out in this book, in over 12 private and public sector organisations and industry associations. Tony has been working with executive management in some organisations and Rob has been working with directors and audit and risk committees in different organisations. The take-up has been incredible.

The moment when the board or executive management team realise what organisation risk management can be, is inspiring to us. We have seen organisation risk management change from a compliance chore to a value-adding component of governance. Excitement has been generated as the power of what can be done emerges—yes risk management excitement is not an oxymoron, it really is occurring.

The underlying frustration with the risk matrix and heat map often does not always immediately surface amongst directors, audit and risk committee members and executive management. There has been a degree of embarrassment in admitting that these tools have been used until something better has been presented.

Not everyone has come on board. Resistance has been encountered from risk matrix junkies who shy away from the high-level strategic thinking that is required for risk value assessment. A few in the resistance still say the matrix is better than nothing ignoring the overpowering agreement of leading academic and industry practitioners to the contrary. These risk bandits will no doubt find accommodating organisations for many years to come.

Just the Beginning

"Risk Bandits" presents an evolutionary path for organisation risk management that otherwise remains stagnant except for the development of more cute tools with the same fundamental flaw; shallow analysis. This book is just the beginning of the evolution in using risk value assessment. As critical mass in its use develops so will the applications, methodologies and tools.

Unlike qualitative risk analysis where survival of the cutest applies, risk value assessment will evolve as organisations better protect and create value from its use. Standard setters, regulators and stock exchanges may well be left behind if they fail to recognise that rudimentary risk tools are an endangered species. The risk management industry with its spread across so many disciplines will probably also move slowly with the more forward-looking professions leading the way. Academia, although still somewhat divided in the qualitative versus quantitative debate, may well be an agent of change with huge opportunities for research and innovation.

Directors will need to lead the way within their organisations, driven by the objective of enhancing shareholder value rather than compliance.

Two Years from Now

The risk bandits that you once tolerated are but a distant memory and the aroma of snake oil and cheap lipstick has almost entirely evaporated. The power of risk management to drive performance in your organisation(s) is now far clearer and your doubts about organisation risk management have been replaced by enthusiasm to have your organisation(s) do it properly. Unless you chose to stay at *Groundhog Day*.

This book is our contribution of intellectual property developed over two working lives to help rescue risk management from tokenism. In the past we have only waged the battle on a small front, and we each have our shortcomings that limited our success. We now realise we should have got together a long time ago to build this battle plan. Our objective is to provide a strategy for our readers to start winning battles on a much broader front.

We encourage you to guide your organisation(s) past the tokenism of the matrix to extract real value from organisation risk management. You now have the foundations to build a strategy to do so.

'The Matrix is everywhere. It is all around us'. 'The Matrix is a system, Neo. That system is our enemy'.

Why not start dismantling risk management tokenism in your organisation(s) today?

Table of Figures

Index